The Labour Party

*An Introduction to its History
Structure and Politics*

Edited by
Chris Cook and **Ian Taylor**

Longman
London and New York

Longman Group Limited London

Associated companies, branches and representatives throughout the world

Published in the United States of America by Longman Inc., New York

© Introduction and Appendix material Granby Research Services Limited and Ian Taylor 1980
© Contributions Longman Group Limited 1980

First published 1980

British Library Cataloguing in Publication Data

The Labour Party
  1. Labour Party-History
  I. Cook, Chris   II. Taylor, Ian
  329.9'41   JN1129.L32   79-41256

  ISBN 0-582-49038-3
  ISBN 0-582-49039-1 Pbk

Set in 10/11pt Comp/Set Times Roman
Printed in Great Britain by
Richard Clay (The Chaucer Press) Ltd, Bungay, Suffolk

Contents

81−1189

Introduction

Now seems to be an appropriate time to review the Labour Party, as it enters a period of opposition, having been in power for half of the post-war period. Although it may be an exaggeration to assert that the Party is entering a new era, or reaching an unusually critical stage in its development, future uncertainties render the present position of the Party particularly interesting. The leadership question is unresolved. The Conservative Party has a comfortable majority in the Commons and, furthermore, appears to be adhering to its contentious Right-wing strategy.

These two factors are of obvious significance when questions concerning the future of the Labour Party are raised. Does the defeat at the May 1979 General Election mean many frustrating years in opposition? Will Labour ever again achieve a healthy majority in Parliament as it did in 1945 and 1966? Will the Party swing more to the Left under a new leader? Is there likely to be an open ideological rift as there was during the 1950s? Will the trade unions and constituency organisations exert more influence on the Party's policies and affairs? An assessment of the Party to date might well illuminate some of these questions which will be answered during the next decade. However, it is unlikely that the answers will be as sharply defined as the questions. They rarely are in British politics.

In recent years it has been suggested that the Labour Party has replaced the Conservative Party as the 'natural' party of government. If this is so, it could well be a sign that the Party has failed to realize its more radical objectives in power. It also indicates that an interventionist political party, committed to more government, is better suited to dealing with industrial, economic and social problems than a free-enterprise party. The State machinery is better understood and manipulated by those who are the most active in creating it. As Labour was crucially instrumental in creating the Welfare State and State-managed economy, it is reasonable to assume that its policies, if maintained, would be effective in the post-war form of modified capitalism. Labour's future as *the* party of government may well be determined by the performance and success of the Conservatives. Already the Conservative Government is attempting to overturn accepted and respected views about post-war party politics. If 'Butskellism' and the convergence theory can be strongly challenged by the Right, how will the Labour Party respond? If the Conservative experiment fails, Labour could be in power for a considerable time.

This reader presents the student of politics and history with a collection of essays on the Labour Party. It covers developments from the origins of the Party to the present day, and provides basic information about Labour's aims, organisation and achievements during the past 80 or so years. It also offers a number of individual analyses and viewpoints about the development of different aspects of the Party. It is designed to provide an additional source to the many texts used widely by students of politics and contemporary history, without concentrating on a particular theme or a specific subject area.

Chapter 1 considers the 'mainstream' ideology of the Party, in relation to the policies advanced at different times. It focuses attention on individual theorists, who are considered to have been influential during the life of the Party, or representative of democratic socialist thought. Chapter 2 examines the organisation of the Party, and deals with the relationship between the different organs of the Party. Chapter 3 discusses the relationship between Labour and the trade unions. It is concerned with factors promoting both 'alliance' and 'stress' in this relationship, paying particular attention to the theme of voluntarism – the voluntary nature of the relationship between the two. Labour's performance in elections is the subject of Chapter 4. This is a helpful statistical guide which also offers an analysis of the significance of Labour's electoral results. There are two chapters covering the eight Labour governments. Chapter 5 deals with the first two minority governments of J. Ramsay MacDonald and considers the reasons why they failed. Chapter 6 discusses the aims and achievements of the post-war governments with accounts of the legislative programmes of each. It also assesses the programmes and performances of these governments in the light of the Party's objectives, and raises constitutional issues thrown up by Labour's years in power. The final chapter (7) examines the Labour Left. It looks not only at ideas on the Left but also its historical position in the Party and assesses its influence.

Chris Cook
Ian Taylor
July 1979

Chapter 1

Ideology and policy

Ian Taylor

> Oh, the world is overburdened
> With the idle and the rich!
> They bask up in the sunshine
> While we plod in the ditch;
> But zounds! we'll put some mettle
> In their fingers and their thumbs,
> For we'll turn things upside down, my lads,
> When the Revolution comes!

(Bruce Glasier, from *We'll Turn Things Upside Down*)

The British Labour Party is described variously as socialist, democratic socialist and social democratic. All are in some measure accurate as titular descriptions of the Party's ideology, yet all may be interpreted differently. The term socialist is a useful umbrella, which may be used to cover either particular doctrines or mere characteristics of socialist ideas or policies. Whilst some members of the Labour Party refer to themselves as socialists, strictly speaking they are democratic socialists, in view of the fact that they accept the political methods of the Party. The method of working within the constitutional confines of the institutional framework of the liberal-democratic State is at the root of the democratic socialist classification. Marxists are loath to describe the Labour Party as socialist, whilst the political Right denounces it as such. The term social democrat is sometimes a self-description of Party supporters who do not wish to be thought of as socialists in a doctrinaire sense. Social democrat is also applied to the Party by those who contend that its ideology has been revised to the extent that its central objective is now the maintenance of the social service State and State-managed economy, rather than more socialistic objectives of industrial democracy and the extensive nationalisation of industries, financial institutions and the land. This essay discusses the development of the Labour Party's mainstream democratic socialist ideology. Ideology is understood to be the synthesis of analysis, prescription and course of action, contained in a body of thought, or in the case of the Labour Party, represented by a number of complementary theories. 'Mainstream' refers to the ideas and practices most generally subscribed to within the Party.

A recurrent problem in the inter-connected studies of political ideas and practical politics is that of determining the influence of the theorist on the politician and the political organisation. Different individuals influence people in a variety of ways and not always to the same degree. Clearly, the interdependent experiences of reading, observing and acting influence greatly the development of political consciousness. A wide-ranging examination of the ideology and policies of a major political Party requires considering the ideas of leading theorists as well as events or periods of particular significances. These events may have initiated the formulation or sometimes reconstruction of basic objectives, as well as changes in policy. In this way, the chapter is something of an incomplete intellectual history of the Party, attended by a description of the policies that were advanced at different times. As the subject is approached historically, it is necessary to consider some of the ideological roots of democratic socialism in Britain.

Of the early nineteenth century British socialist thinkers, Robert Owen was the most influential in a theoretical as well as a practical capacity.[1] His experiment of running the New Lanark woollen mills along humanitarian lines, with production based on co-operation, remains unique. Owen's productive system was working-class based and organised to sustain and benefit the producer. Owen's beliefs that mutual trust was more likely to develop in a society which provided healthy living and working conditions, and that faults displayed by individuals were socially induced rather than 'natural', were pivotal to all socialist theory. His faith in moral, mental and political education as basic stimuli to human progress and social change was shared by both liberal and socialist writers throughout the nineteenth century. The Co-operative Movement owed a great deal to his ideas and the practical example which he set. He was involved in the creation of the Grand National Consolidated Trades Union in 1834, which attempted with very limited success to unite militant trade unions and the still theoretically inspired Co-operative Movement.

The growth of Co-operative societies and trade unionism during the 1820s and 1830s were important in a practical vein. However, there was little agitation of a specifically socialist nature until Chartism, which was the first nation-wide working-class socialist organisation in Britain. The founding of the London Working Men's Association in 1836, and proliferation of public meetings designed to promote a further extension of the franchise contributed to the drafting of the 'People's Charter' in 1837. The Charter demanded universal suffrage, annual parliaments, the secret ballot, equal electoral districts, the abolition of property qualifications for parliamentary candidates and the payment of members. These were all *political* objectives or demands for consti-tutional reform without which working-class political representation and therefore progress were impossible. Whilst peaceful political reform was the first and immediate objective of the Chartists, the use of force was advocated if this failed. Mass demonstrations and provoked violence were integral features of the political methods of the Chartists in their quest for reforms. It is interesting to contrast the mass-movement approach of Chartism with the more idealised principles and tactics of Owenism. Max Beer has commented:

The masses of the working class who adhered to Chartism adopted the social criticism of Owenism, but they rejected its dogmas of salvation, which Owen considered as precisely the most important of his whole system, and he regarded Chartism therefore as a retrograde step.[2]

Chartism collapsed in 1848, but its influence and example remained. As far as progress towards socialism was concerned, the continued development of trade unions and the Co-operative Movement, agitation for, and the eventual extension of, the franchise in 1867, and the filtering through of socialist ideas were individually small, but collectively important contributions. The fertilisation and germination process continued during the mid-nineteenth century and was characterised by some notable developments. Royden Harrison has shown that the relationship between on the one side members of the Positivist School, who adopted Comte's view that the basis of social reform was intellectual reform, in particular through the adaptation of knowledge to political and social questions, and on the other side trade union leaders, was important to the development of the Labour movement.[3] Professor Edward Spencer Beesley, and Frederic Harrison in particular, tried to encourage the trade union leaders to develop a social philosophy based on an understanding of morals in relation to existing society. This belief in working-class ability to understand the nature of productive relations and the importance of concerted political action to induce and stimulate industrial and political change, was the main characteristic of the approach of the Positivists. Later, the involvement of Fabians with the organised working class, and the activities of the Workers' Educational Association and Ruskin College continued the tradition of co-operation between 'academic' and industrial worker.

If Positivism was associated with industrial reform, nineteenth-century liberalism was more closely identified with economic and social reform. John Stuart Mill and Henry George were influential as economists and Thomas Hill Green in the context of social reform. Many of the early Fabians were influenced by Mill's *Principles of Political Economy* and George's *Progress and Poverty*. Both Mill and George were in the tradition of Tom Paine's radical land reformism, believing that the private ownership of land and the accumulated wealth and privilege that accrued from it was the greatest social evil. Mill's principal concern was with land as property, as he believed it to be the basis of all other forms of property.[4] He went further than con-temporary political economists in his insistence that society was based upon privilege, and that the power base of society must be changed since capital was the produce of labour, and the exploited class was the labouring class. He advocated that increased increment in the form of rent should be taxed, and that land should be owned or controlled by the State in the national interest. George argued along similar lines. He claimed that the unequal ownership of land necessitated the unequal distribution of wealth. The remedy was the common ownership of land. He denegrated the utility of rent and capital, because the former was a denial of human rights whilst the latter failed to supply the materials by which labour created wealth.

In 1883 Thomas Davidson founded the 'Fellowship of the New Life', which became the Fabian Society[5] in 1884. Philosophically, the Fabians owed much to Utilitarianism, Positivism, political economy and the ideas of Mill and George on land reform. The Fabian collectivist approach bore a resemblance to the ideas of T. H. Green,[6] the Liberal Idealist philosopher, but there is little evidence to suggest that they owed anything to Green, since they were more utilitarian than Idealist. Green's collectivist theories about remedies for social ills, which demanded more State intervention, not only influenced the development of a more pro State-interventionist wing of the Liberal Party during the late nineteenth and early twentieth centuries, but were also to some extent similar to those advanced later by the Labour Party's most important early twentieth-century figure, J. Ramsay MacDonald. The main difference between Fabians and collectivist Liberals lay in the question of the ownership of wealth. Liberals of all persuasions remained basically hostile to State ownership. Like the Liberal reformist movement, the Fabian Society was middle-class and non-doctrinaire. At the basis of Fabian thinking was the notion that social improvement through the radical transformation of society could best be achieved through education, and an understanding of the process of social change. But the Society lacked cohesion. Norman and Jeanne MacKenzie have written:

Marxists, Socialist Leaguers and anarchists passionately believed in a cause. The early Fabians, on the other hand, were unsure of what they believed, despite the clash of temperaments, they were tolerant of differences to the point of indecision....[7]

The diversity and richness of ideas was brought together in the *Fabian Essays In Socialism* (1889).[8] Of the eight contributors, Sidney Webb was the most important figure in the Fabian Society, in view of his high work rate and his breadth of thinking. He was as much concerned with the minute details of practical policy as with matters of principle. In *Socialism in England* (1890), he underlined that any changes based on socialism would be democratic and therefore acceptable to the majority. They would be gradual, causing no dislocation and would come about by constitutional and peaceful means. Socialism was the collective administration of rent and interest, collective control over the instruments of wealth, the universal obligation of personal service and the replacement of individual conscience by collectivist conscience. He believed that advances towards socialism had been made already, with the development of trade unionism, co-operativism, growth in local government and municipal services, and strike action associated with the New Unionism of the late 1880s.[9]

The most active socialist organisation was the Social Democratic Federation (SDF), which was founded by H. M. Hyndman as the Democratic Federation in 1883. Hyndman was a Marxist, but his highly individualistic and personalised interpretation of Marx's writings led to an estrangement between himself and Frederick Engels, the leading exponent of Marxism. In spite of the organisation's revolutionary tendencies and Marxist leanings, its objectives were similar to those of the Fabian Society and trade union leaders. They included universal suffrage, the abolition of all hereditary authority, the nationalisation of land and the railways, better living and working conditions (including the eight-hour day), free compulsory education and cumulative taxation. A leading figure in the SDF was William Morris. He left in 1887 and formed the Socialist League, which unlike the SDF was anti-parliamentary and more anarchistic than Marxist.

During the 1880s developments such as the selection of trade union candidates for election to Parliament and local councils occurred, and the New Unionism of the late 1880s was one of the most important factors in the development of a working-class socialist party. The objectives of New Unionism were to establish industrial rights for, and the political representation of, the working class. In 1893 the Independent Labour Party was founded to support labour candidates and MPs, to provide an alternative to the Liberal Party for the working class voter and advance socialist policies. Ideologically, the ILP was a synthesis of many different strands of socialist thinking, and had no clearly identifiable ideology. Robert Blatchford's *Merrie England*[10] was an important contribution to socialist thought because in many ways it typified the diversity of the ILP. *Merrie England* was revolutionary in tone, yet anti-revolutionary in doctrine. It contained elements of Marxism, Morris's quest for aesthetics and the anti-temperance moralism of Christian socialism. Although it was ideologically diverse, the ILP's objectives were clear: to obtain mass support from the working class for its socialist policies, and to take the parliamentary road to socialism as far as possible.

Political ideologies and movements and the organised parties which develop from them are not created in isolation from existing institutions, structures and values. They are conceived in and born of them. The limited objectives and diversity of the Labour Representation Committee (LRC), founded in 1900, truly reflected the collage of British socialism at the turn of the century, which was as much the product of a political tradition as the consequence of industrialism and its attendant social forces. In spite of the fact that nineteenth century socialists sought as their central objective the transformation of capitalism by revolutionary or evolutionary means, in Britain at least existing political conventions were accommodated relatively easily. The developing socialist organisations and labour movement were conscious at all stages of a tradition of party-in-Parliament, in contrast to the mass-movement, revolutionary continental approach, although Chartism had embodied both.

The establishment of the Labour Representation Committee, with the objective of creating a cohesive political party to represent the interests of working-class people, was in itself of great political significance. Within the context of ideological development it was important because it illustrated two basic tenets of democratic socialist ideology; the need for a class party but not a class-war party, and a party which was committed to the pursuit of socialism gradually, by parliamentary means. Although there was little actual co-operation between the Fabian Society and the Labour Party in its early years, the gradualist socialism that was expounded by Fabians during the 1880s and 1890s corresponded much more closely with the development of the Labour Representation Committee into a political party than did the class-war thesis, advanced by H. M. Hyndman and the SDF. That the Labour Representation Committee and the early Labour Party had no major programme was due to the fact that its organisation was fragmented, consisting of trade unions, socialist societies, Fabians, the Independent Labour Party (which was the principal Parliamentary group) and the SDF. Broadly speaking, the Party supported the reform measures of the Liberal Government between 1906 and 1911,[11] and did not press for the more radical proposals of the founding manifesto of the LRC, which included the nationalisation of land and the railways.[12]

In the development of a mainstream democratic socialist ideology, the period from 1900 to 1918 was notable for the following. Firstly, the development of a theoretical framework for future policies and goals, which was based on the collectivist view of society and support for a greater role for the State in society. This collectivist approach reduced the importance of class as a barrier to human co-operation and progress, and its principal exponent was Ramsay MacDonald. Another feature was the increasing opposition to the Lib–Lab alliance and the associated growth of syndicalism and guild socialism. Finally, the First World War acted as a catalyst which brought together the industrial, political and intellectual elements of British Labour.

In *Socialism and Society* (1905) MacDonald described society as 'a unified and organised system of relationships in which certain people and classes perform certain functions, and in which individuals find an existence appropriate to their being by becoming parts of the function organs'.[13] This view of society as an evolutionary organism reflected the influence of social Darwinism on MacDonald's ideas. There were, according to MacDonald, incompatible components of society, which resulted in conflict. These were the ownership of land and capital on the one hand, with labour on the other, producer and consumer worker and the instruments of work. However, as society became more democratic, these conflicts would cease, as the form of social organisation became directly dependent on the needs of the community.[14] His adherence to the theory of the organic growth and progressive development of society led MacDonald to criticise utopian socialists, on the grounds that they failed to understand that society developed in accordance with the 'laws of social life'.[15] He also criticised those who adopted the language of Marxism:

> This confusion between thought and action, between words and deeds – this pouring of old wine into new bottles – is the gravest danger which at the present moment threatens from inside the steady advance of Socialism in this country.[16]

Whilst he recognised basic contradictions in capitalist society, and argued that conflict between employer and employee was inevitable, in his view this did not amount to class war. These contradictions were merely imperfections in the social evolutionary scheme. Although he thought that the existence of trade unionism was the 'purest expression' of this antagonism, the Labour Party had been formed precisely because trade unionism had experienced that class war was fruitless.[17] He went further, and implied that any and all progress would lead eventually to socialism, and cited experiments in factory legislation and public health regulation as important steps.[18] Overall, his collectivism was consistent with his belief that Labour should participate in an alliance with the Liberals, and his ideas about progress corresponded with those of the Fabians, who believed that the erosion of conflict through municipalisation, nationalisation and education was the only way forward. The Fabians, however, remained hostile to the idea of establishing a socialist party based upon the support of the organised working class.[19]

MacDonald's commitment to the parliamentary road was shared by most of the Independent Labour Party, but increasingly there was opposition to the tactics of the parliamentary group in general and the leadership in particular. In 1909, the dock-workers' leader Ben Tillett attacked the Parliamentary Party for supporting the Liberals and failing to press for socialist legislation. In *Is the Parliamentary Labour Party a Failure?* he also castigated the 'temperance moralists' in the ILP, especially Henderson, Snowden and Shackleton who criticised working-class indulgence in alcohol. With such tactics and prevalent attitudes, Labour would lose sight of and fail to achieve its objectives if it relied on parliamentary means:

> The safety of a Parliamentary seat is too big a price to pay for the neglect of the millions of homes affected detrimentally by poverty; even at the risk of losing the empty vanity of Parliamentary honours the Labour Party should be rebels in everlasting and open warfare with the powers that be.[20]

A further indication of frustration with the Labour leadership came from within the ILP. A resolution to secede from the Labour Party was defeated at the ILP Conference of 1909. Members of the National Council of the ILP criticised the revisionism of the parliamentary group, claiming that the whole purpose of the ILP was to fight for socialism against both capitalist parties, but that this had been abandoned.[21] Keir Hardie responded to the accusations with his timely *My Confession of Faith in the Labour Alliance*, in which he asserted that the Labour Party had become an acceptable part of Britain's political life, and argued that the difference of opinion between socialists lay not in the *principles* of socialism but in the *methods* of putting socialism to work.[22]

It was for these reasons that syndicalism paraded as an alternative to Labourism and orthodox trade unionism during the period from the Lib–Lab alliance of 1910 to the First World War. Hardie's statement, if considered in conjunction with the aims of syndicalism, showed that it was precisely *because* Labour had become a familiar and 'acceptable' part of the political and institutional establishment that it was considered to be bankrupt as a vehicle to benefit the interests of the industrial worker directly. As for the methods of putting socialism to work, it could have been claimed quite legitimately that differences in method and tactics were more directly the result of differences in principle. This was how the syndicalists saw the situation. Syndicalism was essentially a direct-action, non-theoretical movement (although its theoretical roots lay in nineteenth century French syndicalism, anarcho-syndicalism and co-operativism) which sought to establish control over the means of production by the workers themselves. Instead of conceptualising society as collectivist and capable of being transformed through the State, syndicalists revolted against virtually all traditional socialist doctrines. Strikes in the coal mines, the engineering and building industries and on the railways between 1910 and 1914 were syndicalist inspired. However, in spite of syndicalism, the increased support of trade unions for the ILP during this period greatly strengthened the Labour Party.[23]

The support of trade unions was vital to the expansion of the Labour Party, and the ILP leadership responded to the threat from the syndicalists. Philip Snowden discounted syndicalism as a viable alternative to parliamentary socialism[24] and in *The Socialist Movement* (1911) Ramsay MacDonald restated his collectivist philosophy and set out his objections to revolution and the materialist conception of history. Revolution, he asserted, could never bring about socialism, because the social transformation that socialists contemplated was one which would 'affect every fibre of society, and which must therefore be an organic process'.[25] Revolution was the end, not the means to the end.[26] He maintained that the materialist conception of history was not essential to socialist theory because it contained too many general-isations, like the theory of the class war.[27] In spite of the reactions of the parliamentarians to the syndicalist alternative of revolutionary class politics, Graham Wallas claimed justifiably that there was nothing new about syndicalism,[28] and L. T. Hobhouse argued that syndicalism was intelligible as a despairing protest against the lack of progress made by a cumbersome party machine.[29]

The First World War was a significant chapter in the development of the Labour Party as a mass party, and was not without relevance in the development of a mainstream ideology. J. M. Winter has written:

That the Labour Party lacked an ideology was an often-repeated – and valid – judgement among socialists in the years before 1914. What they meant was that the party had operated without a coherent idea of its political function. The experience of war corroborated this charge and exposed the consequences of the party's absence of purpose.[30]

The creation of the War Emergency Workers' Committee brought the principal Fabian spokesman Sidney Webb into direct involvement with organised labour, and led to closer ties between himself and Arthur Henderson, the Party's Chairman.[31] This war-time alliance of the official ILP, Fabians, and trade unions and the growth in size and bargaining power of the trade unions during the war, increased the credibility of a mass party and laid the foundations for the Labour Party's Constitution of 1918 and the programme 'Labour and The New Social Order'.

Winter has argued that it was not the theory but the practical activity and influence of British socialism that changed during the war.[32] Certainly, the principles proclaimed in the programme and objectives underlined in the Constitution were products of the period from the 1880s to the First World War. The orthodox, traditionalist nature of British trade unionism and the evolutionism of the two dominant strands in Labour's developing ideology, the collectivism and State interventionism of Fabianism and the parliamentarism of the ILP leadership, ensured that the objectives of the programme and organisational structure adopted by the Constitution reflected the fusion of interests. Arguably, having reached this juncture, the Labour Party was destined to be a reformist socialist rather than a transformist socialist party. Ralph Miliband has described the 1918 programme as 'a Fabian reformist blueprint', which represented the establishment of the ideology of 'Labourism', rather than socialism.[33]

Labour and The New Social Order stated that the new social order must be built on fraternity, and the planned co-operation in production and distribution for the benefit of hand and brain workers on a 'systematic approach towards a healthy equality of material circumstance' for everyone, based upon political and economic freedom and consent. The new 'House' of society would be erected upon four pillars: the universal enforcement of the national minimum; the democratic control of industry; a revolution in national finance; and the distribution of surplus wealth for the common good.[34] Labour would press for a minimum wage for all adult workers, introduce legislation to amend and consolidate the Factory Acts, re-settle the de-mobilised in industry and schemes of municipally controlled public works, establish the 48 hour week, raise the school-leaving age to 16, extend State unemployment insurance and raise the weekly benefit.[35] These proposals were aimed at establishing a national minimum standard of living. The programme called for progressive taxation, including taxes on profits, unearned increments on land and minerals and increased death duties. A capital levy would be charged on all property and the surplus wealth created by such a fiscal policy would be utilised to increase national expenditure on the public services.[36] In international affairs, Labour would support the claims of all nations seeking democractic self-government.[37]

As far as changing the relationship between capital and labour was concerned, and altering the power structure of British society, the programme was vague:

What the Labour Party looks to is a genuinely scientific reorganisation of the nation's industry, no longer deflected by individual profiteering, on the basis of the Common Ownership of the Means of Production.[38]

In addition, the proceeds of industry would be equitably distributed and machinery would be set up to ensure that the administration and control of industry was in the public interest. Land would be nationalised, along with the railways, coalmines, electrical power, and municipal control over services would be extended.[39] State ownership and control reflected the Fabian influence, and indicated that the form that public ownership was likely to take would be State and municipal, not participatory control by the workers themselves. This was also reflected in the Constitution. Whilst the document was more concerned with the organisation of the Party than principles and objectives, Clause Four stated the need to maintain a party in Parliament and the country, to co-operate with the Trades Union Congress and other 'Kindred Organisations'. The Party's object was as follows:

To secure for the workers by hand or by brain the full fruits of their industry and the most equitable distribution thereof that may be possible upon the basis of the common ownership of the means of production, distribution, and exchange, and the best obtainable system of popular administration and control of each industry or service.[40]

Other objects included the promotion of the political, social and economic emancipation of the people, and international co-operation with labour and socialist organisations in other countries.

The importance of the 1918 Programme was its conveyance of the broad objectives of democratic socialism into specific proposals, some of which, like the nationalisation of land and democratic control over industry, still appear in Party programmes. However, the open-endedness of both the Programme and Clause Four with regard to the ownership and control of industry, indicated the Party's unwillingness to commit itself to action which might not, under certain circumstances, be consistent with the over-riding objective of transforming society through conventional, parliamentary methods. In fact, the issue of industrial democracy and worker control was re-vitalised during the war, after the failure of syndicalism to make much headway. G. D. H. Cole, a Fabian who did not share the Fabian faith in the growth of

State power and municipalisation, advocated guild socialism, less revolutionary than syndicalism, although it shared some of its characteristics. Cole's thesis was that the only way to grant effective control to the workers in an industrial system was through guilds organised on socialist lines. In *The World of Labour* (1917) he contended that the basic weakness of the Labour Party was that it was neither a wing of liberalism, nor in any sense an independent socialist party.[41] Cole's guild socialism was independent within a democratic-socialist, non-revolutionary framework, to the extent that he advocated direct political action by trade unions, through the strike, to secure control over the means of production. This view, that political and economic action were inseparable,[42] represented a break from the liberal-democratic conception of the strike as a last resort, to be used by workers only to obtain basic rights in the productive sphere. In *Self Government in Industry* (1917) he elaborated his theories, claiming that not only would guilds be the only alternatives to collectivism and syndicalism,[43] but through their extension and inter-action, they would embrace questions of wider interest to the community and co-ordinate producer interests in association with co-operatives and State services.

Cole was not alone in his belief that a collectivist philosphy, if allied to extensions of State control through Parliament, would not necessarily benefit industrial workers. In *The Science of Wealth* (1911) J. A. Hobson argued that the worker would set a definite meaning upon his trade, and gather a notion of how his trade stood in relation to others if the machinery of industrial control was more localised.[44] Graham Wallas, in *The Great Society* (1914), reasoned that the continued growth of collectivism depended upon the efficiency and acceptability of the machinery of the collective will, and argued that there was growing dissatisfaction with the existing methods of representation.[45] In view of the fact that the State-interventionist, centralist tendency in Labour's strategy depended upon, or had elected to depend upon, the traditional institutions of Party and Parliament, these reservations about collectivism and the strengthening of the State were well founded.

Cole's functionalist, direct-action strategy was answered by MacDonald in *Parliament and Revolution* (1919) and *Parliament and Democracy* (1921). In *Parliament and Revolution* he maintained that, during the war, capitalism as the ruling power had been challenged. This was particularly true in terms of the increase of State intervention and the growth of trade union power.[46] His reply to Cole was that there were two kinds of strikes, the legitimate or industrial (limited objective) strike and the illegitimate or political strike.[47] In *Parliament and Democracy* he stated that the ILP favoured the notion of State sovereignty over the idea of the functional society (as in guilds and co-operatives), as society was multi-functional.[48] He also criticised the Bolsheviks, and argued that the Russian Revolution was bound to fail because it attempted to establish socialism by force. He believed that a parliamentary election victory would give Labour all the power that Lenin had achieved by revolution.[49]

By the early 1920s the mainstream ideology of the Labour Party was well established and consisted of a gradualist, collectivist-based reformist type of socialism, in which the State was the main agent of social and economic change. This ideology was embodied in a number of Party documents and in the ideas and writings of leading politicians and intellectuals. If one individual encapsulated democratic socialism, it was R. H. Tawney, although it must be said that Christianity rather than particular socialist doctrines was the basis of his thought. In *The Acquisitive Society* he provided democratic socialists with one of the most comprehensive analyses of contemporary capitalism and expositions of democratic socialism to date.

Tawney contended that there had been an historical progression towards the acquisitive society, which the eighteenth century had defined and which the twentieth century had largely obtained, or was at least capable of attaining. The acquisitive society was geared towards the acquisition of wealth, an activity which was leading the individual to become the centre of his universe. This simplified the problem of social life and the need to respond to a collective conscience. This was the result of the individual being relieved from the necessity of discriminating between different types of economic activity and different sources of wealth.[50] He argued that the criterion of social function ought to be more important than that of wealth, because the application of a notion of function would make it clear that remuneration was based upon service, rather than on the privilege and power which accrued from the dependence on profit.[51]

In contemporary industrial systems, he argued, man was considered to exist for industry rather than industry for man. This 'desert of unnatural dreariness'[52] which ensued condemned activities which failed to serve the dominant economic interests. Private property, whose existence was pivotal to the existence of socialism, was uncreative. Tawney contrasted starkly the fact that the most hideous places in the country produced the greatest wealth (which was consumed by the most luxurious), with the way in which the ruling class traditionally lived:

A public school and then club life in Oxford and Cambridge, and then another club in town; London in June when London is pleasant, the moors in August, and pheasants in October, Cannes in December and hunting in February and March; and a whole world of rising bourgeoisie eager to imitate them, sedulous to make their expensive watches keep time with this preposterous calendar.[53]

Such 'gut reaction' socialism, based upon anti-privilege for its own sake and a revulsion with the low quality of life which capitalist systems created for the vast majority, was reminiscent of Blatchford's *Merrie England*. In expressing his socialism in this way, Tawney offered a form of ethical socialism to his readers, which it seemed that the Labour alliance of ILP, trade unions and Fabians had lost sight of.

Tawney advocated the creation of a functional society, which would be organised primarily for the performance of duties and the protection of rights, which were necessary for the discharge of social obligations. In order for such a society to operate, the following changes were necessary. The owners of property and industry must be dispensed with and industry become a more worthy profession, with the responsibility for its maintenance in the hands of those who undertook the work.[54] He recognised that nationalisation and the creation of guilds were alternative forms of organisation, but unlike MacDonald he was confident that the two could work side by side. Nationalisation did not simply involve placing industries under the machinery of the State (civil servants and ministers). The authorities to which industries were entrusted should consist of representatives of consumers, work-force, professional associations and State officials. The administrative autonomy of each industry was essential, and if the principle behind industry was function instead of profit and acquisition, disputes would be less likely because those employed in the industry would be more likely to identify with the common cause.[55]

Throughout the 1920s, the mainstream ideology of the Labour Party embodied its long-term objective, the creation of a socialist society step by step; its method, which constituted winning a sufficient number of seats in the House of Commons in order to command a majority large enough to ensure the passage of its programme; its policies of State control and ownership of the means of production, and the provision of a wide range of State social services. The dominance of Fabianism, the limited objectives of M.P.s and trade unionists and the absence of a potent intellectual Left wing, indicated that radical deviations from this strategy and policy were unlikely. This was epitomised by Sidney Webb's Presidential Address to the 1923 Labour Party Conference, in which he uttered the celebrated statement:

First let me insist on what our opponents habitually ignore, and indeed, what they seem intellectually incapable of understanding, namely, the inevitability of our scheme of gradualness.[56]

The 'inevitability of gradualness' not only reflected the development of the Party's mainstream ideology to date, but to this day has symbolised the impact of Fabianism on the Labour Party.

During the 1920s there was a predictable consistency between what the Party stood for in ideological terms and how it responded to events. In 1920, the Party's leaders and the majority of the Party rejected the proposal of the Left wing of the ILP that Labour should affiliate to the Third International. A section of the ILP was critical of the hostility shown towards Lenin by the Labour leadership over the affiliation, particularly Snowden and MacDonald.[57] The British Communist Party's request for affiliation to the Party was rejected in 1920. Labour's brief experience in power demonstrated that it would be impossible to advance its more socialistic legislative proposals until it had a substantial overall majority in the Commons.

The General Strike was probably the most significant event of the 1920s, because it exhibited the unwillingness of the leadership to become involved in an issue which was fought strictly along class lines, even though it did not constitute MacDonald's notion of a political strike. The Right saw the Strike as a constitutional threat, which challenged the stability of the liberal-democratic State and parliamentary system of government. Whilst Labour's mainstream ideology precluded the possibility of the Party supporting a general strike as a revolutionary weapon (which the 1926 Strike clearly wasn't), it still begged the question as to where the Party would stand in the event of an overt class-struggle issue, and how far it would be prepared to go to provide political support and leadership for the trade unions. The events of 1926 alienated the ILP further, although by this time it was but a sizeable Left wing pressure group in the Party, which protested about the diluted socialism of the leaders. In 1927 the policy-document *Labour and the Nation* reiterated the policies of the leadership by emphasising the need for State intervention and control, to ensure the extension of the social services and the public ownership of basic industries.

The political crisis of 1931 raised a number of issues concerning the strategy of the Labour Party, but more notably it was responsible for restoring an awareness that there were certain limits beyond which a democratic socialist party, which supposedly represented the interests of working class people, could not go. When MacDonald and the Labour leadership in the Cabinet were faced with splitting the Party, by agreeing to the request of the international financial community to reduce unemployment benefit and cut public spending, or alternatively resigning, MacDonald formed the notorious 'National' Government with the Conservative and Liberal parties. His betrayal not only lost the support of the Labour Party and trade union movement, but came to symbolise the dangers of compromising fundamental principles for the sake of office. That his Party's support should be forfeited on matters of principle, notably collaboration with parties of capitalism to reduce the standard of living of the working class, was a foregone conclusion. It was true that MacDonald betrayed the Party by forming a coalition, but it is much more questionable as to whether or not he betrayed his own beliefs. Whilst the ideology of Labour was essentially that of MacDonald, the Labour leader's conviction that Labour in office under almost any conditions was more likely to lead to progress than Labour in opposition,[58] and his blind adherence to collectivist principles and non-sectarian 'national' interests, were in keeping with his action in 1931. Bernard Barker has argued that the events of 1931 blinkered the Party to the extent that MacDonald's ideas prevailed still in Labour politics, and that his actions were consistent with gradualism.[59] Miliband has argued that the experience of 1931 did not cause any major transformations in the political thought of the Party.[60] Both impressions are accurate, although the impact of 1931 fired the determination of the new leaders to work towards a major electoral victory for the Party, which would in itself be an effective weapon against hostility to its socialist policies. It also led to a re-statement of basic objectives in a decade that was rich in socialist rhetoric.

Opposition during the 1930s enabled the Party to take stock of its policies and gave the leaders the opportunity to express and define the Party's purpose in the many books, pamphlets and policy statements issued by, or published under the auspices of, the Party. Ultimately, the policies that were advanced during this period reflected a degree of compromise between, on the one hand, the trade-union dominated industrial wing and, on the other, the influence of Marxism, which was more evident during the 1930s than at any previous time. In spite of this influence, Fabianism remained the dominant strand in the mainstream ideology, and despite the popularity of the Left Book Club and appeal of Harold Laski and John Strachey, it was the ideas of Fabians such as Hugh Dalton, Clement Attlee, Herbert Morrison, G. D. H. Cole and E. F. M. Durbin, that reflected and to some extent influenced the climate of opinion in the Party. One reason why Marxism failed to become a force in policy-making was the cautionary, gradualist ideology adhered to by most leading figures in the trade union movement. Marxism could not offer convincing and practical guarantees to many trade unionists, that a viable programme which would produce higher wages, better living conditions and full employment could be constructed from the doctrine's class war, revolutionary assumptions.

The leading exponents of democratic socialism reflected the views of their predecessors. Attlee, who became leader in 1935, believed that socialism depended upon collective action, through which the socialist objective of granting freedom to the individual could be realised. Such societal action would establish the Socialist Commonwealth.[61] Dalton maintained that the relative strength of socialism could be assessed by measuring the extent to which a community was socialist by the relative strengths of the socialised and private sectors in its economic life.[62] Morrison's socialism was also orientated towards the collective (public) ownership of the land and means of production, which would be administered efficiently in the interests of the community.[63] The most comprehensive re-statement of democratic socialism was Evan Durbin's *The Politics of Democratic Socialism*. Durbin referred to recent changes in capitalism, including the strengthening of the bargaining power of trade unions, the growth of State social services, the increase of State control and the proliferation of State-organised monopolies and higher taxation. These had led to developments in the social fabric, notably the rise to power of the intermediate classes, the conversion of the proletariat into a class with similar interests to the petit bourgeoisie and the sub-division of the 'grand bourgeoisie' into three groups, director-ate, shareholder and management.[64] Significantly, he maintained that two components of socialism were less relevant, property and freedom of enterprise.[65] He criticised the Marxian materialist interpretation of history, which claimed that acquisitiveness was the sole force operating in society at any time. Other forces, he argued, were present. These were based upon the emotional and preference responses of individuals.[66] By distinguishing between economic and other forces, Durbin demonstrated a fundamental difference between democratic socialist thought and Marxism, although he differed from Tawney in his understanding of the influence on human psychology of the economic forces inherent in capitalist, acquisitive society. By appealing for changes in capitalism to be taken into account and criticising the Marxian interpretation of capitalist development, Durbin can be regarded as a precursor of 'revisionism'.[67]

Labour's mainstream ideology, which was typified by Durbin, held less attraction for the Labour Left. The ILP seceded from the Party in 1932. The caution of the Party's leaders, together with their belief that socialist measures in general and nationalisation in particular could be achieved constitutionally through the mandate and Parliament, met opposition from the Left. The Socialist League[68] and supporters of the United Front[69] argued that nationalisation would be a sufficient threat to the vested economic interests, for the ruling class in the political shape of the Conservative Party and House of Lords, to resort to unconstitutional action to block Labour legislation. Sir Stafford Cripps argued that, if necessary, Labour should be prepared to invoke emergency powers to implement its policies.[70] Harold Laski warned that the Parliamentary road might well contain obstacles, and argued that the events of 1931 had driven the Party towards more thorough socialist measures, which might well persuade the Conservative Party to employ extra-constitutional opposition methods.[72] This view was an exaggeration, for whilst the Party adopted a Leftist tone during the 1930s, its commitment to the parliamentary road and winning popular support for its programme ensured that whilst every major industry might well be a target for nationalisation, its objectives for a normal period in power would be manageable and limited.

An important development during the 1930s was the extent to which the concept of planning became a basic feature of policy statements. Attlee, Dalton and Durbin[73] maintained that planning, as a means to an end, was a vital component of any socialist programme. Without an economic plan, urged Dalton, the Party would be unable to control and direct economic resources towards social priorities.[74] G. D. H. Cole was the principal advocate for planning,[75] contending that it was impossible to advance towards socialism without a plan, and that it would be necessary for a Labour Government to establish planning machinery as soon as it came to power. In effect, planning encompassed State control over production, the distribution of wealth and the provision of services. In terms of policy, this meant nationalisation, the provision of a comprehensive range of social services and the control and regulation of finance to ensure industrial development and full employment. The slow recovery from economic depression, and what was known of the Soviet Five Year Plans, which aroused the enthusiasm of the Webbs, added impetus to the demand for planning, so that by the end of the decade planning was an integral facet of Labour's mainstream ideology. The policy documents *For Socialism and Peace* (1934) and *Labour's Immediate Programme* (1937) both reflected the resurgence of socialist rhetoric and the demand for planning. *For Socialism and Peace* restated many of the objectives of *Labour and The New Social Order*, but it also committed the Labour Party to the nationalisation and public control of the following concerns: transport, water, coal, gas, electricity, land, iron and steel, ship-building, engineering, textiles, chemicals, banking and credit and insurance.[76] The *Immediate Programme* was of more direct significance because it set out what a Labour Government could expect to achieve in a five-year period in office. It was a cautious programme, which struck a balance between on the one hand the Socialist League's demands for extensive nationalisation along the lines of the 1934 proposals, and on the other the need to promote the extension of the social services as the major priority. It stated that the Party's goal was the 'Socialist Commonwealth', the aims of which were peace and democracy.[77] The Bank of England was to be nationalised and a National Investment Board would be set up to control and direct investment into key industries. The railways and fuel and power industries were to be nationalised. Finance would be controlled more strictly and food production and land would be controlled in the public interest. The principal social policy objectives were the raising of the school leaving age to 16, improved pensions, a new Workmen's Compensation Bill, the extension of the health services and the abolition of the Means Test. State responsibility for the future location of industry was to be an essential aspect of the Party's policy for the distressed areas.[78]

The years between 1931 and the outbreak of war were significant as far as the relationship between ideology and policy was concerned. A number of principles were re-enforced. A Labour Government would plan in future through economic controls, nationalise basic industries and services (with the public corporation as the administrative organ), extend the social services and promote international co-operation. In view of the problems that minority Labour governments had faced, it was considered to be important that the Party should establish as priorities a number of specific objectives which by their nature excluded the possibility of coalition, yet were not sufficiently Left wing to alienate the 'middle ground' of potential Labour voters. Whilst there was a high degree of unity between the Party's leaders and influential trade unionists like Ernest Bevin and Walter Citrine, the expulsion from the Party of such eminent figures as Cripps, Aneurin Bevan and George Strauss[79] indicated that there was by no means unanimity about the Party's immediate priorities.

A significant development in British society during the Second World

War was the massive extension of State control over the economy in general, and in particular over finance, industry, agriculture and the social services. As the principal employer of labour, purchaser of raw materials and manufactured goods, and controller of imports and exports, the Government assumed control not only over production, but over the day-to-day lives of millions of people. Government departments were enlarged, and new ones like the Ministries of Supply and Production were created. The proposals of the Beveridge, Barlow, Scott and Uthwatt reports [80] all called for extensions of State control over a number of areas, notably the social services, industrial development, investment and the use of land. The Government responded with White Papers on 'Employment Policy', 'Social Insurance', 'Workmen's Compensation', 'A National Health Service' and 'Educational Reconstruction'. Many of their proposals were in keeping with those previously advanced by the Labour Party, whose post-war reconstruction policy-committees adopted and often extended the Coalition Government's often tentative reform proposals.[81]

In view of the fact that Labour's early-war policy documents called upon the Party to take advantage of the revolutionary potential of the War,[82] the Party's 1945 manifesto, *Let Us Face the Future*, was surprisingly similar to the *Immediate Programme* of 1937. The nationalisation of steel was the sole addition to the public ownership list. This factor above all illustrated the extent to which the leadership was in control of the Party's policy,[83] as well as the fact that the policies advanced during the 1930s were still considered to be sufficient to lay the foundations of the 'Socialist Commonwealth'. During the war, governmental responsibility for managing the economy, maintaining full employment and providing social services became the norm, so that Labour's 1945 proposals did not appear as threatening to the vested interests as they did during the mid-1930s. Also, the collectivism of wartime and influence of J. M. Keynes and William Beveridge were in part responsible for this.

The main problem facing the Labour Party after the war and in particular after 1951, was where to go to next. The Attlee Government nationalised the Bank of England, the coal-mines, gas and electricity, the railways, iron and steel and sections of civil aviation and road transport. There was a national health service, a unified system of health and unemployment insurance, and the reform of the educational system was well under way by the time Labour left office. There was more governmental control over the economy, and the redistributive taxation system which was strengthened during the war had been extended. The issues that confronted Party members and supporters throughout the next decade revolved around these related questions: to what extent had capitalism been transformed, and how far ought the Party to go towards accepting that a transformation had taken place, and adapt its policies accordingly?

The portrayal of the ideological division in the Party during the 1950s as being between the 'revisionist' Gaitskellites on the one side and the 'fundamentalist' Bevanites on the other is an over-simplification. It implies that the Party divided neatly into Left–Right categories on most major issues, which was not the case. It is necessary to assert that 'revisionism' was always a force in Labour politics. The very nature of the Party demanded that it adapted to different conditions, and in the process diluted its socialism in order to accommodate the machinations of the political system, and a variety of economic circumstances. It was almost inevitable that once Labour's basic or primary objectives were realised, that a section of the Party would want to change direction, or question the value of sacred assumptions. What was significant was that the challenge to certain components of the mainstream ideology came from the Right, not the Left; from an influential section of the leadership, not the rank-and-file. This was not unexpected, as the rising leaders such as Hugh Gaitskell, Roy Jenkins, Anthony Crosland and Douglas Jay were influenced by the people they were gradually replacing; Attlee, Dalton and Morrison. Most were Oxford educated, well-versed in 'PPE', middle-class and Keynesians.

The Keep Left movement of the late 1940s was the first organised attempt on the part of the Left and centre-Left to influence a change in the policies of the leadership. In particular, the Keep Left group tried to persuade the leaders, and Foreign Secretary Bevin specifically, to pursue an independent international role for Britain.[84] The challenge of the Left was unsuccessful, if measured against the adoption of the insipid programme *Labour Believes in Britain* (1949), which was particularly non-committal on nationalisation. However, the potential for division in the Party and the prospect of the development of a large and rebellious Leftist force was signalled by the resignation of three Ministers from Attlee's second administration. Bevan, John Freeman and Harold Wilson resigned over Gaitskell's imposition of charges for teeth and spectacles in 1951, a factor which in itself illustrated that the party leaders were sacrificing basic principles, and that to be 'Left' in this context meant little. This identified Bevan as the unequivocal leader of the Left, and Wilson as 'of the Left'.

The observation most central to 'revisionism' was that as a result of the Second World War and the implementation of the Party's 1945 Programme, the structure of capitalist society and nature of capitalism had changed. In *The Transition from Capitalism*,[85] Anthony Crosland asserted that if by capitalism was meant an advanced industrial society in which privately owned concerns operated with little governmental interference, then capitalism had been transformed since 1945.[86] There were, according to Crosland, eight essential features of this 'new society' which distinguished it from the traditional conception of a capitalist society. Individual property rights no longer constituted the basis of economic and social power; power previously wielded by property owners had passed largely into the hands of managers; the power of the State had increased enormously; there existed a comprehensive range of social services; a high level of employment had resulted from the comprehension of Keynesian techniques; there was an upward trend in the standard of living; the class structure was more diversified than ever; ideologically, the dominant emphasis had ceased to be on property rights.[87] Not only had capitalism changed, claimed Crosland, but the Labour Party had failed to realise it. Labour, he argued, should now place more emphasis upon the classless society and equality as objectives, and reject the widely-held notions about the need to pursue certain policies which consituted the 'essence of good socialism'.[88] This questioning of the relevance of nationalisation as an at-all-costs priority was shared by Roy Jenkins,[89] R. H. Tawney,[90] and John Strachey,[91] who within a period of ten years had swung from Marxist intellectual to 'revisionist' exponent. All maintained that capitalism had changed, and that Labour should revise its policies towards creating equality, not through nationalisation for its own sake, but through the redistribution of wealth, and in the case of Jenkins[92] and Austen Albu[93] through more direct worker participation in the running of industry.

Aneurin Bevan's *In Place of Fear* (1952) challenged the view that post-1945 developments were significant enough to induce a revision of Labour's more traditional objectives. He argued that whilst the changes had benefited everyone (although not working-class people in particular), the basic class and power structure of Britain had hardly been touched. Even though there was more State intervention, the main problem still related to the unwillingness of private enterprise to concede that the disposal of the economic surplus was a function that should belong to collective (public) action.[94] Public expenditure, for example, was still regarded as an infringement of private, and individual commercialism still conflicted with collective social values. The attitudes that capitalism generated, he maintained, were still the same.[95] He believed that democratic socialism was much more than merely a middle-way between capitalism and communism, because the consideration of principle with respect to modern conditions was an important feature of democratic socialism, which should be the determining factor in all policy-making.[96] If the Party had made a mistake, then it was in compromising by asserting that public ownership was a major, but not the only step in the direction of securing public control and industrial democracy.[97]

An important contribution to the debate about democratic socialism was Richard Crossman's *Towards a New Philosophy of Socialism*, in which he stated that following the achievement of the limited objectives of 1945 there had been a loss of momentum in British socialism. Labour wasn't sure of its future course.[98] He believed that a number of questions which were being avoided must be faced. What, for example, was socialist about free dentures if people still had to pay for travel, and was the centralised public corporation a more socialist method of running a nationalised industry than municipal or co-operative ownership?[99] Labour had 'capsulated its theory into a number of measures'. By this he implied that at one time there had been a theory to which policy conformed, rather than vice-versa. This supported his claim that the absence of a theoretical base for practical programmes was one reason why the 1945–51 Labour Government 'marked the end of a century of social reform and not, as its socialist supporters had hoped, the beginning of a new epoch'.[100]

Crosland's *The Future of Socialism* (1956) encapsulated 'revisionism'. In addition to re-stating that to refer to capitalism was misleading, Crosland developed the increasingly popular view on Labour's Right wing that the 'ownership of the means of production' was becoming a more irrelevant issue.[101] In his view, there were two principal sources of inspiration in British socialism. The first was ethical and was based on the principle of equality. The second was practical, and was founded upon a basic antagonism towards capitalism and the evils it engendered. In view of the recent past, a high proportion of practical objectives were now obsolete. However, socialists were paying too little attention, in his view, to equality.[102] In order to achieve a situation of equality, socialists should be concerned with utilising public expenditure to alleviate social inequities, and obtain social equality through the redistribution of rewards, equal opportunities and equality of status, to ensure social justice.[103] Labour's priorities should be comprehensive education, higher personal consumption, an increase in the ratio of public to private property, the reform of the taxation system which would include a direct property tax, the taxation of capital gains and a heavier discrimination against unearned, compared with earned, incomes.[104] There should be changes in the structure of industry, with more worker participation and joint consultation.[105] Public ownership should be more cautious and selective. There should be heavy taxation to limit profits and dividends, and planning to ensure high investment.[106]

The importance of *The Future of Socialism* was that it re-stated that equality was the over-riding socialist objective, but emphasised that its attainment should not be governed by whether or not the means of production were publicly owned, but by the promotion of economic growth by the expansion of the social and productive elements of the public sector, and the regulation of the private. Revisionism accepted the existence of the Welfare State and State-managed economy as the structure through which future Labour Governments would be implementing their programmes. The Party, they believed, must adapt its policies to this reality which it had helped to create. Apart from this, many of the objectives of revisionism were also held by the Left. Both favoured heavier direct taxation on wealth, increased public expenditure, the reform of the education system, the abolition of poverty and the creation of some form of industrial democracy. The difference lay in their respective interpretations of changes that had taken place in the distribution of industrial and economic power. The Right believed that the balance of power had shifted from the private to the public sufficiently to place less emphasis upon public ownership for its own sake. The Left argued that the so-called 'managerial revolution' and State intervention of the post-war years indicated that capitalism had merely changed its clothes.

Labour's defeat at the 1959 General Election was the precursor to a short period of paranoia, during which the conflict between revisionism and mainstream traditionalism reached its peak. The Right maintained that defeat was the consequence of the out-dated, working-class image of the Party[107] and too much emphasis on public ownership. The spectacle of the Leader of the Labour Party discounting the possibility of the Party changing its name or breaking with the unions at the Labour Party Conference of 1959 illustrated graphically this self doubt in the Party's strategy and ability by members of the Right wing and leadership.[108] Of more immediate impact were Gaitskell's remarks about the need to reform Clause Four of the Party's Constitution, on the grounds that it was inadequate as a statement of the Party's objectives, because it implied that public ownership was an end, instead of a means to an end.[109] He failed to realise, or chose not to demonstrate, that both means and ends display values.

The suggested revision of the 'socialist' clause was a direct challenge to the Left by the Right, and represented a lack of faith in the Party's fundamental constitutional objective. In any case, moves to amend Clause Four were unnecessary, in view of the fact that Party Conference resolutions and policy documents of the 1950s, if not revisionist, had certainly relegated nationalisation in importance if compared with the situation in the 1930s. Gaitskell was obliged to drop his pursuit of constitutional revision in view of the likely combination of trade union and constituency opposition at the 1960 Annual Conference. In view of the fact that Clause Four was guaranteed to remain unamended, but to all intents and purposes obsolete, Richard Crossman called for a new approach to public ownership, which decentralised its oligarchical tendencies and credence, to the democratic control of industry.[110] He pointed out that revisionism had reflected Britain's political mood over the last eight years, but questioned its adequacy as a socialist philosophy for the next decade, as a more vigorous socialist opposition would have more influence upon the electorate.[111]

The defeat of the leadership's defence policy at the 1960 Conference and its reversal the following year, and the establishment of the Campaign for Democratic Socialism[112] as an identifiable Rightist, pro-Gaitskell caucus in the Party marked the end of ten years of sporadically bitter intra-Party conflict. In 1961, a new policy-statement, *Signposts For The Sixties*, reflected and to some extent introduced a new image and purpose. Its tone was modernist, non-rhetorical and conciliatory. It contained the following statement:

We live in a Scientific revolution. In the sixteen years since the war ended, man's knowledge and his power over nature – to create or to destroy – have grown more than in the previous century.[113]

This essentially neutral, 'scientific' interpretation of change was supported by policy proposals which contained revisionist as well as more traditional objectives. The domestic needs to be catered to were planning and economic expansion, the use of land, a new approach to social security, equality of educational opportunity and fair taxation. It recommended the establishment of a National Industrial Planning Board to plan industrial development and investment, and a Land Commission to plan and control the use of land. This corresponded to the pre-war proposals to set up a National Investment Board and a Land Commission. The education system was to be expanded and re-organised. In industry, iron and steel would be re-nationalised, otherwise forms of public ownership would 'vary widely'.[114]

With the death of Gaitskell and accession of Wilson, Labour passed from an era of ideological conflict to one of pragmatism and compromise. Wilson's tone was Leftist, yet he was really of the centre, a distinct advantage in winning support from the Left and trade union leaders. At the 1963 Annual Conference, he expanded the 'technological revolution' theme. In his view, the increase in automation had 'put the whole argument about industry and economics and socialism into a new perspective'. He continued:

The problem is this. Since technological progress left to the mechanism of private industry and private property can lead only to high profits for a few, a high rate of employment for a few, and to mass redundancies for the many, if there has never been a case for socialism before, automation would have created it. Because only if technological progress becomes part of our national planning can that progress be directed to national ends.[115]

The key to socialist advancement and technological progress was education, but the scientific revolution would not become a reality unless people were prepared to change their social and economic attitudes. This would permeate the whole of society.[116]

As far as ideology and policy were concerned, the Right/Left division of the 1950s and early 1960s did not lead to a marked change in direction. The Party that Wilson inherited in 1963 was really no more or less revisionist or fundamentalist than it had been during the 1940s and 1950s. The importance of the conflict was that it made the mainstream ideology more difficult to identify during the 1950s. It is important to question the extent to which the Left was more Left than it was before, and whether the Right was more Right. Whilst revisionism challenged the relevance of traditional objectives, this was by no means a deviation from a particular Labourite form of democratic socialism. It was in accord with it. The Left appeared to be stronger than it actually was, partly because in Bevan it had a leader of stature, but also because the issues that were raised had more impact on the centre. This led to a greater identification with the Party's Left wing, without strengthening it greatly in any long-term sense.

This tends to be supported by the Party's policy objectives during the late 1950s and early 1960s, as well as the actual experience of the Wilson governments. The election manifestos of 1959 and 1964, as well as *Signposts For The Sixties* placed relatively little emphasis on nationalisation, between them only advocating the public ownership of the water supply industry[117] and the re-nationalisation of steel and road haulage.[118] The 1964 manifesto regarded the nationalised industries as being vital to Labour's National Plan.[119] Wilson's governments of 1964–70 contained many Gaitskellites, including George Brown, Denis Healey, Douglas Jay, Anthony Crosland and Roy Jenkins. Richard Crossman and Barbara Castle of the old Centre-Left and Left respectively were notable exceptions. There was relatively little ideological debate during the 1960s, partly because many of the 'theorists' were too preoccupied with governmental business, but also because the Left had been appeased by the promise of what was to come, or discovered that it had little fire and too few able politicians to permeate the pragmatism of Labour policy. Opposition to the Vietnam War and *In Place of Strife* revitalised the Left towards the end of the decade. Throughout, the Tribune Group demanded defence cuts, more public expenditure on social services and further nationalisation measures, traditional demands when Labour is out of office, even on the part of the leaders.

Only Anthony Wedgwood Benn emerged as a thinker of some foresight and influence during the 1960s and early 1970s. In *The New Politics* (1970) he argued for a reconnaisance of various issues arising from the industrial and technical changes of the 1960s.[120] Benn maintained that the result of applying technology to society had not created the sort of society that Harold Wilson had envisaged, because the institutions had not adapted to the new conceptions of change.[121] In fact, people had less control over their lives than before, due to the proliferation and dominance of multi-national corporations and the increased centralisation of control and production in business, industry, the militia and growth of government.[122] He called for worker control over their produce, and direct action against bureaucracy and a move towards more open government. He claimed that one reason why Labour lost the 1970 General Election was because it failed to emphasise the need for greater equality, industrial democracy, the ending of privilege and an increase in public expenditure.[123]

Opposition gave the Party time to re-think policy and in particular to concentrate upon issues like industrial democracy, and the public accountability of industries. These traditional objectives had been neglected during the Party's period in power. The outcome was *Labour's Programme* (1973),[124] the most socialistic policy document since *For Socialism And Peace*. 'We are a democratic socialist Party and proud of it', the Programme proclaimed, and restated Labour's socialist objectives as: a fundamental shift in the balance of power and wealth in favour of working people and their families; to make power fully accountable to the community; to eliminate poverty; to achieve greater economic equality; to increase social equality by a substantial shift in the emphasis put on job creation, housing, education and social benefits; to improve the environment. The most radical proposals were for the nationalisation of North Sea Oil, shipbuilding, financial institutions and the docks. Industrial democracy would be extended, and a 'social contract' between the workers in industry and a Labour Government would be formed. Labour would set up a National Enterprise Board, which would have the functions of job creation, investment promotion, technological development, the growth of exports, the promotion of Government price policies, tackling the spread of multi-nationals, industrial democracy and import substitutions.[125] The view that an organisation like the National Enterprise Board was required to control the development of British industry in the public interest was a reflection of the belief that the so-called 'mixed economy' of the post-war years wasn't really a fair mix, since the State had assisted capitalism by undertaking the unprofitable infrastructure of the economy, which had provided a base for private profit-making.[126] Labour's February 1974 manifesto reflected the approach of the 1973 Programme, calling for the public ownership of land required for development, ship-building, ship-repairing, marine engineering, ports, the manufacture of airframes and aeroengines. Labour would not confine the extension of the public sector to unprofitable concerns, but would take over the profitable sections or individual firms in vital industries to control prices, stimulate investment, boost exports and create and protect jobs.[127] The Party's 1976 Programme continued the Leftward trend.

References to capitalism in official programmes, and the recognition that the 'mixed' economy was dominated by the private sector, which for the most part was able to operate outside the boundary of what a Labour Government considered to be for the common good, heralded a more positive attitude on the part of the leadership to control the development of the British economy. This did not necessarily mean more socialist measures. In *Socialism Now*, Crosland claimed that there was no need for revisionists to revise their definition of socialism,[128] and argued as before that nationalisation would make little contribution to the objective of equality.[129] A contrasting view was that of Stuart Holland, who, in the most complete rejection of revisionism yet undertaken,[130] asserted that the conception of the mixed economy and indeed the basis of Keynesian economics and sovereignty of the capitalist nation State had been undermined by the proliferation of multinational corporations.[131] He contended that Labour's National Plan of the 1960s lacked the instruments for controlling expansion, and had to resort to fiscal measures to cut back expansion. It had also failed to control the strategic sectors of the economy, because of its inability to control the private sector:

It is on the key question of state power, and government control that the Crosland analysis has been proved wrong, and with it the 'revisionist' thesis of which he has remained the foremost advocate in post-war Britain[132]

He believed that Labour's Programme of 1973 and the manifestos of 1974 embodied a strategy which made a democratic transition to socialism in Britain possible.[133]

Looking back at Labour's programmes of 1934 and 1918, it could also be said that they too promised a great deal but delivered little. The policies which were 'forced' upon the Labour Government of 1974–79 marked a retreat from many of the most simple and fundamental objectives of democratic socialism. Cut-backs in proposed public expenditure in order to obtain a financial loan from the International Monetary Fund, high unemployment, a pact with the Liberal Party and restrictions on wage increases might have looked to an outsider like 1931 all over again. The leadership's justification was that the need to reduce inflation was vital if in the long term the social services were to be maintained, production and consumption were to increase and jobs were to be found. If the most that democratic socialism can ever achieve is to make life a little easier for the disinherited, then it should admit to its limitations. Are the hand and brain workers any closer to obtaining control over their produce in 1979 than they were 60 years ago? Is socialism any nearer now than it was in 1918? These and other questions can only be answered in the light of a clear conception of what a socialist society created by democratic socialist methods would look like. The essence of democratic socialism is that there is no such conception.

The Labour Party is a complex organism, comprising a number of ideological standpoints on the Left. Whilst there has been an identifiable mainstream democratic socialist ideology at least since 1918, there has never been uniformity about priorities or immediate strategy. The key word 'democratic' denotes that the supporters of the Party believe that unless, or possibly until, the conditions of life in an advanced capitalist society can no longer be sustained adequately, that physical, moral, social, intellectual, spiritual and environmental progress can be achieved in some measure through the existing constitutional means. They occupy the middle ground in British politics.

An important intra-Party issue is whether or not the difference between ideological perspectives displayed by the so-called Right and Left wings of the Party are more apparent than real. The mass media (with few exceptions) chooses to emphasise the rift between them. There are clearly differences. The Left sounds the more traditional socialist objectives of the Party, arguing that it is still the Party of the producer of wealth, fighting the privileged and economically powerful. Class identification and doctrine are still very relevant. The Right does not deny the importance of this broad line of approach, but maintains that existing economic conditions prevent rapid progress or the pursuit of policies which might be electorally unpopular. On the one hand it is contended that unless the Party is socialist now, prevailing conditions will not in any case change. On the other, that if only conditions were more favourable the Party could afford to be more socialistic. The Labour Party can afford to lose the ideologically confused and morally bankrupt to Conservatism, but it cannot afford to lose or fail to win the support of genuine socialists. Without its Left wing (and one must always be careful in the use of this term), the Party would flounder ideologically. It would lose sight of its 1918 objectives which to some are outdated or have been modified by changed circumstances, but to many have yet to be fulfilled. The mainstream ideology of the Party has so far accommodated both views, if at times uneasily.

Notes

1. R. Owen, *A New View of Society* (London) 1820.
2. M. Beer, *A History of British Socialism* Vol. II, G. Bell & Sons (London) 1919, p. 46.
3. R. Harrison, *Before the Socialists*, Routledge (London) 1965.
4. J. S. Mill, *Principles of Political Economy* (London) 1859, p. 140.
5. Named 'Fabian' after the Roman General Fabius Maximus, the 'Delayer'.
6. See T. H. Green, *Lectures on the Principles of Political Obligation* (London) 1874.
7. N. and J. MacKenzie, *The First Fabians*, Weidenfeld & Nicolson (London) 1977, p. 71.
8. G. B. Shaw (Ed.), *Fabian Essays in Socialism* (1889). The contributors were: G. B. Shaw, William Clarke, Sidney Olivier, Graham Wallas, Hubert Bland, Annie Besant and Sidney Webb.
9. S. Webb, *Socialism in England* (London) 1890, p. 48.
10. R. Blatchford, *Merrie England* (London) 1894.
11. Notably social insurance legislation, old-age pensions, the reversal of the Taff Vale judgment, the reform of the House of Lords.
12. F. W. S. Craig, *British General Election Manifestos 1900–1974*, Macmillan (London) 1975.
13. J. Ramsay MacDonald, *Socialism and Society*, Socialist Library (London) 1905, p. 36. For an excellent biographical study of MacDonald see D. Marquand *Ramsay MacDonald*, Cape (London) 1977.
14. Ramsay MacDonald, op.cit. (1905), p. 70.
15. Ibid., p. 82.
16. Ibid., p. 16.
17. Ibid., pp. 129–37.
18. Ibid., pp. 146–7.
19. M. Cole, 'Beatrice and Sidney Webb' in M. Katanka (Ed), *Radicals, Reformers and Socialists*, Charles Knight (London) 1973, p. 228. The author described how the Webbs in particular disliked the ILP of Ramsay MacDonald and Keir Hardie.
20. Ben Tillett, *Is the Parliamentary Labour Party a Failure?*, Twentieth Century Press (London) 1909, p. 11.
21. ILP, *Let Us Reform the Labour Party* ILP (London) 1910.
22. Keir Hardie, *My Confession of Faith in the Labour Alliance*, ILP (London) 1910, pp. 5–6.
23. Tom Mann was largely responsible for the founding of the Industrial Syndicalist Education League in 1910. Its aim was to bring trade unionists and syndicalist activists into contact. For an account of the syndicalist

28   *The Labour Party*

movement, see Bob Holton, *British Syndicalism 1900–1914*, Pluto Press (London) 1976.
24. Philip Snowden, *Socialism and Syndicalism*, Collins (London) 1913.
25. J. Ramsay MacDonald, *The Socialist Movement*, Williams & Norgate (London) 1911, p. 103.
26. Ibid., p. 105.
27. Ibid., p. 146.
28. G. Wallas, *The Great Society*, Macmillan (London) 1914, p. 327. He cited Owen, Blanc, Lasalle, Marx and Morris as having syndicalist ideas.
29. L. T. Hobhouse, *The Labour Movement*, Fisher Unwin (London) 1912, p. 5. This was a revised edition of his original 1893 publication.
30. J. M. Winter, *Socialism And The Challenge of War*, Routledge (London) 1974, p. 273.
31. The ILP leadership was opposed to the war. Henderson joined the Coalition Government in 1916.
32. J. M. Winter, op. cit., p. 270.
33. R. Miliband, *Parliamentary Socialism*, Merlin Press (London) 1961, pp. 61–2.
34. Labour Party, *Labour and The New Social Order*, Labour Party (London) 1918, p. 4.
35. Ibid., pp. 6–9.
36. Ibid., pp. 14–15.
37. Ibid., p. 18.
38. Ibid., p. 10.
39. Ibid., pp. 10–13.
40. Labour Party Constitution (1918). Clause IV, Sub Section 4. This is regarded as the 'socialist' Clause in the Constitution.
41. G. D. H. Cole, *The World of Labour*, G. Bell & Sons (London) 1917, p. 397.
42. Ibid., pp. 403–5.
43. G. D. H. Cole, *Self Government in Industry*, G. Bell & Sons (London) 1917, p. 17.
44. J. A. Hobson, *The Science of Wealth*, Williams & Norgate (London) 1911, pp. 1–7.
45. G. Wallas, op.cit., p. 316.
46. J. Ramsay MacDonald, *Parliament and Revolution*, National Labour Press (Manchester) 1919, pp. 11–12.
47. Ibid., pp. 76–7.
48. J. Ramsay MacDonald, *Parliament and Democracy*, Social Studies Press (London) 1921, pp. 35–7.
49. J. Ramsay MacDonald, *Parliament and Revolution*, op. cit., p. 92.
50. R. H. Tawney, *The Acquisitive Society*, G. Bell & Sons (London) 1921, pp. 33–4.
51. Ibid., p. 41.
52. Ibid., p. 45.
53. Ibid., p. 36.
54. Ibid., p. 97.
55. Ibid., p. 133.
56. Labour Party Annual Conference Report, 1923, p. 178.
57. Executive Committee of the Communist International, 'Moscow's Reply to the ILP'. Published by the 'Left-Wing Group' of the ILP (Glasgow) 1920.
58. See this chapter; account of *Socialism and Society*.
59. B. Barker, *Ramsay MacDonald's Political Writings*, Allen Lane (London) 1972, p. 10.

60. R. Miliband, op. cit., p. 183.
61. C. R. Attlee, *The Labour Party in Perspective*, Gollancz (London) 1937, p. 124.
62. H. Dalton, *Practical Socialism For Britain*, Routledge (London) 1935, p. 27.
63. H. Morrison, *An Easy Outline of Modern Socialism*, Labour Party (London) 1935, p. 4.
64. E. F. M. Durbin, *The Politics of Democratic Socialism*, Routledge (London) 1940, pp. 133–4.
65. Ibid., pp. 134–5.
66. Ibid., pp. 174–7.
67. 'Revisionism' is discussed later in this chapter.
68. The Socialist League was founded in 1932. It comprised leftist elements, including former members of the ILP who wanted to remain in the Labour Party. It was fairly successful at the Party's Annual Conferences, where it probed the leaders and pressed for more nationalisation measures to be included in the official policy documents. Harold Laski and Sir Stafford Cripps were amongst its most notable figures.
69. A United Front against Fascism was proposed by the ILP, Socialist League and Communist Party. Labour's National Executive Committee refused to commit the Party to such co-operation.
70. Sir Stafford Cripps, *Can Socialism Come by Constitutional Methods?*, (London) 1934, p. 4.
71. H. Laski, *The Crisis and the Constitution*, L. & V. Woolf, Fabian Society (London) 1932, pp. 8–9.
72. H. Laski, *The State in Theory and Practice*, Allen & Unwin (London) 1935.
73. See C. R. Attlee, *Labour's Aims* (London) 1937, p. 5.
H. Dalton, op. cit., pp. 246–7; Durbin, op. cit., p. 326.
74. H. Dalton, op. cit., p. 243.
75. G. D. H. Cole, *The Principles of Economic Planning*, Macmillan (London) 1935;
The Machinery of Socialist Planning, Hogarth Press (London) 1938;
Plan for Democratic Britain, Labour Book Service (London) 1939.
76. Labour Party, *For Socialism and Peace*, Labour Party (London) 1934, p. 15.
77. Labour Party, *Labour's Immediate Programme*, Labour Party (London) 1937, p. 2.
78. Ibid., pp. 3–4.
79. They were expelled for their open hostility to the leadership's attitude towards the United Front.
80. Beveridge called for a comprehensive unified system of health and unemployment insurance, a national health service and family allowances; Barlow recommended more governmental control of the location of industry; Uthwatt and Scott proposed increased State control over the use and development of land, in both urban and rural areas.
81. For an account of the work of the sub-committees of the Labour Party's Central Committee on Post-War Reconstruction Problems, see the author's Ph. D. thesis: 'War and the Development of Labour's Domestic Programme, 1939–45' (University of London, 1977). The best account of politics in war-time is Paul Addison's *The Road to 1945*, Cape (London) 1976.
82. See for example: Labour Party, *The War and After, Labour's Home Policy*, 1940; *Labour's Peace Aims*, 1940; *The Old World and The New Society*, 1942, all published by the Labour Party (London).

83. The Executive's defeat at the 1944 Annual Conference virtually committed the Party to extensive nationalisation. The ensuing manifesto did not.
84. Supporters of the so-called 'Third Force' included Richard Crossman, Ian Mikardo and Barbara Castle.
85. C. A. R. Crosland, 'The Transition from Capitalism', in R. H. S. Crossman (Ed.), *New Fabian Essays*, Turnstile Press (London) 1953.
86. Ibid., p. 23.
87. Ibid., pp. 38–40.
88. Ibid., pp. 61–3.
89. Roy Jenkins, 'Equality', in Crossman, op. cit., pp. 71–2.
90. R. H. Tawney, 'British Socialism Today', in *The Radical Tradition*, Allen & Unwin (London) 1964, pp. 170–5.
91. J. Strachey, 'Tasks and Achievements of British Labour', in R. H. S. Crossman (Ed.), op. cit., p. 182.
92. R. Jenkins, *The Pursuit of Progress*, Heinemann (London) 1953, pp. 171–3.
93. A. Albu, 'The Organisation of Industry', in R. H. S. Crossman (Ed.), op. cit., pp. 129–36.
94. A. Bevan, *In Place of Fear*, Heinemann (London) 1952, pp. 79–80.
95. Ibid., pp. 80–98.
96. Ibid., p. 124.
97. Ibid., pp. 125–28.
98. R. H. S. Crossman, 'Towards a New Philosophy of Socialism', in *Planning for Freedom*, Hamish Hamilton (London) 1965, p. 36. First published in *New Fabian Essays*, 1953.
99. Ibid., p. 37.
100. Ibid., p. 39.
101. C. A. R. Crosland, *The Future of Socialism*, Cape (London) 1956, p. 69.
102. Ibid., pp. 90–9.
103. Ibid., pp. 112–13.
104. Ibid., pp. 258–320.
105. Ibid., pp. 339–48.
106. Ibid., p. 511.
107. S. Haseler, *The Gaitskellites*, Macmillan (London) 1969, p. 163.
108. Labour Party Annual Conference Report, 1959, p. 85.
109. Ibid., pp. 111–12.
110. R. H. S. Crossman, 'The Clause Four Controversy' (1960), in *Planning For Freedom*, op. cit., p. 115.
111. Ibid., p. 117.
112. For an account of the activities of the C. D. S., see S. Haseler, op. cit., pp. 209–36.
113. Labour Party, *Signposts For The Sixties*, Labour Party (London) 1961, p. 7.
114. Ibid., p. 18.
115. Labour Party Annual Conference Report, 1963, p. 135.
116. Ibid., p. 140.
117. Labour Party, 'Let's Go With Labour for the New Britain', in F. W. S. Craig, op. cit., p. 255.
118. These were included in 1959 and 1964.
119. See D. Steel's section on Labour in Office, 1964–70, pp. 134–9.
120. A. Wedgwood Benn, *The New Politics*, Fabian Society (London) 1970, p. 1.
121. Ibid., pp. 1–3.
122. Ibid., pp. 4–5.
123. Ibid., pp. 16–28.

124. Labour Party, *Labour's Programme 1973*, Labour Party (London) 1973, p. 7.
125. Ibid., p. 33.
126. Ibid., p. 31.
127. Labour Party, 'Let Us Work Together – Labour's Way Out of the Crisis', in F. W. S. Craig, op. cit., pp. 402–3.
128. C. A. R. Crosland, *Socialism Now*, Cape (London) 1974, p. 15.
129. Ibid., pp. 35–7.
130. S. Holland, *The Socialist Challenge*, Quartet (London) 1975.
131. Ibid., p. 99.
132. Ibid., p. 26.
133. Ibid., pp. 9–10.

Chapter 2

Party organisation

Iain McLean

The history of any political party can tell us a great deal about the reasons for its internal structure. All modern mass parties are superficially similar. They have large numbers of individual paid-up members all over the country, whose main job is to help their party win elections by paying money to campaign funds and by helping to canvass voters and bring them to the polls. Party members normally also have a role in two other activities: formulating the Party's policies and selecting its candidates for public office. But this is where the historical differences loom largest. Relations between individual party members, policy-formers and public representatives vary enormously according to whether the party grew from 'the top down' or 'the bottom up': whether it started as a group of M.P.s who created a supporting organisation for themselves or as a group of like-minded people who created an organisation to elect M.P.s sympathetic to themselves.

The Northumberland Voters' Association is a good example of a 'top down' party.[1] Traditionally, councillors were elected to Northumberland County Council without Party labels or organisation: usually they would be 'local notables' from a village in their electoral division. Then, after the First World War, a Labour Party organisation appeared in the coalfield, and a disciplined Labour group emerged on the County Council. In reaction to this, most of the existing councillors formed a 'non-political' grouping to retain control of the County Council. As if to emphasise that they thought that they were not a political party, they made no efforts to recruit members or discuss policy outside the council chamber. When the wife of one of the councillors was mistakenly asked for a subscription she became the only voter ever to join the Northumberland Voters' Association.

This sort of party is commoner than students often realise. In Britain there were examples in, for instance, Edinburgh, Glasgow, Bristol and South Shields. In France, the Radical Party, which was at the heart of the Third and Fourth Republics, and was therefore in government for most of the period from 1871 to 1958, was almost as purely a 'top-down' party as these local government examples. You did not become an important local figure because you were an M.P.; you became an M.P. because you were an important local figure. So Radical M.P.s would not have taken kindly to candidate-selection meetings or policy-making conferences.

The 'bottom-up' party is easier to understand. The National Front is a 'bottom-up' party; so is the Workers' Revolutionary Party. Both want to get their way by (among other things) electing M.P.s. So they recruit members whose subscriptions and door-knocking energies are applied to putting up parliamentary candidates (though of course both money and energy are applied to many other activities as well). And they hold annual conferences at which the membership (at least nominally) determines the policy of the Party.

Neither the Conservative nor the Labour Party is a pure example of either type. But if we remember that the Conservatives are *essentially* a 'top-down' party and Labour is *essentially* a 'bottom-up' party, we can explain most of the differences between their internal arrangements at a stroke. In 1867 the franchise was extended so that for the first time a substantial part of the working class had the vote. Conservative M.P.s immediately set up the National Union of Conservative and Unionist Associations to help make sure that as many of the new voters as possible had the Tory message put in front of them and were chivvied to the polling stations by local Conservatives. There was no suggestion that the new body would be responsible for either selecting candidates or deciding party policy: it was to be a handmaid to the party', not a body to 'usurp the functions of party leadership'. A later Conservative leader, A. J. Balfour, allegedly once said that he would 'as soon take advice from his valet' as consult the National Union.[2] Before long, some scholars were alarmed that the National Union and its Liberal counterpart had become constitutional monsters which were wresting policy decisions from Parliament and the people.[3] They were wrong. No Conservative leader has ever accepted that the Party organisation outside Parliament has any right to decide Party policy, although it is true that the extra-parliamentary Party does have almost complete autonomy in selecting Conservative candidates for Parliament and local government.

The Labour Party was quite different. It began life as the Labour Representation Committee, whose purpose was defined clearly in the resolution calling its first conference: 'to devise ways and means for securing the return of an increased number of labour members to the next Parliament'.[4] The wording captured the changing mood of trade unionists in 1900. Seven years earlier, Keir Hardie had founded the Independent Labour Party as a vehicle to elect socialist M.P.s to Parliament. It got little trade union support and failed all round in the 1895 General Election. Most trade union leaders thought that industrial and social welfare was a matter for collective bargaining, not legislation. If miners wanted an eight-hour day, they should negotiate for it with their employers, not try to get it through Act of Parliament. This view appealed to the dominant groups in the TUC – the miners, the textile workers and the engineers. But their complacency was shaken by the failure of strikes involving two of the strongest unions – the engineers and the South Wales miners – in 1897 and 1898. At the same time, various court judgments were depriving trade unions of some of the civil rights and privileges they thought they had.

These events led several trade union leaders to change their minds about Hardie and the ILP, and to swing round in support of the Labour Representation Committee, whose foundation conference was in February 1900. The title was significant. It was not a socialist party; it was certainly not socialist, and by no means everyone present was even convinced that it ought to be a Party.

It was not a 'bottom-up' Party in the pure sense, because it was an indirect body: a pressure-group set up for the specific function of electing 'labour' – i.e. working-class – M.P.s. You could not join the Labour Representation Committee; you could only join a body which sent delegates to it, such as your trade union or the ILP. This was a favourite format for trade union-dominated pressure groups. If union members wanted to do something that was outside their union's terms of reference, they would set up a committee to do the job, and invite affiliations from other unions. Thus most of the trade unionists in the Memorial Hall, London, on 27 February 1900 envisaged a single-issue pressure group with indirect membership and (maybe) a relatively short life, such as the Labour Electoral Association of the 1880s.

The ILP had other ideas. For a start, it was a socialist Party; secondly, its 'labourism' – its commitment to a disciplined *party* of working class M.P.s – was much more thorough-going than the trade unions'. But the ILP tacticians, Hardie and Ramsay MacDonald, approached the 1900 conference very warily. They knew they could not afford to alienate the trade unions who had far more money to sponsor parliamentary candidates than the ILP could ever have. Therefore Hardie squashed the idea of the ILP proposing a socialist programme for the new committee. He did, however, get it to agree that it would campaign for 'a distinct Labour Group in Parliament, who shall have their own whips, and agree upon their policy'. The ILP also got a representation on the committee out of all proportion to its membership or financial contribution, and had its best organiser, Ramsay MacDonald, unanimously appointed secretary to the new body.

There was nothing inevitable about the rise of the Labour Party. These manoeuvres around an unimportant committee in 1900 mattered only in retrospect. Only the Taff Vale affair and the Gladstone–MacDonald pact, described in other chapters of this book, saved the Labour Representation Committee from dying in the obscurity in which it had been born. But by 1906 the Committee, now renamed the Labour Party, had got its 'distinct Labour Group in Parliament'. The Party constitution, conceived as a compromise between weak socialists and indifferent trade unionists, became, and has remained, an important feature of British politics. Like the American Constitution, the Labour Party Constitution was as important for what it did not say as for what it did say. The silence of the Party Constitution on the relationship between M.P.s and the Party's policy-forming bodies was as eloquent as the unspoken questions of 1787 (such as whether a State could secede from the Union). The next three sections of this chapter will examine the evolution of the 1900 Constitution in each of the three essential areas of activity: mass membership; candidate selection; and policy formation.

Mass membership

In the beginning, the LRC was scarcely a Party at all; political activists could support it only indirectly through the ILP. And the ILP was, of course, a puny organisation compared to the National Liberal Federation and the National Union of Conservative and Unionist Associations. In 1906, for instance, it affiliated to the LRC on a nominal membership of 16,000, which was almost certainly much higher than the true figure.[5] Furthermore, it lost its marked over-representation on the executive of the LRC in 1903. At *constituency* level, individual activists were vital; many constituencies or towns had local Labour Represent- ation Committees, active ILP branches or other, more informal, groupings of labourists and socialists whose money and canvassing support were essential if any serious campaign was to be run. The early leaders of the Labour Party often regarded the presence or absence of a strong local Party as the single most important factor in helping them to decide whether or not to contest a seat; it was particularly crucial at by- elections. But these groups never coalesced into a *national* Party before 1918. The ILP could never become a truly national Party. There were many reasons for this. Its socialism never really appealed to trade union leaders of the day. Parts of the country where working-class politics was mostly channelled into local union branches (Co. Durham and South Wales for instance) were much weaker in ILP membership than in Labour support at the polls. Furthermore, the ILP was identified with the evangelistic, religious nonconformist approach to socialism both in doctrine and in style. Philip Snowden's impassioned appeals for socialism to the workers of the West Riding were half-jokingly called 'Philip's Come to Jesus'.[6] This was all very well in Wesleyan Bradford or Presbyterian Glasgow; it cut no ice in Anglican Lancashire or in godless London, or among Catholics anywhere. Only with the introduction of individual direct membership, in 1918, could the Labour Party become any sort of nationwide mass movement. Direct membership confirmed the long decline of the ILP; but it gave the Labour Party its modern shape.

The membership statistics which the party prints every year in the Conference Report are familiar, and so are many of the difficulties in interpreting them. Total membership of the Party rose from 375,931 in 1900 to a peak of 6,498,027 in 1954 and has now declined slightly to hover around the 6 million mark. But the vast majority of these people are trade unionists who are Party members by virtue of their union's affiliation. In the beginning, unions simply based their affiliation fee to the LRC on their membership, or a proportion of it arbitrarily decided by themselves. But in 1909 a Liberal trade unionist called W. V. Osborne successfully obtained a judgement that compulsory levies on union members to support the Labour Party were illegal. The effect of this was reversed by the Trade Union Act of 1913, which allowed unions to set up political funds on condition that they were kept separate from general funds and that members who wanted to could contract out of the political levy. After the General Strike, the Conservatives changed the rule to 'contracting-in' in 1927; Labour changed it back to 'contracting-out' in 1946. The aftermath of both of these changes shows that inertia not conviction makes many trade unionists into Labour Party members. Between 1927 and 1928 affiliated membership of the party dropped from 3.2 million to 2.0 million. Between 1946 and 1947 it rose from 2.6 million to 4.4 million. These two quantum leaps can have only one interpretation. If any more evidence is needed, it is that a recent survey of members of the Union of Post Office Workers showed that only about half of those who were paying the political levy realised that they were doing so.[7]

Thus the only worthwhile index of the mass membership of the Labour Party is the list of individual members. The official statistics start in 1928 (before then, statistics would have been misleading in any case as many activists would still have joined the ILP rather than the Labour Party direct) at 215,000. The peak year was 1952, with just over a million members, since when there has been a steady decline to an official figure of between 600,000 and 700,000 in recent years. But this is a vast exaggeration, since constituency parties have since 1963 only been allowed to affiliate on a basis of at least 1,000 members; almost every constituency now affiliates on precisely 1,000, and their real membership is obviously far less. Just how much less is unclear, and commentators' guesses as to the real individual membership of the Labour Party are heavily influenced by the purpose of the axe they are grinding. One careful study distinguishes three levels of membership: the number recorded in the official statistics (almost always 1,000 per constituency), the number in the local records and the number who both believe themselves to be and actually are paid-up members.[8] The last of these is of course the smallest but the truest category of 'Labour Party members'. Their numbers have been shown in various constituencies to vary from about 600 to as low as 50, with the lowest numbers to be found in safe Labour seats in big cities. There is no guarantee that the constituencies examined are representative of the country as a whole, and therefore the often-quoted extrapolation from figures like these to a true figure of 150,000 to 200,000 Labour Party members may be wildly inaccurate. However, in the absence of further information it will have to do.

This information is often discussed by Labour supporters in an atmosphere of deep gloom. The percentage of members to voters in the British Labour Party is far lower than in any other European social democratic party. The Labour Party's paid-up membership is about 6 per cent of its parliamentary vote. (But suppose a researcher found out that the Workers' Revolutionary Party had 50 per cent as many members as it ever got parliamentary votes. Would that make it eight times healthier than the Labour Party?) The steady decline in the number of paid agents has also often been noticed. In 1951, when the Party bureaucracy had already been attacked by Harold Wilson as a 'penny-farthing machine in a jet age', there were 296 constituency full-time agents. There are now less than 100.

Why has membership, and with it, the resources available to pay a Party bureaucracy, declined? There are many explanations, and the most complete as well as the most frequently heard is the more or less Marxist view that membership has declined because Labour govern-ments have not satisfied, and cannot satisfy, their working-class supporters. If capitalism is doomed, then a Party which tries to work for the working class within the capitalist system is bound to fail. More specifically, it is argued that the working classes have ceased to be active supporters of the Party, and that in the ensuing middle-class takeover the Party has lost its original radicalism.[9]

There are some quite good arguments for the Hindess thesis but not many of them are used by Hindess. He established that the ward Labour parties he studied in Liverpool are dominated by small middle-class groups but not that they have usurped a mass working-class movement, nor that their takeover has shifted the Party to the Right. Furthermore, Hindess and other Marxist writers presume that the Labour Party was once socialist but no longer is. If this presumption is false, then not only are their explanations weak but it is not clear whether there is anything to be explained.

The most dubious factual part of the argument is that Labour grass-roots activists have moved to the Right. There could hardly be a worse place than Liverpool to try to establish such a claim, as it is only in the last 20 years that the power of an extremely Right-wing, Catholic *and working-class* caucus has been broken in Labour politics in that city.[10] In Liverpool, a middle-class takeover could hardly fail to move the party to the *Left*, not the Right. Most of the evidence shows that Labour Party activists are more middle-class than they used to be – although the 'embourgeoisement' of party activists should not be exaggerated: many of them always were middle-class. However, grass-roots opinion has moved not Right but Left. There are both empirical and *a priori* reasons for expecting it to be always to the Left of the opinions of both the Party leadership and the Labour-voting electorate. This is a point which will be examined later in this chapter.[11]

Though mass membership of the Labour Party (and the Conservative Party as well) has undoubtedly declined, it is probably still comparable with its level at any time until the late 1930s. So perhaps it is not the abnormally low membership now that needs explaining but the abnormally high membership for a few years between 1947 and 1954. We might, then, interpret the membership statistics as follows. From the beginning of individual membership in 1918 until the 1945 Labour Government, Labour was breaking out of its regional, religious and occupational heartlands to become a truly nationwide class Party. The effect of this on membership statistics was accentuated by two things: the well-known collapse of the ILP, and the success of a body called the Constituency Parties Movement, which had been totally forgotten until it was recently resurrected by Ben Pimlott.[12] The ILP's membership was steadily falling from 1918 to 1932, when its leaders took the suicidal decision of disaffiliating from the Labour Party. This pushed most of its remaining members into direct membership of the Labour Party.

The Constituency Parties Movement arose out of individual members' discontent at the way the NEC was elected. Up to 1937 candidates for Party office were voted on by the whole Annual Conference. But since trade union block votes comprised up to 90 per cent of the votes available, they could if they wished dictate the entire membership of the Executive. In 1937 the rules were changed. Elections to the NEC are now split into constituencies so that 12 members are elected only by the trade unions, seven only by constituency parties and one by socialist societies. There are also a Party treasurer and five women members of the Executive (a piece of 'tokenism' that the Women's Movement has not yet eradicated) elected by the whole conference and thus, in effect, by the trade unions.

Encouraged by these improved conditions, the growth of individual membership continued between the wars. The process was never completed, and in the last ten years it has gone into reverse, but class–Party correlations were highest in the 1945, 1950 and 1951 General Elections. As old rural–urban, Protestant–Catholic and centre-periphery divisions faded away[13] so the appeal of Labour to rural workers, London workers and Catholic labourers differed less and less from its appeal to Methodist millwrights in Brighouse, hence a steady rise in individual membership to its 1952 peak. The rise may have been speeded by the intense popular interest in current affairs during the Second World War, typified (but exaggerated) by the Army Bureau of Current Affairs.[14] The downhill slide that followed resulted from changes in society, not changes in politics. Except for a few intense partisans, Party activism has never been an exciting end in itself – membership was much more a matter of expressing community or class feeling and arranging social activities among like-minded people. On the British Left, this point was grasped brilliantly in the 1890s by the wayward publicist Robert Blatchford. Blatchford founded a Clarion Fellowship and a Clarion Cycling Club which were much more enduring and more influential than any political organisation he ever ran. The early ILP ran rambling clubs, choirs and drama groups (the Glasgow Orpheus Choir and the Newcastle People's Theatre are two well-known examples that outlived their environments). As one might expect, the German and Austrian Social Democratic parties had a much more thorough structure of allied fringe groups, so that one could live one's whole social life among socialist singers and socialist stamp collectors without being infected by bourgeois ideology.

But the environment that spanned these organisations is dead. People no longer live in such close-knit, economically homogeneous communities as they once did. Nowadays, close-knit communities – like Caernarvon – are not one-class, and one-class communities – like Dagenham – are not close-knit. Durham and South Wales mining villages are survivors of the old working-class communities but even they are breaking up with the decline of coal. The Durham Miners Gala – the 'Big Meeting' on the third Saturday of July – is Britain's last remaining genuinely working-class political festival, and it is a ghost of what it was.

There are many reasons for changes like these. Three obvious ones are television, contraception and automation (with its accompanying decline in traditional 'blue-collar' working-class jobs). Much of the decline of Labour Party membership can be put down to the death of the sort of society which made people want to join the Clarion Cycling Club.

All this said, there remains an irreducible kernel of truth in the Marxist argument about the reasons for decline in the mass membership of the Labour Party. Party members *are* more militant than their leaders; they *have* been consistently disappointed and have seen their policies consistently rejected by the leadership. There are, as we shall see, good theoretical reasons for expecting this to be a continuing fact of life. It follows that the prognosis for the health of the mass membership is very poor. This also entails a bleak future for the Party 'machine' manned by full-time Party employees. About 80 per cent of the central funds and half of the local funds of the Labour Party are provided by trade unions, but their contribution has declined in real terms with inflation – fundamentally because they have not been prepared to let their membership subscriptions rise in money terms enough to remain constant in real terms. And the rest of the Party's funds – those provided by individual members – have been even more vulnerable. Does this not cripple the Labour Party as a vote-winning organisation?

Not necessarily. Many of the Party agents who have now disappeared spent most of their time arranging the non-political life of the Party, and in particular doing the fund-raising that provided their own salaries. The loss of such jobs is only a technical, not a real, decline in Party efficiency (and in GNP). It is also notorious that the degree of Party organisation seems to make very little difference to election results in marginal seats: when regional Party managers are asked immediately before an election to identify constituencies where their Party organisation is unusually good (or bad), the seats they pick out rarely deviate from the general trends.[15] Swing, like rain, falls indifferently on the just and the unjust.

But one traditional electioneering activity *does* matter. This is the organisation of the postal vote. The old, the sick, those who have recently moved and those whose jobs make it likely that they will be away on polling day are all entitled to postal votes. (Holidaymakers, though, are not, for no very obvious reason.) But the onus is on the individual to register himself for a postal vote. Left to themselves, very few people would bother to do so outside an election period, and when an election is called – the very time when the ordinary voter might suddenly realise that he ought to have a postal vote – it is too late to apply for one. Thus many, probably hundreds of thousands, of voters entitled to postal votes are disenfranchised because they fail to apply for them. Labour suffers more than the Conservatives from this for obvious reasons. Applying for a postal vote is the sort of bureaucratic procedure that comes more naturally to a retired stockbroker than to a retired miner's widow. Labour are more likely to be penalised than Conservatives by failing to claim their postal votes.

Voter registration was always the main task of Party machines when the onus was on the elector to put his own name down. The Victorian Liberal and Conservative parties spent huge sums of money registering their own supporters and challenging those of their opponents. In many parts of the United States the Republicans and Democrats still do. In Britain the onus of compiling the register was shifted to the State in the Representation of the People Act of 1918, and most of the occasion for the traditional sort of Party organisation disappeared – except for the registering of postal votes. Here the Conservatives have always compounded their natural advantage over Labour by having a richer and more efficient agency organisation. The Conservative agency service is declining as well as the Labour one; but there is no evidence that it is declining *faster*, so the Conservatives may expect to retain their relative advantage in the postal vote.

In most British General Election results there are about 12 or 15 Conservative marginals where the winning margin was less than the number of postal votes cast, and half a dozen where it was so small that the postal vote would have been decisive even if it was only 60 : 40 in favour of the Conservatives. This may not seem much, but a swing of six seats means a difference of 12 in the winning Party's lead: a swing which could make narrow results like 1951 and both 1974 elections look very different. In this area at least, the long steady decline of the Labour Party's organisation may prove important.

Candidate selection

A 'top-down' party like the French Radicals could never exercise much control over recruitment of new M.P.s because their election depended on their status as local notables and not on anything the party could do for them. In British national politics, the decline of the local notable began earlier, and the Liberal and Tory Party 'caucuses' spent a lot of time finding suitable candidates for seats, and (sometimes) suitable seats for candidates. This work was done on behalf of the Parliamentary Party – its purpose was to ensure that new M.P.s would be assets to the Party. There were frequent conflicts with constituency activists, who were more likely to be seduced by the man who offered to pay all his election expenses than by the next Prime Minister but three. But in the Conservative Party what central control there was, was (and still is) exercised by a committee controlled by Conservative M.P.s – now the Standing Advisory Committee on candidates. It was not primarily a job for the extra-parliamentary Party.

Because of its extra-parliamentary origins the Labour Party is again different. In the 1900 Constitution, and the practice of the early years, the responsibility for proposing Labour candidates lay primarily with local parties. But a parliamentary candidature could not go ahead unless it was approved by the National Executive. They had to bear in mind several factors: could the Party afford a contest? Was the proposed candidate acceptable? And, from 1903 to 1906, did the proposal violate the secret MacDonald–Gladstone pact with the Liberals, allowing each party a clear run in a number of seats? Without the MacDonald–Gladstone pact, the Labour Party would have got nowhere by 1914. The most important thing that either Hardie or MacDonald ever did for the Party was therefore to keep it a secret, as, if its existence had been admitted, it would have collapsed under pressure from Party militants in both parties.

Thus already in the first decade of the Labour Party there was tension between the grassroots and the leadership, tension which was pointed by the refusal of the Party to endorse Victor Grayson as a Labour candidate in the Colne Valley constituency in 1907. (He won, but lost in January 1910 to the leadership's barely disguised relief.) However, there was still a big difference from the Conservative position. The central control in the Labour Party was, and still is, *extra-Parliamentary* control. The ultimate arbiter of candidates' acceptability, and of overall electoral strategy, is the National Executive (NEC) and the Annual Conference. The leader and deputy leader of the Parliamentary Labour Party (PLP) are ex-officio members of the NEC, and some M.P.s are always elected members of it, but their power to take part in candidate selection derives from their status as NEC members, not as M.P.s.

The power to select, reselect and refuse to reselect is potentially very great. Since 1867, parliamentary electorates have been too big for a candidate to win purely through force of personality, social standing or bribery; electors have voted primarily for the Party, not the man, and therefore getting and keeping Party endorsement has been essential for every aspiring M.P. Until recently, the record of Party rebels in modern politics was very poor: when M.P.s deserted, or were deserted by, their parties, they usually lost very heavily to an official Party candidate in the ensuing general election. Four recent Labour rebels (S. O. Davies,

Merthyr Tydfil, 1970; Dick Taverne, Lincoln, 1973–74; Eddie Milne, Blyth, 1974; and Eddie Griffiths, Sheffield Brightside 1974) are partial exceptions. All quarrelled with their local parties and were refused re-adoption as official candidates. All stood against their official opponents with some success. Taverne won twice but lost at the third try. Milne won in February 1974 but lost in October. Davies won, but died in office; and Griffiths did not win, but his 27.9 per cent of the vote in October 1974 was easily the highest for an unsuccessful Labour rebel in recent times.[16]

But no Labour rebel has yet successfully completed a full parliamentary term, and not every rebel even now is as successful as these four. (The former Labour M.P. for Keighley, standing as a Tavernite, got 0.8 per cent of the vote in his old seat in February 1974.) In local government, with smaller electorates, the chances of a Party rebel keeping his seat against official opposition are much higher because voters may know the candidates well enough to judge between the man and the Party. But for parliamentary elections, selection and reselection remain as important as ever.

The arrangements have not changed much since they were well described a decade ago in two books to which readers wishing to know more may refer.[17] Transport House maintains two lists of potential parliamentary candidates who have been proposed by an affiliated organisation. Some of these organisations, such as the AUEW, vet applicants to decide whether they think they are suitable before proposing them. Most do not, and neither, normally, does Transport House. List 'A' is of those sponsored by affiliated organisations, usually trade unions. Sponsorship mainly entails a guarantee to pay some of the candidate's election expenses. The Party Constitution forbids any mention at a selection conference of whether or not candidates are sponsored – it wants constituencies to select the best, not the richest, candidate – but it is in practice impossible for selectors to ignore the financial benefits of sponsorship. List 'B' is of unsponsored candidates, mostly proposed by constituency Labour parties. Although most constituencies draw up their candidate shortlists from the 'A' and 'B' lists, there is nothing in the rules to stop them looking elsewhere, and safe seats particularly sometimes adopt local 'favourite sons' who are not on the lists.

Candidate selection is the one area of Party politics where constituency activists undoubtedly come into their own. Their role has been rudely attacked – Conservative selection conferences as 'government by greengrocers' and Labour ones as dominated by unrepresentative militants. Whether the attack is justified or not depends on what one means by 'representative', but there is no doubt that those who go to selection conferences are more Left wing than any other organised group of Labour supporters: Party members, or Labour voters or Labour M.P.s. A selection conference is a special meeting of the General Management Committee (now officially renamed General Committee) of the constituency, an indirect body to which wards and trade unions appoint delegates; the shortlist is drawn up by the Executive Committee, also an indirect body elected partly by the wards and the unions and partly from the GMC. The NEC has powers to intervene in selection conferences, but very rarely uses them. Most of the few occasions it has used them have arisen over candidates it judged too Left wing, an event much less likely to arise now that the NEC has itself shifted markedly to the Left. In by-elections, however, the constitution requires national and regional party officers to play a bigger part, because more national attention is then focussed on a single contest and the Party machine would be more embarrassed by a bad or extreme candidate.

The present selection system is attacked by both Right and Left-wing pressure groups in the Party. The Right wants selection conferences to be open to all paid-up Party members, because it thinks (probably correctly) that they would be more Right wing than the present 'selectorate'. The Left wants sitting Labour M.P.s to be automatically required to submit themselves for reselection before each new General Election, because it thinks (certainly correctly) that this would increase the influence of Left-wing groups within constituency GMCs. Given the present composition of the NEC and Annual Conference (which is constitutionally responsible) the first reform has no chance of enactment but the second rather more. Given the small size of many GMCs, even the Left-wing M.P.s on the NEC, who might be expected to support automatic reselection, are probably too worried about their own vulnerability to 'raiding' by extreme Left groups to support the proposal. However, an arrangement for reviewing the position of sitting M.P.s if their constituency GMCs are dissatisfied with them has been recently introduced. It contains a provision for appeal by the M.P. to the NEC if his constituency votes to dismiss him. The NEC has the last word, and would be doubtless influenced by its judgement of how likely the 'sacked' M.P. would be to win if, like Davies, Taverne and Milne, he took on his former Party at the polls. It is impossible to generalise: some M.P.s might be at risk because of alleged laziness or incompetence, not political incompatibility with their GMCs, and people in such cases would be much less likely to 'do a Taverne' with success.

In general, there is no doubt that candidate selection is the area of Labour Party politics where individual members have most real power. The move to the Left among constituency activists has certainly radicalised recent cohorts of new M.P.s, but it is too early to say whether this will in the long run move the PLP to the Left or not. The power of the grass roots is much more dubious in the realm of policy formation, to which we must now turn.

Policy formation

The LRC was ambiguous about this at its very first conference, and the

Labour Party still is. Many conference and executive leaders – an early example was Ben Tillett – saw the issue as being quite straightforward. The LRC was a committee to get working-class M.P.s into Parliament. People who wished the LRC's help had to assure it that they supported its programme, and (from 1903) that they were not supporters of either the Liberal or the Conservative Party. Such people would not get elected but for the activities of their organised supporters. Surely those who paid the piper had a right to call the tune, and mandate Labour M.P.s to support the policies of the Labour Party Conference?

But no parliamentary Labour leader has taken this view, not even Keir Hardie. Look again at the policy statement which Hardie got the LRC foundation conference to adopt: 'a distinct Labour Group in Parliament, who shall have their own Whips, *and agree upon their policy*' (my emphasis). No question here of taking instructions from Conference or the NEC. In 1907 the issue came to the fore when both the ILP and the Labour Party conferences criticised Hardie and the Labour M.P.s for their handling of the women's suffrage question. Hardie angrily refused to accept that the conferences had a right to instruct M.P.s what to do. He was even unwilling to concede them any right to give advice if he did not approve of it. His threats to resign ensured that the issue was not forced.

But it would not go away. Conference delegates have always demanded some say in policy formation in return for their voluntary work and fundraising. No parliamentary leader except George Lansbury has ever made a serious concession, and when Lansbury did appeal to Conference in 1935 he was brutally attacked by Ernest Bevin for abdicating his responsibilities as Party leader. Lansbury was a pacifist, whereas most of the PLP in 1935 were prepared to back 'collective security' through the League of Nations against aggressors. Lansbury went to Conference and offered to resign as leader, in the clear hope that Conference would reject his resignation and allow him to stay. But Bevin destroyed him: 'It is placing the Executive and the Movement in an absolutely wrong position to be hawking your conscience round from body to body to be told what you ought to do with it.'

Thus the one Labour leader who actually sought policy instructions from Conference was rebuffed. Two other leaders have treated Conference's claim to be the party's supreme policy-maker with some respect: Attlee and Gaitskell. In 1937, Attlee said that 'The Labour Party Conference lays down the policy of the Party, and issues instructions which must be carried out by the Executive, the affiliated organisations, and its representatives in Parliament and local authorities',[18] (p.93). But he had changed his mind by 1945. Before the election campaign, Harold Laski, as Chairman of the National Executive, had said that the Labour Party would not necessarily be bound by foreign commitments made by Attlee as a member of the government. This was seized on by Churchill, who argued that voting Labour would be voting for a Party at the beck and call of an extreme, unelected body. Attlee rejected the charge. To Churchill, he wrote: 'At no time . . . has the National Executive Committee ever sought to give, or given, instruction to the Parliamentary Labour Party'. To Laski, he is said to have written crisply, 'A period of silence from you would be welcome.'[19] Gaitskell was the only modern Labour Party leader to tackle a hostile Conference head-on.

In 1959, he decided that Clause Four of the Party's Constitution, committing it to the nationalisation of the means of production, distribution and exchange, was an electoral liability, and tried unsuccessfully to get a special Conference to annul it. This was the prelude to a much bigger fight over unilateral nuclear disarmament, which Conference supported at Scarborough in 1960. Gaitskell angrily promised to 'fight and fight and fight again to save the party we love', which for him meant reversing the Conference decision because he and the majority of the PLP disapproved of it. He succeeded; the 1961 Conference rejected unilateralism.

Both of his successors – Harold Wilson and James Callaghan – have suffered much more damaging defeats in Conference for PLP or Government policy. But unlike Gaitskell they have not paid Conference the compliment of taking any notice. They have simply continued with their policies, on Vietnam for instance, and incomes policy, as if nothing had happened. Since the Party Constitution is silent on this point, there is nothing Conference or the NEC can do about it. A resolution demanding that M.P.s should pay more attention to Conference resolutions has no more force than any other conference resolution.

The Party Constitution does give Conference and the NEC a say in drawing up the Party manifesto. Resolutions passed at Conference by a two-thirds majority are deemed to have become part of the 'Party Programme'. This does not necessarily mean that they will ever be put to the public as Party policy, though. There is a further hurdle. A joint committee of the NEC and the Cabinet (NEC and the Shadow Cabinet when Labour is in opposition) is responsible for selecting those items from the Party programme which are to go in the manifesto for each General Election. This is the stage at which Labour leaders will insist on the exclusion of items which their private opinion polls tell them are electoral liabilities. The nationalisation of the building industry is part of the Labour Party programme; but it is a safe bet that it will never appear in a Labour election manifesto.

Does all this matter? Surely nobody except other politicians and telly dons ever reads an election manifesto, and hostile politicians who read those can also find out what is in the Party programme, and taunt Labour candidates with it if they think it is to their advantage? In fact, however, the distinction is important. The Election Manifesto is a published document, the Party programme is not. And though few people read the manifesto itself, most Labour candidates draw the political content of their own election literature from it, so that it is mostly ideas from the manifesto which are put to the public in order to win votes. And since Labour candidates exist to win votes from the public, whereas conference delegates exist to win votes from other conference delegates, it is the candidates who must pay much more attention to *public* opinion, and play down the aspects of Party policy which they know, or think, the electorate dislikes.

Here lies the basic reason for tension between Party militants and parliamentarians. It is a quite general point, but it can be seen clearly in the Labour Party case. It is best illustrated through Anthony Downs's famous spatial theory of Party competition.[20] Downs argued that parties trying to win votes were like entrepreneurs deciding where to set up shops. If Acacia Avenue has 99 identically-spaced houses, nos. 1 to 99, all on the same side of the road, then a rational shopkeeper must set up at no. 50. If he starts up anywhere else (at no. 33, say), then a rival need only put a shop at 34 to get all the trade from houses 34 to 99 inclusive. But if the first to choose chooses no. 50, then his rival can only, at best, choose no. 49 or 51. Either way the first chooser will get 50/99 of the trade, and the second 49/99. By analogy, Downs argues that political parties will always converge on the middle – more precisely, that they will always tend to express the policy preferences of the median elector on a linearly-scalable issue.

Downs's theory is too simple and abstract to apply to the real world

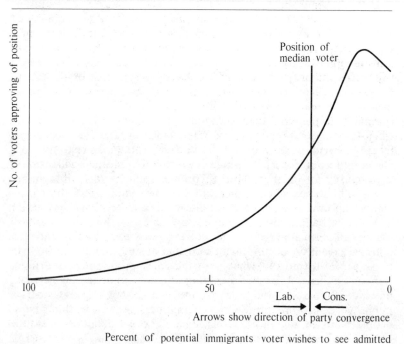

Fig 1 A skewed distribution of opinion

without modification. But, used with proper caution, it can tell us a great deal about the dynamics of Labour and Conservative policy formation. The simple form of the theory assumes that there is a two-Party system. This is substantially true for England (if less so for the rest of the UK). It assumes that there is a clear spectrum of opinion among both politicians and voters, which can be measured from one extreme through a central position to the opposite extreme. This is true for a limited range of issues, such as race relations and the level of public spending. It is true in a qualified way of central issues like incomes policy. It is not true of a wide range of political issues, because they are not measurable along a single line, or because voters have no strong views, or for both reasons. But the issues which do fit the conditions are key ones, and Downs's theory can be applied to them. The parties *have* converged on the centre on most central economic issues, and on some non-economic ones such as coloured immigration. Notice that 'centre' means 'the position of the median voter'. This will not be the same as the centre position if the distribution of opinion is 'skewed' as it is on immigration (see Fig. 1). Here, the 'centre' towards which the parties have converged was not the central position of letting in one in every two coloured immigrants who wanted to enter Britain; it was the position of the voter who had exactly as many other voters to his 'left' as to his 'right' and hence much more restrictive.

Thus if parties want to win elections, they ought to move towards the centre on those issues which matter to the electorate. But their own activists will always tend to pull the other way. To see why, let us consider an issue where public opinion is more normally distributed: policy towards redistribution of income and wealth (see Fig. 2). Let us suppose that the median voter is happy with the status quo: he wishes neither more redistribution nor more restoration of eroded differentials. Then the competition to win the election will, on the face of it, draw both competing parties to this position. But consider the effect of the presence of potential political activists. If I am an activist with views on the issue, what do I do about it? If my views are to the 'right' of the median, I certainly do not join the Labour Party – I belong with the Conservatives. If they are on the median, there is no need for me to do anything: the parties will converge on my views without my assistance, so why should I bother to spend scarce time or money on bringing about something that will happen anyway? If they are to the 'left' of the median, then I do have an incentive to join the Labour Party to try to pull it away from convergence towards my own position. And the further 'left' my own views, the keener I will be on getting my party to adopt them.

This is a gross oversimplification of a very sophisticated argument, an argument which stands up well to the many criticisms with which I have no room to deal. It shows that Labour activists will always tend to be to the Left of both the electorate and their own leadership on those issues where such a scale can be meaningfully established. And the Party will always be torn between satisfying its supporters at the risk of losing elections and winning elections at the cost of disillusioning its active supporters. That is why the issue of 'Who decides policy?' has always been disputed between Conference delegates and parliamentary leaders. It is a tension which often comes to the fore in candidate selection, when aspiring M.P.s pretend to be much more Left wing than they actually are, in order to capture the hearts of the Party faithful. And it is certainly one reason for the continuing decline in membership, as the leadership has consistently put winning elections higher among its policies than satisfying Party activists. In short, it permeates every level of the Party organisation. It is muscle and sinew which makes the dry bones of Party organisation move. Thus there is nothing pathological about the conditions we have listed in this chapter: they are a normal part of the functioning of the body politic.

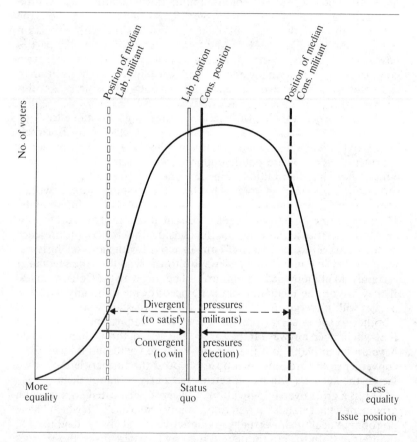

Fig. 2 Downsian convergence for a normal distribution of opinion

Notes

1. A. J. Beith, 'An Anti-Labour Caucus: The Case of the Northumberland Voters' Association', *Policy and Politics*, Vol. 2, pp. 153–65.
2. R. T. McKenzie, *British Political Parties*, 2nd edn, p. 146, Heinemann (London) 1963. See also R. T. McKenzie and A. Silver, *Angels in Marble*, Heinemann (London) 1968.
3. M. Ostrogorski, *Democracy and the Organisation of Political Parties*, Vol. 1, Macmillan (London) 1902.
4. H. M. Pelling, *Origins of the Labour Party*, 2nd edn, p. 205, OUP (London) 1965; see also I. McLean, *Keir Hardie*, pp. 79–80, Allen Lane (London) 1975.
5. H. M. Pelling, op. cit., p. 226.
6. C. Cross, *Philip Snowden*, ch. 3–5, Barrie & Rockliff (London) 1966.
7. M. Moran, *The Union of Post Office Workers: A Study in Political Sociology*, Macmillan (London) 1974.
8. T. Forester, *The Labour Party and the Working Class*, Heinemann (London) 1976.
9. B. Hindess, *The Decline of Working Class Politics*, Paladin (London) 1971.
10. R. J. Baxter 'The Working Class and Labour Politics', *Political Studies*, Vol. 20, pp. 97–107.
11. T. Forester, op. cit., but see also R. Rose, *The Problem of Party Government*, Macmillan (London) 1974.
12. B. J. Pimlott, *Labour and the Left in the 1930s*, CUP (Cambridge) 1977.
13. I. McLean, *Elections* (esp. ch. 4), Longman (London) 1976; and also I. McLean 'The Politics of Nationalism and Devolution', *Political Studies*, Vol. 25, pp. 425–30.
14. P. Addison, *The Road to 1945*, Jonathan Cape (London) 1975.
15. See D. Butler and D. Kavanagh, *The British General Election of February 1974*, Macmillan (London) 1974.
16. See J. Ramsden and R. Jay in C. Cook and J. Ramsden (Eds), *By-Elections in British Politics*, Macmillan (London) 1973. See also E. Milne, *No Shining Armour*, John Calder (London) 1976.
17. A. Ranney, *Pathways to Parliament*, Macmillan (London) 1965; and M. Rush *The Selection of Parliamentary Candidates*, Nelson (London) 1969.
18. C. R. Attlee, *The Labour Party in Perspective*, Gollancz (London) 1937.
19. H. M. Pelling, *A Short History of the Labour Party*, 2nd edn, Macmillan (London) 1965.
20. A. Downs, *An Economic Theory of Democracy*, Harper and Row (New York) 1957.

Chapter 3
Labour and the trade unions

Anthony Fenley

'A political or ideological tradition, especially if it sums up genuine patterns of practical activity in the past, or is embodied in stable institutions, has an independent life and force, and must affect the behaviour of political movements.' *Hobsbawm*[1]

'In so far as one can speak of any common ideology shaping or reinforcing the attitudes of British trade unions to the State, it is not socialism or the class struggle, but a devotion to what is called the voluntary system or sometimes free collective bargaining.' *A. Flanders*[2]

To what extent can British trade unions be said to have an ideological tradition; and how has this shaped the extent and nature of their political activity?

The philosophy of trade unions is usually encapsulated in the obscure concept of 'voluntarism'. Before elaborating on its facets in more detail, it can be described succinctly as a relative low profile for the Government in industrial relations, but a relatively interventionist role for the Government in other areas of the economy and society. However, such a definition only hints at what is an essentially ambivalent attitude to the role of the modern State.

Although the concept of voluntarism is a unifying ideology and is a useful common denominator for describing organised labour's traditional outlook, it allows a plurality of other ideologies to flourish and permits them to use the magic word voluntarism as an instrument of convenience. It acts, therefore, as a façade for masking a range of ideological proclivities and trends within the unions. It is within this framework that contradictions within the British trade union movement manifest themselves; and considerably influence relations with the Labour Party. For instance, the notion of voluntarism can be utilised by trade unionists whose sole concern is the instrumental pursuit of their own sectional, quite often selfish interest, a concentration on immediate goals within the context of the firm; often this is termed 'business unionism'. The concept also has advantages to Marxist–Leninists who place 'the political class tasks of the trade unions higher than the private corporative tasks'.[3]

First, it provides a means by which they can attempt to destabilise the economy and society through collective bargaining, but it also allows an indolent self deception because whereas working men may support the Marxist–Leninist in his voluntarist hat as a bargainer, when he raises the basic political fundamentals of his own ideology he is denied mass support. Similarly, the Syndicalist who believes in overthrowing capitalism through industrial action may gain support for his methods, but these fit into a voluntarist pattern, and are not dissimilar from those of the instrumentalist, whilst receiving no support whatsoever for his economic and social ends.[4]

Further confusion is caused by those who are committed to 'voluntarism', but who are also 'democratic socialists'. They quite sincerely believe that: 'the most effective redistributor of wealth and incomes in the community is . . . the militant stand of the Trade Union Movement. . . .'[5] In addition there is a socialist strand whose concept of the labour movement is one which 'looks outside itself to the good of society as well as its own betterment, and to a national fellowship as well as its own membership'.[6] It is this final trend which provides the fundamental link between the trade union movement and the Labour Party.

Nevertheless, the close relationship of the unions to the Party is both changeable and complex, because the contradictions within trade unionism are amplified in their political commitments which arise from, and are sustained by, the voluntarist tradition. In 1961 it was stated that: 'The TUC did not and could not start its examination of any problem as a Socialist, Liberal, Conservative, or Communist. We start as trade unionists, and we end as trade unionists.'[7] This view is highly incongruent in the light of hard political facts given that, 'the structure and procedure, and financial base of the Labour Party indicate a degree of integration with and dependence on the TUs that places the party in a category apart from any other in Europe'.[8] Indeed the assertion that the 'Labour Party came out of the bowels of the TUC' was not uttered by someone on the periphery of party politics.[9]

Voluntarism

The fundamental proposition of this essay is that trade union political activity must be seen in terms of the defence of the doctrine of voluntarism: and that union–Party relations must be considered within that context. It is contended that when governments have no longer been prepared to accommodate the voluntarist ideology of the trade union movement that trade unions have extended their political activity both in its scope and content. The defence of voluntarism has provided the dialectics of change both within the movement, and within the State.

There is no metaphysical base to voluntarism; but a distinguishable and tested theory of trade unionism has developed as the ad hoc response of men to particular situations. The tenets of voluntarist thought are basically simple, but allow an understanding of the complexity of the labour movement, and the manifold contradictions of its development. The defence of voluntarism is the key to understanding both cohesion and conflict in Party–union relations.

The three basic principles of voluntarism are a preference for collective bargaining as opposed to State legislation; complete autonomy for the parties; and a non-legalistic type of collective bargaining. The value of voluntarism is that it permits trade unions to give priority to their industrial objectives. It is a doctrine which gives trade unions a flexible political framework within which to operate, to the extent that it places both maximum and minimum constraints on their political activities. The minimum constraints are the maintenance of a legal and economic framework within which they can flourish, whilst the upper limits prevent them from pursuing objectives which might endanger their industrial unity, and continuation as organisations.[10]

There are other reasons why the ideology of voluntarism recommends itself to trade unions. First, it permits trade unions to come to terms with the exigencies of the modern industrial State whilst maintaining their traditional bargaining role. Second, this in turn secures the allegiance of their members, thereby permitting trade unions to retain their identity as organisations. Third, it allows trade unions to express 'class feelings' without having to engage in an irreconcilable type of class conflict, thereby reflecting the social stratification of British society.[11] Fourth, the doctrine serves an operational function in terms of maintaining the unity of the union; externally it can be used against either managerial or political opponents. Internally, it can be used against 'non unionists', dissidents or political factions whose aims could threaten the union's industrial unity and effectiveness; at the same time it permits Marxist, Collectivist and Syndicalist traditions to exist in British trade unions, without dominating them. Nevertheless, voluntarism rejects Marxist and Collectivist theories of trade unionism which perceive of trade unions as instruments of political mobilisation; who, once a political transformation had taken place, would have a role subordinate to that of the Party and the State.

The voluntarist tradition was apparent during the last quarter of the nineteenth century when a *modus vivendi* had been reached between the governing classes and labour. Legislation passed in the 1870s by the Conservative Party provided unions with a framework of immunities, in respect of striking and picketing that were not only consistent with the dominant economic doctrines, but were also a recognition of the responsible role that it was thought trade unions would play in industry and society.[12]

The recommendation of the 1894 Royal Commission on Labour endorsed these sentiments and quite clearly showed the State's acceptance of voluntary principles; this was entirely in keeping with the trade unions' preference for collective bargaining, and limited political action.[13] At the time the chief political characteristic of British workers was the absence of their own independent socialist party; Engels described the working class merely as the 'tail of the great Liberal Party'.[14]

The creation of the Labour Party

Developments within the trade union movement that led to the creation of an independent political party can be interpreted as either a tentative step towards socialism; or as a prerequisite of a safeguarded voluntarist framework. Amongst historians the viewpoint has been expressed that the development of the new unionism in the 1880s and 1890s marked a shift towards the Left and to collectivist ideals.[15] It has also been pointed out that within the established unions 'socialists increased their influence' by identifying themselves with the industrial unrest generated by Britain's economic decline, and technological change.[16]

Because of the threat of these developments the entrenched minority amongst the aristocracy of labour increasingly questioned the traditional trade unionists' reliance on 'collective self help'. In addition the new entrants amongst the ranks of organised labour needed direct parliamentary legislation to secure objectives they could not achieve by collective bargaining. To the general unions this meant improved economic status for their members; to the Railway Servants it meant having a say in the parliamentary legislation which affected their employment, and securing recognition from their employers.[17]

This apparent retreat from voluntarist ideology must be placed in perspective. Even in the new unions the value and priority of effective collective bargaining has been emphasised; and it has been suggested that socialist leaders were accepted in spite of their socialism, not because of it.[18] At the same time the influence of the traditional Lib–Lab view of political action was not easily relinquished. The ASE and the textile workers did not affiliate to the LRC until 1903, and the miners not until 1909. The older trade unionists moreover retarded socialist influence at the TUC during the 1890s by excluding Trades Councils, initiating the bloc vote and restricting delegates to either trade union officials or workers at the trade.[19]

However, at the 1899 Congress a motion was passed instructing the Parliamentary Committee to call a conference to examine ways and means of securing an increased number of labour representatives in Parliament. The Railway Servants Union's motion was only narrowly carried, and although the resolution was discreet on the question of political independence, it still met opposition from the miners and the unions of textile workers. Although less than half the TUC sent delegates to the meeting in 1900 which led to the formation of the LRC, Keir Hardie, by steering a middle course between the rigid Marxism of the SDF and the vacillations of the Lib–Lab delegates, secured the principle of establishing a distinct labour group in Parliament.[20]

Apart from providing most of the initial support, it is arguable that the new unions had a pivotal role to play in the events leading to the establishment of an independent Labour Party. Where trade unions could not obtain recognition, or were in a weak position, they relied on devices such as the closed shop and picketing, which in the eyes of the ruling classes and employers led to disturbingly overt forms of conflict. Although the middle classes had conceived of trade unions as a means of socialising the poor and welcomed the 1889 Dock Strike, this sympathy developed into hostility.[21]

Employers organised themselves in the parliamentary sphere, and a further ominous sign was the establishment of Collison's National Free Labour Association, a body designed to break strikes. Although the notion of an employer's offensive has been placed in perspective by Clegg,[22] during the 1890s the engineers, shoe operatives and railway workers all suffered industrial defeats. A campaign was mounted in *The Times* blaming Britain's woes on worker organisations; a further manifestation of the ruling classes' mood of discontent. However, the most disquieting aspect of the new climate was the judicial incursion into the voluntarist traditions of British trade unionism.[23]

Although legal judgments did not always go against trade unions, it is clear that during the 1890s a series of court decisions circumscribed the industrial activities of trade unions; the culmination of this was the Taff Vale decision in 1901 which held trade unions to be liable for losses caused to employers as a result of trade disputes. The old immunities had disappeared. The response of union leaders was mixed, but the TUC's counsel saw it as an attempt to 'establish principles of law against trade unions'.[24] The TUC's Parliamentary Committee's inability to obtain redress, and an unfavourable division in the House convinced many unions to expand their political activities, with the result that trade union membership of the LRC expanded from 376,000 in 1901 to 861,000 in 1903.[25]

Legal incursions, political impediments and industrial battles are vital to an understanding of the increased trade union commitment to the LRC. Clearly, no satisfaction could be obtained from the Conservatives. In spite of the Lib–Lab pact, it was increasingly apparent that the Liberals were unsatisfactory bedfellows also. The vital clauses of the 1906 Trade Disputes Act which restored immunities to trade unions resulted from amendments by the Labour Party; the original Liberal Bill had maintained certain restrictions on unions.[26] At the local level, the unwillingness of local Liberal Associations to adopt workingmen as candidates increasingly alienated trade unionists, even those of Lib–Lab sentiments. Loyalty to one's union preceded loyalty to a political party.[27]

The Liberals were no longer able to accommodate the grievances and aspirations of workers. Many important Liberals were employers, and a number of socialist contemporaries believed it was incongruous to oppose them industrially, but embrace them politically. Although the relationship between industrial militancy and the rise of the Labour Party is an area where more systematic research is needed, there are examples of industrial events giving a spur to Labour's advancement. Support in the coalfields and amongst textile workers are examples of this.[28]

Labour activists often presented parliamentary activity in terms of an extension of industrial issues. Robert Blatchford wrote:

A Labour Party is a kind of political trade union, and to defend trade unionism is to defend Labour representation. If an employer's interests are opposed to your interests in business what reason have you for supposing that his interests and yours are not opposed in politics?[29]

MacDonald also emphasised that industry was organising politically and that trade unions needed to do the same in self-defence.[30]

These experiences support the view that trade union political action was seen as the defence of voluntarism. The greater part of the PLP's efforts were concerned with issues of direct interest to trade unions, and with the accession to the party of the cotton workers and mineworkers Keir Hardie was fearful that their interests would dominate the Party and eclipse the broader political work.[31] In anticipation of these fears the Parliamentary Party had adopted in 1906 a 'conscience clause' for those who felt difficulty in accepting a majority decision. Whilst at the 1907 Conference union attempts to control the PLP were defeated, the Parliamentary Party was to heed the opinion of conference, but had discretion in the implementation of resolutions.

By 1914 over 1.5 million trade unionists were affiliated to the Labour Party through their unions, and this in spite of the Osborne judgement, 1910, which had prevented trade unions from using their funds for political purposes.[32] This judicial incursion was remedied by the 1913 Trade Union Act which held that any trade union wishing to engage in political activity had first to secure a majority in favour in a ballot of the membership. The ballot results showed almost unanimous support amongst unions for the political fund and supporting the Labour Party, despite abstentions and significant opposing minorities amongst the membership.[33]

At the outbreak of war trades councils and union organisation formed the backbone of party organisation; electorally the Party did well in areas where unions were well organised, in addition the unions provided the Party's financial support. Despite this degree of commitment by the unions to the Party other developments were a potential incubus on the relationship. The first of these was the PLP's wish to appear respectable; parliamentary leaders were denounced as 'sheer hypocrites' who 'for five and ten guineas at a time will lie with the best'.[34] Sidney Webb noted 'The desire to enjoy the amenities of the House of Commons is the weakness of Labour members – if they are going to pose as a party.'[35] Secondly, unions were concerned to retain their organisational autonomy, hence they supported the contributory principle on Social Insurance; in opposition to many in the Party. It was claimed that the unions were not concerned with unorganised workers; nor did they wish to arouse the excessive expectations of the proletariat.[36] They were suspicious that socialists were attempting to manipulate unions for their own ends, and at the 1905 Conference an unsuccessful attempt was made to disaffiliate the socialist societies. The third development was the increasing tension in relations between unions and the State. Ironically, at the very time when labour established a Party that one day might become the Government, workers were engaged in activities that might at some stage lead to direct confrontation with the Government.[37]

Before the war levels of industrial unrest reached unprecedented scales; and although the workers may not have had Syndicalist objectives, they did employ Syndicalist methods. Although the Triple Alliance was organised for effective collective bargaining, and not revolution, the prospect of a conflict with the Government was always possible. This was something that did not escape the attention of Parliamentarians such as MacDonald, who criticised Syndicalist methods and ends; whilst in 1911 Arthur Henderson tabled a Bill attempting to outlaw strikes unless 30 days' notice had been given, a move condemned by the 1911 TUC Conference.[38]

By 1914 it was apparent that the Labour Party gave unions a voice in Parliament of such a kind that would have been increasingly unavailable to them; and was instrumental therefore in defending voluntarist ideology. The Party obtained, in return, financial support, an effective organisation and an established electoral base. But areas of stress were already apparent, and were to be a recurring feature of the alliance in the future.

The First World War

With the advent of war the trade union movement soon realised that it was faced with a war on two fronts. It wished to support the Government and defeat German militarism, whilst avoiding the entrenchment of those interests engaged in exploiting and profiteering at the expense of the working class. An additional complication was that many political socialists objected to the war, in contrast to the patriotic sentiments of the trade unionists.[39]

The dilemma this presented for the trade union movement led to a highly varied situation, where the many intricacies of union opinion can be best described as ambivalent. The unions conceded many of their traditional rights to the State, and participated in the wartime Government, ranging from Arthur Henderson's inclusion in the Cabinet to the involvement of trade unionists in many of the 2,000 wartime committees.[40]

Trade union co-operation was illustrated by the renunciation of the use of trade unions' bargaining power, and by proclaiming an industrial as well as a political truce.[41] Unions willingly set aside their rules and customs, and made an immediate attempt to terminate all trade disputes. They also supported the Government's recruiting campaign, and were party to the Treasury Agreement which allowed for the dilution of labour. This led to their acceptance of the 1915 Munitions Act, which prohibited strikes, and imposed compulsory arbitration. The Act saw the innovation of 'controlled establishments', no increases in wages were allowed without the Minister's permission and leaving certificates were initiated. Together with the Defence of the Realm Act, the vast increase in State intervention represented a new chapter in the curtailment of individual liberty.[42]

Despite organised labour's co-operative attitude the tradition of anti-statism found continuity in the shop stewards' movement. Increasingly the future role of the State in the post-war world was questioned as a result of Government intervention. Many shop stewards regarded 'Wartime Collectivism' as a 'stage in the construction of state capitalism' more onerous than nineteenth century individualism. This contrasted with the opinion of those who believed the 'experience of war thus seemed to bear out the Fabian doctrine that socialism would arise ... not out of the prosecution of the class struggle, but as an administrative necessity – as the only feasible response to the problems of production and distribution confronting the State.'[43]

The views of the mainstream of the labour movement are to be located somewhere in between these conflicting interpretations; they were much more varied and reflected the pragmatic nature of trade unionism. This was best exemplified in the attitude of Ernest Bevin, who had objected to the outbreak of war, but decided to do his 'best to preserve the economic unity of the men' that he represented and 'accept passively the opinion of the majority of the men' he led. He believed, 'the only safe weapon for the workers, slow as it is at times, is the trade union form of organisation which has stood the test every time'.[44]

The pragmatic approach of labour was illustrated in the work of the War Emergency Workers National Committee, which precluded all debate about the merits of the war, and concentrated exclusively on the social consequences. The Council initiated the 1916 special TUC Conference which called for a repeal of all legislation of a compulsory type on the 'mankind of the nation'. In 1917 they mounted a 'conscription of riches' campaign as a counter by the Labour movement to the Munitions Act; this permitted a response by the unions to State intervention in their freedoms, whilst still avoiding an overt conflict with the Government.

State incursions into the voluntarist tradition had obliged labour once more to extend the horizons of their political activities. Wartime collectivism had opened the eyes of many trade unionists to the possibilities of a regulated society;[45] but that does not explain why the unions gave their support to a Party which adopted a socialist

constitution. Samuel Beer has suggested that the adoption of Clause
Four resulted from the development of trade union organisation and
increasing class consciousness which the Liberals were unable to
accommodate; in his view, 'the adoption of socialism as an ideology'
was 'functional to the choice of political independence'.[46] Harrison, on
the other hand, has suggested that Clause Four of the Labour Party's
constitution, rather than being the common objective that Beer
believed, accommodated and concealed a large diversity of particular
concerns. Clause Four, in fact, was a rallying point around which many
different ideologies and interests assembled; and this viewpoint has
found general acceptance.[47]

Winter has pointed out the role that the Russian Revolution and the
'Doormat' incident played in realigning Henderson's viewpoint. He
recognised the limitations to the links with Lloyd George's Liberals, the
new role the State had to play in society and the new democratic
consciousness amongst the working classes.[48] McKibbin has shown that
Henderson persuaded the unions to support the new constitution and
individual membership by assuaging their fears over the socialists and
liberal emigrés. The commitment of the trade unions was retained
because they kept control of the elections to the NEC and maintained
the block vote at Party conference. Clause Four was simply a sentiment,
with which some agreed and some disagreed; the apparatus and
structure was what mattered and the unions retained hegemony over
that.[49]

Post-war developments

The adoption of a new constitution and 'Labour and the New Social
Order' were indicative of an enhanced alliance between the Party and
the trade unions. The unions provided the Party with an organisational
infrastructure and a social base;[50] but, paradoxically, 'the ideological
character of the party, which had always been eclectic, became even
more so',[51] and contributed towards the differentiation between
political and industrial spheres of activity. A great many socialists were
unhappy with the potential dominance by the unions; MacDonald
always believed the unions were 'a terrible incubus'.[52] In addition, there
was an influx of liberal emigrés, unloved by the unionists, who were
hardly likely to ascribe to the virile class symbolism unashamedly
displayed by organised labour. A further blemish on the alliance was the
unions' concern with immediate issues, and their reliance on industrial
action.

The post-war period was one of intense industrial conflict, with
famous strikes by the police and railwaymen, and the miners' disputes
which culminated in the 1926 General Strike. Although the period
marked the demise of the Triple Alliance, it witnessed the rise of the
TUC General Council as an expression of the new group activities at

work in society.[53] In addition, in 1920 organised labour was mobilised through Councils of Action to prevent military assistance to the Poles against Russia: in May London dockers had refused to load the *Jolly George* with armaments for Poland. Bevin warned that 'the whole industrial power of the organised workers will be used to defeat this war'.[54] In confronting the State over the question of foreign policy the unions had gone beyond voluntarist doctrine, an exception that proves the rule; it was also an occasion when, 'for once . . . public opinion, was on the side of unconstitutional action'.[55] Nevertheless, the incident illustrated the priority organised labour gave to 'industrial' as opposed to 'political' methods.[56]

This was equally true when the first Labour Government took office in 1924; the unions exploited favourable economic conditions in their negotiations with employers regardless of the Government's political complexion. MacDonald's administration threatened on occasions to use the Emergency Powers Act, and dealt with disputes as any other government might. Bevin condemned the intrusion into industrial affairs – and at the 1925 TUC Conference criticism was made of those with, 'the mistaken view of regarding the political labour movement as an alternative instead of an auxiliary to the trade union movement. Such an attitude is extremely dangerous . . . the best safeguard for our political liberties is to be found in a vigilant and active Labour movement'.[57]

The commitment of trade unions to voluntarist doctrine, and the consequences of this for relations with the Labour Government, was not totally lost on contemporaries. A delegate to the 1925 TUC Conference noted:

Even with a complete labour majority in the House, and with a Labour government which was stable and secure, there would be a permanent difference in point of view between the government on one hand and the trade unions on the other . . . the trade unions have different functions to perform than the functions of government.[58]

The attitude of the Party leaders towards direct action was predictably critical. Clynes had warned that the Councils of Action were undemocratic, and forecast that they would strain the loyalty of workers; in addition to creating a precedent for other sections of the community should a Labour Government be elected. When a Labour Government was elected in 1924 Clynes spoke of a 'National and not a class government'.[59] MacDonald had never hesitated to show his disdain for trade unionists: they were poorly represented in the Government, and treated unfavourably. The Government had little liaison with the TUC; the machinery of the NJC established in 1921 for this express purpose remained largely moribund.[60] But by the same token the emphasis the trade union leaders gave to the industrial sphere was displayed in their unwillingness to take up political roles; the ablest leaders preferred to serve on the General Council.[61]

Despite these divergences Bevin's attempt at the 1925 Labour Party Conference to prevent a future minority government taking office was defeated, when most of the large unions supported MacDonald. Co-operation between the Government and the unions was not unknown; for example, the Building Workers Union co-operated with Wheatley's Housing Bill by agreeing to expand the labour force. However, events did nothing to allay the fears of labour politicians about direct action, and they continued to show their concern with constitutional proprieties. Of the General Strike Clynes wrote: 'Labour M.P.s did all they could to counsel moderation, and not only keep the men within the law, but advise them to have a care for public convenience and national well being'.[62] The unions, fickle as usual, preferred the PLP to keep out of industrial matters, were critical when the PLP did not speak up for the miners, and hurt when politicians made unfavourable comments.

The aftermath of the General Strike

The defeat of the General Strike in 1926 revealed to the unions the limits of industrial action, and had a significant impact on future attitudes.[63] In Aneurin Bevan's words they had 'forged a revolutionary weapon without having a revolutionary intention'.[64] Trade unionists realised the inadequacy of their approach to political activity, and the 1927 Trades Dispute Act, which placed new restrictions on trade unions, emphasised once more the need for effective legislative channels. Trade unions could only achieve their industrial objectives within a sympathetic socio-economic and legal framework; voluntarism as an ideology was dependent on the commitment of governments and employers to the institution of collective bargaining.

Beatrice Webb believed the 1926 collapse would 'explode the inflation of the trade union ideal characteristic of the last few years',[65] but, in fact, recognition of the need for political action did not eclipse the priority given to traditional trade unionism. The eclipse of the strike and subsequent events indicated that capitalism was not breaking down. Industrially, conciliatory lines were pursued through the Mond–Turner talks, which were designed to place employer–union relations on a better footing. Wedderburn has referred to this new understanding as a period when 'the big battalions of Labour and Capital stood together, respectively, against the small union or producer'.[66]

The distinction between the industrial and political spheres was further emphasised when in 1926 the Joint Research bodies established in 1922 were wound up, and each wing became responsible for its own research. The unions remained highly sensitive to what they regarded as political trespass by the Party into their affairs; and in particular they resented those factions who wished to use the trade unions as political instruments, thereby transgressing the inviolable principles of volun-tarism. The ILP's revelations that they had formed industrial branches within unions, and their proposals for a Minimum Living Wage, were perceived as intrusions into legitimate trade union business.[67] The legal setting of wages would upset traditional wage patterns, and complicate or destroy the unions' functions. It might destabilise the economy which would weaken their bargaining power; in addition it would stretch the loyalties of many unionists who were not socialists – it was important that political objectives should not split the unions' industrial unity. Policies which curtailed the trade union function or jeopardised the bargaining environment were a constant *bête noire* to the unions, as was soon to be shown.

When the second Labour Government was elected in 1929 trade-union sponsored M.P.s formed less than half the PLP, largely because of Labour's gains in the marginal seats. Again trade unions were poorly represented, there was a general lack of liaison, and complaints that they were not consulted on important policy issues and legislation. The chairman of the General Council felt that the Labour Government had 'not been as fair as some of the other governments'.[68] Morrison's refusal to countenance direct worker representation on the London Passenger Transport Board was also a contentious issue with some unions, although union views on this subject were, and even today are, still diverse.

The split between the Labour Government and the trade unions in 1931 rested on the MacDonald Cabinet decision to implement cuts in unemployment benefit. MacDonald had wished to present the Party as a responsible party of government, which entailed remaining in office and initiating stringencies in accordance with economic orthodoxy; whereas the unions saw the Party as representing the interests of working people, whose wellbeing was jeopardised by the cuts. In addition, evolutionary socialists such as MacDonald and Snowden saw the Depression as an inevitable feature of capitalism which the workers would have to endure; but the trade unions were concerned with the immediate situation and believed that economic remedies were available which did not require deflationary policies.

Apart from the direct effects on those concerned, cuts in unemployment benefit weakened trade union bargaining power. Trade unionists, such as Bevin, who had served on the Economic Advisory Council and the MacMillan Committee, were far more aware of alternative economic policies than labour politicians, having been exposed to Keynes' ideas. They could contend that specific class interests were not incompatible with the general interests of the nation.[69]

MacDonald's formation of a National Government, in defiance of Party opinion, was the second bitter lesson the trade union movement had learned in the space of five years. The events of 1926 may have placed restraints on industrial action; but 1931 was to place limits on the political licence that unions were willing to give to a Labour Government. In many ways the political parameters within which the movement operated were established in those years.

The aftermath of the 1931 crisis

For philosophical and practical reasons the unions became the custodian of the Party; ironically the electoral disaster of 1931 meant that the majority of 51 M.P.s were union sponsored, and of relatively low calibre; in these circumstances the General Council took the initiative. This degree of influence found institutional expression in the National Joint Council, a joint body consisting of the General Council, National Executive and PLP which had met only rarely in the 1920s. It was now reconstituted, the General Council having 50 per cent of the places, plus the chairmanship. The NJC was the institutional cornerstone of trade union political activity but voluntarist doctrine provided the ideological fountainhead and a basis for action that was both tangible and effective.

The huge parliamentary majority of the National Government and the economic climate of the 1930s placed constraints on the political leverage and industrial strength available to the trade union movement. In these circumstances the unions adopted a defensive strategy described by Miliband as a belief in 'institutionalised co-operation' with the State and management, 'supplemented by the parliamentary pressure of the Labour Party for legislation beneficial to the working classes'.[70]

Walter Citrine believed that, 'the General Council should be regarded as having an integral right to initiate and participate in any political matter which it deems to be of direct concern to its constituents'.[71] Elsewhere, he noted,

The GC . . . did not seek in any shape or form to say what the Party was to do, but they did ask that the primary purpose of the creation of the Party should not be forgotten. It was created by the Trade Union movement to do those things in parliament which the Trade Union movement found ineffectively performed by the two party system.[72]

Arguably this was a precedent for future relations between the Party and unions; however, the peculiar circumstances of the 1930s need to be noted. First, the fundamental weaknesses of the PLP. Second, the widespread economic depression and the ominous spectre of dictatorship. Third, trade union incursions into politics, including their initiatives on foreign policy, were not a cavalier departure, but were concerned with established union objectives and the defence of voluntarism.

The commitment of the unions to the party was reflected in the work of the National Joint Council (renamed the National Council of Labour), which met consistently throughout the 1930s, and issued numerous policy statements.[73] The National Executive and its sub-committees were responsible for details, but followed the lines established by the NCL. The NEC was, until 1937 of course, elected by the trade union block vote.

A new party programme evolved and was set forth in *For Socialism and Peace* (1934), and *Labour's Immediate Programme* (1937). The TUC and the Party collaborated on a number of policy documents, including statements on the socialisation of the cotton and coal industries. The unions also gave initial but brief support to the NFRB and SSIP research bodies concerned with constructing and disseminating a long-term socialist programme.[74]

The new cohesion in union–Party relations did not deter the unions from seeking a co-operative relationship with employers and the Government. Their behaviour was quite consistent with the defence of voluntarism, and friction within the Party evolved around attempts to upset this established tradition. 'Mondism' – conciliatory bargaining rather than industrial action – determined relations with employers.[75] Trade union concern was with maintaining themselves as organisations. This was apparent in the inter-union rivalries to recruit workers in the new industries. Similarly, in many non-union areas the initiative for collective bargaining came from the rank and file. Only then did managements recognise the value of unions as managers of discontent.[76]

This trend was also apparent in the attitude to unemployed workers, and the reluctance of unions to engage in direct action on their behalf. Although the General Council recommended local Unemployed Associations, they were 'not intended as instruments of unemployed agitation'. The one body that did agitate fiercely was viewed disdainfully as a Communist Front.[77] Pollard has noted how after 1933 the TUC appeared to adapt to having 2 million unemployed.[78] The relative insularity of the trade unions was exemplified in their attitude to the Invergordon mutiny, where the protesting sailors were isolated from the main stream of the labour movement.[79]

For voluntarist ideology to survive unions required not only the co-operation of employers, but the goodwill of governments. A mark of success was the presentation of a knighthood to Walter Citrine, the TUC's General Secretary, in 1935. A more practical indication was the limited representation the movement obtained on government committees; governments also consulted them on the reorganisation of industry – although the amount of influence exercised remains to be seen.[80] The trade unions, in an essentially defensive position, had established a new equilibrium in their relations with both the Government and employers, but it was important that the content of long-term political initiatives designed to regulate the economy and society should not unbalance these relationships. This is the key to understanding the causes of stress between the unions and certain factions within the Party during this period.

Objections to factional elements within the movement became increasingly apparent during the late 1920s. In 1927 Bevin and Citrine had turned against the Anglo-Soviet trade union council, and by 1933 their denunciations of both communists and fascists were enunciated in *Dictatorships and the Trade Union Movement* (1933), and the *Communist*

Solar System (1933). These leaflets emphasised democracy and civil liberties; and the sentiments were translated into action when the Black circulars were issued recommending sanctions against communists.[81]

This opprobrium extended to communist fronts, to the minority movements in various industries and to bodies such as the Socialist League. The latter resulted from the transformation of the SSIP into an independent faction within the Party, replacing the ILP which had seceded in 1932; the League's sentiments, which were well to the left of the Party, were unacceptable to trade unionists. An amplification of this standpoint was the expulsion of Sir Stafford Cripps and his 'Bloomsbury Revolutionaries', because his calls for a 'Popular' and 'Common' Front not only might have allowed the communists opportunities for disruption; but they were also in defiance of the collective decisions of the movement.[82]

Trade union objections to factionalism rested on three assumptions. First, the policies and tactics pursued would undermine the industrial unity of the unions. Second, the faction's substantive policies would upset the delicate political balance within which trade unions operated. Third, the policies would lead to dictatorial political regimes which would eliminate free trade unions.

British trade unionists were well aware of the threat fascism posed to worker organisations. In 1936 Bevin had asked 'which is the first institution that victorious fascism wipes out? It is the trade union movement. ...'[83] The previous year he had savaged Lansbury's pacifist sentiments when the latter opposed the NCL's policy on the use of sanctions by the League of Nations. However, a divergence of viewpoint remained between the PLP, who supported collective security but opposed rearmament, and the trade unions, who regarded this as just as incongruous as collective bargaining without the strike sanction. It was only at the 1937 Party Conference that rearmament became the adopted policy of the Party following collusion between Bevin and Hugh Dalton, after the ground had been carefully laid by the NCL, and at the annual TUC Conference. Trade union concern with foreign policy was concern with defending free trade unionism; it was not an international crusade.

One final source of tension remains to be considered. In the nine years up to 1937 individual membership of the Party within the constituencies had doubled, but the card vote meant that the trade unions had control over the election of constituency members to the NEC. Not surprisingly the discontent of individual members within the constituencies grew, and Ben Greene formed the Constituencies Party Movement to remedy the situation. The trade unions were zealous of their custodianship of the Party; however, because the Constituencies Party Movement sought change through constitutional channels, the unions agreed to a rules alteration at the 1937 Conference. In future, seven constituency representatives were to be elected by the constituency parties; unions were persuaded to accept these reforms because they were procedural not substantive.[84]

Miliband has described the policies adopted by the trade unions as 'Labour's tragedy' because, they believed, 'there was little they could do to force the Government out of its ways'.[85] Pollard, on the other hand, has argued that the unions stood up to the traumas affecting them remarkably well; at one level seeking common ground with employers, and at another focusing their attention on alternative forms of economic regulation and planning.[86] Others have emphasised the tangible benefits that the TUC gained for the working class (which meant that the trade unions pursued policies that essentially preserved the working class movement).[87]

Relations between the unions and the Party during the 1930s must be considered within the context of this debate, although by 1937 'the party was behaving more like a potential government than ever before'.[88] The trade unions had in no way relinquished their commitment to voluntarism. Bevin noted: 'Our movement is a voluntary one, and the claim for State regulation must not be carried too far. It might easily lead onto the slippery slope of the totalitarian state under capitalist control.'[89] The view was expressed that the unions' 'guiding principle for more than a hundred years' was 'by means of voluntary agreements with the employers', and that Britain had produced 'a logically complete system of voluntary regulation'. That system, and the unions' relations with Labour Ministers, were soon to be put to the test.[90]

The Second World War

Although the unions had supported rearmament and collective security, they were critical of Chamberlain's policies. A further fear was that the Treasury, at variance with the Ministry of Labour, desired direct controls over the movement of labour and wages. The unions also disliked the imposition of conscription, when they had sought voluntary agreement through the Schedule of Reserved Occupations. Nor did Churchill escape criticism; in 1940 Bevin listed six actions taken by Churchill in previous years that had been detrimental to labour.[91]

Although co-operation did take place, for example in engineering, neither the unions nor the Party flew into the war administration's arms; they had no desire to be held captive in the way that Lloyd George had held them. In fact the number of strikes was half that of the First World War and the Labour Party had finally entered the Government on its own terms, as a full partner, under a new Premier.[92] Bevin became Minister of Labour, and generally managed to retain a voluntarist approach to industrial relations whilst fulfilling the country's manpower and industrial requirements. In addition, the TUC had access and influence on Government committees on a wide range of social and economic issues.

Despite some differences on detail, and a not necessarily sympathetic attitude to unions, William Beveridge described the TUC as the 'Godfathers of the Beveridge Report'.[93] In addition Labour Ministers had considerable discretion with which to encourage professionals and groups to initiate policies on social and economic reform. The compatability of these policies with the union viewpoint sustained a healthy relationship with the Party. There were few rifts, although on one occasion the PLP annoyed Bevin, who thereafter behaved as a trade union delegate to the Cabinet rather than as a Labour M.P.

Bevin showed a remarkable capacity to sustain the treasured voluntarist doctrine during a total war situation.[94] The Government did intervene in industrial affairs, but in a way that strengthened rather than undermined trade union organisation and collective bargaining; and maintained workers' rights and interests. A framework for co-operation was established at the national level through the Joint Consultative Committee, and at the workplace through joint works committees.[95]

The advent of compulsory arbitration through Regulation 1305 and the establishment of a National Arbitration Board rather than usurping trade union functions, in fact enhanced membership and organisation; it was a 'collective agreement given the clothing of law'.[96] Similarly, although the General Provisions Order of March 1941 permitted the direction of labour to essential services, it also laid down minimum employment conditions, whilst restrictions on workers' rights to leave were balanced by dismissal rights. The Defence Regulation Act (IAA), which made it an indictable offence to 'instigate or incite' a stoppage of work, was directed against Trotskyist agitators, that is, against unofficial factions; and therefore was in general keeping with the precepts of voluntarism.

Pelling has noted the 'remarkable fact . . . that the peace time system of collective bargaining was never superseded'.[97] The continuation of traditional trade unionism together with developments in economic and social policy meant that the unions and the Party could face the 1945 election united around the proposals for reform contained in *Let Us Face the Future*. At the 1946 TUC Conference Sir Walter Citrine spoke of the unions passing from 'an era of propaganda to one of responsibility'.[98]

During the 1940s trade unions were regarded as becoming the fifth estate of the realm, an integral part of a consensus polity and society. But it is questionable how many of the fundamental issues affecting relations between governments and unions were resolved in this period; it is arguable that both the Party and the unions engaged in a certain amount of self deception and the politics of convenience.

The Attlee legacy

The significance of the Attlee administration was that it established the contours within which post-war politics and trade unionism would operate. It was thought that the Government as a manager, spender and employer, through its commitment to Keynesian economics and limited public ownership, could achieve its economic objectives of growth, full employment, price stability and a healthy trade balance. The establishment of a Welfare State would safeguard the social wellbeing of citizens; and this was thought to be entirely compatible with the continuation of free collective bargaining and voluntarist industrial relations.

Relations between the unions and the Labour Government during this period can be divided into one of three interpretations: the 'goodwill' theory; the 'obstructionist' theory; and the 'progressive' theory. The 'goodwill' theory emphasises the smooth working relationship established between Attlee and Bevin with Arthur Deakin (TGWU), Tom Williamson (NUGMW) and Will Lawther (Miners) and provided a stable rapport between the industrial and political wings.[99] The repeal of the 1927 Trades Dispute and Trade Union Act and the social and economic policies, including the extent and nature of nationalisation, initiated by the Government won the support of the unions for voluntary wage restraint and responsible bargaining. According to this viewpoint, only the pressure on wages of the Korean War and subsequent price rises, led to a rank and file revolt, and the defeat of the General Council's policy at the 1951 TUC Conference.

The 'obstructionist' interpretation held that whilst the unions accepted social and economic reform, they prevented any reforms which affected their traditional functions and methods. Before the war the unions had stressed their industrial independence and expressed their unwillingness to 'hang onto the coattails of the Labour Party'.[100] Irving Richter has emphasised the unions' commitment to traditional wage bargaining, and the maintenance of differentials. The unions' main concern was with maintaining the bargaining system in the context of a mixed economy; therefore they retarded attempts at a planned economy.[101] Beer has also noted the trade unions' rejection of manpower planning as the key to overall planning.[102]

Panitch, on the other hand, has implied that the unions were more progressive than the Party in their attitude to planning. He argues that socialists such as Attlee and Jay were committed to a mixed economy and a traditional role for unions. His contention is that some unions were calling for socialist planning measures in excess of those proposed by the Government; but the unwillingness of the administration to innovate led to opposition to income restraint from both militant and moderate unionists.[103]

An accurate analysis of the situation is complicated not just by inter-union–Party divergencies, but also by intra-party and intra-union differences. This period is one to which historians need to give renewed attention, since the implication of the arguments is that developments during the six years of the Attlee administration trammelled the future development of the Labour movement.

Despite this controversy at least two trends were apparent. First, union leaders were under pressure to oppose policies of wage restraint; second, there was increasing concern with factional elements to which the call for expulsion of communists stood testimony – they trespassed a cardinal principle of voluntarism, allowing 'democratically determined policy to be deflected at the behest of an outside body'.[104] During the early 1950s the concern with factionalism, and the resulting tension within the movement, centred on Bevanite controversy.

Aneurin Bevan and his supporters were in fundamental disagreement with the Party on the issues of nationalisation, defence and foreign policy. The unions feared that Bevan and his policies would become a catalyst for dissident factions within their own unions, creating alternative power bases, and organisational disunity. Bevan claimed to be as representative of union members as much as their leaders were; and this was something that clashed entirely with the outlook of the trade union leaders.[105]

The rifts in the 1950s

The early 1950s was a good environment for voluntarist ideology; the unions had already made clear to the Labour Government in 1950 and 1951 their opposition to a National Wages Board and wage restraint,[106] whilst the Conservative Government elected in 1951 did not seek wage restrictions – it sought an amiable relationship with the unions, a policy the TUC was anxious to reciprocate.[107] Unions were able to secure reasonable wage increases in the annual negotiating rounds, facilitated by greater price stability. Voluntarism, therefore, prospered in the framework of consensus politics. 'Bevanite' policies were conceived as destabilising the political balance.

The General Council, as a rule, supported the Labour leadership opposing excessive nationalisation, in support of German rearmament and against workers' control. Arthur Deakin denounced proposals for the engineering industry as 'just a mumbo jumbo of meaningless words and phrases', warning delegates 'not to drive us into the position of falling out and breaking with the party on such an issue as this'.[108] Deakin also sought Bevan's expulsion from the Party for what he regarded as 'indiscipline'. Stress in union–Party relations centred on opposition to what was regarded as a destabilising factionalism.[109]

However, during the late 1950s stress in union–Party relations emanated from opposition to the Party leadership; although the extent of loyalist sentiments should not be underestimated. The source of tension was both internal developments within the Party, and the Conservative Government's initiatives in collective bargaining; both of which were perceived as a threat to traditional trade unionism. Although the British had 'never had it so good' the growth of industrial conflict and economic problems prompted the Tory Government to interfere in bargaining in the public sector. The 'trade union' problem became part of conventional political wisdom especially when the Committee on Prices, Productivity and Incomes blamed inflation on the 'cost push' effects of union bargaining. Union dismay at the 'politicisation of industrial relations' became increasingly apparent.[110]

Matters were exacerbated by the development within the Labour movement of a 'revisionist' school of socialism. Until the 1950s, broadly speaking, the Party and the unions had clear spheres of influence; the Party did not interfere in union matters, whilst the unions stayed out of less direct political matters. However, Tony Crosland in his *Future of Socialism* decried the class nature and industrial militancy of the unions. The 'revisionists', unlike the old Labour Right, were initiators of change; and in attacking the 'class consciousness' of unionists they were perceived by the unions as criticising a key concept of voluntarism, and aroused the sensitivity of trade unions.[111] Following Labour's third successive electoral defeat in 1959 the revisionist school were increasingly anxious to disassociate the Party from the 'cloth cap' image which the links with the unions gave it. In addition they criticised union control over the Party, and decision making within unions, although at no stage did they wish to jettison the industrial wing.[112]

The unions were not only critical of what they regarded as 'dilettante socialist' policies;[113] they were also anxious to show their political independence and their autonomy to negotiate on behalf of their members, at a time when they felt increasingly threatened by the Conservative Government. The inevitable conflict between the party 'revisionists', including Hugh Gaitskell, and disaffected elements within the unions centred on the 'Clause Four' and 'Unilateral Disarmament' debates.

Gaitskell wished to qualify Clause Four with declarations of socialist values other than nationalisation, and which implied acceptance of the 'mixed economy'. Miliband has suggested the opposition to Gaitskell on these proposals and on defence policy was indicative of currents within the movement in pursuit of more radical policies. At the 1959 Conference 'speaker after speaker rose to pour scorn on the acceptance of a mixed economy'.[114] An alternative view is that union opposition to amending Clause Four represented the innate conservatism and sentimentality of the union leadership. They opposed the 'revisionists' as they opposed the 'Bevanites' because they were initiating change, and unsettling the Party's traditions.[115] It has also been argued that the unions' policy on 'unilateral' disarmament was concerned not with defence policy, but the leadership question, including resentment at Gaitskell's initiative on Clause Four.[116]

It is possible to substantiate this view by comparing the unions' unanimous opposition to the Clause Four initiative with the considerably less than unanimous support for unilateral disarmament. Unions could be on the Right without being revisionist, because the latter was perceived as threatening voluntarism, whilst the former was not. This explains the capacity of the Campaign for Democratic Socialism (CDS) to help change union conference decisions in 1961. The CDS generally avoided the charge of factionalism not only because of its subtle methods, but also because it 'tapped' the inherent loyalty within the unions.[117] By the time the 'defence' issue was resolved the Clause Four debate had been settled, whilst Gaitskell had emphatically defeated Wilson in the leadership ballot. The containment of the revisionists on the Clause Four question meant that voluntarism was no longer overtly under internal attack, Gaitskell's position was secure – therefore there was no point in challenging Defence Policy.

The real motives of unions to these contentious issues is an area historians should reconsider with vigour. However, by the early 1960s the threat from the Conservative administration to traditional unionism was reflected in the pay pause of 1962, and Chancellor Selwyn Lloyd's 'guiding light' of $2\frac{1}{2}$ per cent for wage increases; whilst in January 1964 the House of Lords decision in *Rookes* v. *Barnard* posed a new threat to the traditional legal immunities of trades unions. The post-war parameters within which voluntarism had operated were receding; the 'shadow of the State' once again loomed ominously. This explains, in part, why the unions donated £600,000 to the Labour Party at the 1964 election, an increase of 84 per cent over 1959.[118]

Despite this tangible symbol of alliance unionists were not as committed as Labour politicians to the need for an incomes policy; but mutual acceptance of a 'planned growth in incomes' through economic growth camouflaged these differences. The deceptive cohesion provided by Harold Wilson's leadership did not prevent increasing functional differentiations in Party–union relations. After 1960 there were no more joint Labour Party–TUC statements, in 1962 only individual members of the Party could qualify as union delegates to the Party Conference; whilst during the 1960s meetings of the National Council of Labour, so influential in the 1930s and 1945–51, diminished considerably.[119] When the Labour Party won the 1964 General Election with its commitment to the 'white hot heat' of the technological revolution, the union movement had, in effect, opened the lid on Pandora's Box.

The threat to voluntarism

The Wilson administration's policies of 'positive interventionism' led to the most dramatic incursions into the traditions of voluntarism; involvement in collective bargaining was spearheaded through a Prices and Incomes Board, and attempts were made to reform industrial relations through legislation. Initially the Government secured the consent of the trade unions to a voluntary incomes policy; the Party presented itself as the progenitor of technological revolution which would lead to sustained and real growth. Accordingly both employers and unions signed a Declaration of Intent on Productivity, Prices and

Incomes, agreeing to the P & I Board, and wage norms. With the exception of the giant TGWU, the administration enjoyed the co-operation and goodwill of the unions.[120] However, because of economic exigencies and external pressures the Government gave the PIB compulsory powers to delay and vet wage increases, and to apply fines against recalcitrant strikers. Frank Cousins, the TGWU's leader, who had been Minister of Technology in the Government, resigned, and described the issue as the most important facing the unions this century.[121]

Nevertheless during a six months income freeze and a subsequent period of severe restraint union leaders continued to give their support to the Government. However, by 1968 increasing disaffection within the wider labour movement was apparent; and at the TUC and Party Conferences of that year motions opposing incomes legislation won overwhelming support.[122] Increasing signs of dissent were also apparent within the PLP. To make matters worse there were instances of unions and union branches disaffiliating from the Party; whilst in 1966 the numbers paying the political levy fell by 192,000 (the biggest drop since 1928).[123]

The issue of incomes intervention was resolved when the Government decided in 1969 that prices and incomes policies were no longer acceptable to its supporters. A General Election was in sight, and the Government needed the support of trade unionists, its traditional social base, to stay in power. In addition, the Government had yielded to a number of strikes, for example the dockers and dustmen, thus undermining the precept of their own wages policy. This was set against the backcloth of popular debates about strikes and industrial unrest, and the growing predominance of the belief that strikes were a cause rather than a symptom of the UK's economic problems.

A recurrent theme in Government–union relations was the Party's desire to court a broad range of opinion contrasting with the unions' need to represent their specific interests. Nowhere was this better highlighted than in the *In Place of Strife* proposals. Despite the 1968 Royal Commission's preference for the procedural and structural reform of industrial relations and its objections to statutory inter-vention, a White Paper was published proposing, amongst other things and in certain situations, conciliation pauses, compulsory strike ballots and the Ministerial settlement of inter-union disputes.

The General Council of the TUC opposed the Bill, including Right wingers such as Jim Conway (AEU), who believed the penal clauses sounded 'the death toll of British trade unionism, they drive a wedge between the Labour Party and the trade unions'.[124] Rank and file opposition was apparent in token strikes called by the Liaison Committee for the Defence of Trade Unions. The Ford strike of 1969 further illustrated objections to penalty clauses in bargaining agree-ments.

It was also clear that opposition to the Bill was not confined to the

TUC. In March, 53 M.P.s, including members of the normally loyal TU group, voted against the Government; in addition the NEC voiced its opposition, including the Home Secretary, Jim Callaghan. Rumours of a coup on the leadership abounded, and by May it was clear a majority of the Cabinet opposed the Prime Minister's stance.[125]

The unions' desire was not to unseat the Government, but to maintain the voluntarist system intact. At a special TUC Conference in 1969 a 'Programme for Action' had been devised whereby the TUC was to adopt a more positive role in unofficial disputes; the TUC also hoped to accommodate the PLP to these proposals. Eventually, the Chief Whip impressed on Wilson the extent of the PLP's opposition, and the Premier agreed to accept the TUC's proposals which were endorsed by a 'solemn and binding undertaking' and the Bill's clauses were dropped.

Despite the stress in relations between the unions and the Party the TUC sought a realistic solution with the Government; Ministers showed a willingness to negotiate. Wilson sensibly left himself room for manoeuvre and could claim that the TUC had moved more in one month than in 40 years. However, the Labour movement had lived through and survived its most important crisis since 1931.[126]

Incomes Policy and industrial relations reform had been advocated not only by those in the Party who saw it as an integral part of a mixed economy acceptable to international financiers and the general public, but also by those, such as Castle and Crossman, who saw it as a prerequisite of a socialist society. Union opposition was directed against both these viewpoints; it was they, not the Government or the PLP, that represented working class interests. By 1966 only 32 per cent of Labour M.P.s had working class origins; the Chairman of the PLP felt, 'that too many Labour Ministers are removed by education and life's experience from the great mass of the movement. . . . They appear at times to be alienated from working class thinking'.[127] Frank Cousins noted, 'It is not Harold Wilson's Labour Party, it is ours'.[128]

Starting from this premise it followed that trade unions wished to maintain their autonomy as organisations. State intervention in collective bargaining appeared to abnegate, to a great extent, the trade unions' organisational role. These fears were substantiated by some of the biggest yearly falls in trade union membership in the post-war period.[129] The philosophy of the new leaders of the Transport and Engineering Unions – Jack Jones and Hugh Scanlon – emphasised strong workplace bargaining and the devolution of power to shop stewards. They opposed 'Woodcockism'; that is, trade unions having too close an association with the Government, including the operation of an incomes policy.[130]

The unions wished to retain their collective bargaining prerogatives because of what they regarded as inequities in other areas of the economy; they claimed to be disappointed at the lack of growth and planning, and what they perceived to be the more favourable treatment of dividends and capital. The Wilson administration also came unstuck on its harsher treatment of the public rather than the private sector; pressures on the low paid were compounded by increases in import prices, and the incidence of the poverty trap.[131]

The development of a social contract

The 1969 Labour Party Conference, despite opposition from the TGWU and the AEU, gave support to 'Agenda for a Generation' which contained a commitment to incomes policy; the same Conference also passed a motion favouring a 'voluntary policy'; but relations between the union and the Party were still strained.[132] The repercussions of this were apparent in the 1970 Election result, where conflicting interpretations suggest that Labour lost because many of the Party's regular supporters abstained in disgust at Government incursions into voluntarism. Alternatively, it has been argued that the Conservatives capitalised on the Government's failure to take firm action.[133]

Clearly the Party needed the industrial and political support of the unions to sustain itself. The lessons for the unions were as yet unclear and only became increasingly apparent in the four years of the Heath administration. By 1974 a new cohesion had been reached in union–Party relations, to appreciate why attention must be paid to relations with the Conservative Government.[134]

The 'Selsdon Man' policies of the Heath administration consisted of giving greater breadth to market forces, and, if necessary, allowing unemployment to rise. Wages in the public sector would be strictly controlled by a 'N–1' policy; whilst trade unions would be brought under the rule of law by the provisions of the Industrial Relations Act. The provisions of this legislation allowed for judicial incursions into the traditions of voluntarism on an unprecedented scale, far in excess of the *In Place of Strife* proposals.

However, the unions refused to recognise the institutions created by the Industrial Relations Act and adopted a non co-operative stance; famous cases involving the TGWU and the AUEW illustrated, what in effect, was a policy of civil disobedience. Threats of a general strike in 1972 following the imprisonment of five dockers (the Pentonville five) illustrated the prudence of the past traditions of non-intervention.[135] The Act's inadequacy in the face of the railwaymen and miners' strikes amplified the futility of using the judicial apparatus of the State to achieve economic goals.

The policy of 'Cabinet laissez faire' also failed. Although by January 1972 the number unemployed was over 1 million, trade union bargaining power had not diminished. Sit-ins at UCS and Rolls Royce illustrated the workers' unwillingness to accept mass redundancies and closures. Discontent with the public sector wage policy led to a number of strikes, and culminated in the successful miners' strike of 1972.

The final irony was that the Tory Prime Minister who had seemingly renunciated the pragmatism that had been the traditional strength of British Conservatism, aptly enough, Janus like, did an about turn. In August 1972 he initiated tripartite talks and proposed a concordat to management and trade unions. Despite Tory opposition to an Incomes Policy in 1970, the Government eventually imposed a wage freeze, and subsequently a statutory incomes policy.

The 'Tripartite' talks were largely unsuccessful. The Government was restricted by constitutional proprieties and Conservative principles; the unions felt the emphasis had been on consultation rather than negotiations, nor were they too anxious to become involved with the Conservative administration.

Mr Heath's 'Selsdon Man' policies provided the crucible within which the social contract developed, and are a prerequisite to understanding the new mutuality achieved between the Party and the unions in this period.[136] The response of the unions to the initiatives of the Conservative Government (and previously the Wilson Government) meant that union leaders had to seriously consider and confront the dilemmas facing their predecessors in the 1920s and 1930s. The nature of voluntarist doctrine, and the unions' relations with the Labour Party, meant that there was a built-in ambivalence in union attitudes to the role of the State in society.

This rested on the belief that the State should not interfere with collective bargaining; on the other hand it allocated the State a positive role, which involved using the Government to establish a floor of rights at the workplace, and the enactment of legislation beneficial to the working classes. Whilst voluntarism was a convenient ideology it was also a doctrine with a built-in dilemma. It was something more than business unionism, but it was not a Marxist–Leninist conception of trade unionism.

The shadow cast by the State in the form of incomes policy and industrial legislation meant that trade unions, as never before, had to clarify their attitudes to the Government. How were they to define the areas of non-State intervention; and those areas of positive intervention? The traditional contours of British politics were more malleable than at any time since the war. We will have to wait until memoirs are published, and records revealed; but there is evidence to suggest that trade unions were fearful of either a fascist backlash, or its cosmetic offspring, a 'national government'. This was true at the time of both the Heath and third Wilson administration.[137]

The policies of industrial conflict and civil disobedience placed the trade unions in a potential cleft stick situation. Either the unions overthrew the State, or the State imposed its hegemony over the unions; or alternatively the unions discovered a political initiative and created positive outlets for channelling their fears and aspirations. Fortunately the unions had both the will power and the intelligence to choose the third of these alternatives. They were assisted to a considerable extent by the inept Mr Heath, who had forgotten 'the fundamental political fact of modern Britain, namely, that this country could not be run in flat defiance of its working class majority'.[138]

Mr Heath fell between two stools; he was not flexible enough to concede an increase to the miners outside the norms of incomes policy, and lacked the will power and instinct that no doubt a latter day Lord Birkenhead would have shown. In an attempt to emulate Baldwin, the Premier defined the problem as one of 'Who governs Britain'; but whereas Baldwin had presented the 1926 strike as a threat against the State, Heath presented it in terms of a challenge to the Government (a subtle, but important, difference). Worse still, he actually gave the people an opportunity to judge. Unfortunately, for him, the scales of justice tilted slightly Left. The return of a Labour Government in 1974 owed much to the perspicacity of Harold Wilson; but more important, the wisdom and statesmanship of Jack Jones.

During the early 1970s the concept of a 'social contract' had gained credence within the Labour movement. Lord Balogh, the Labour economist, had floated the notion in *Labour and Inflation*, and union leaders such as David Basnett (GMWU) spoke of the need for agreement 'on the broad lines of an equitable economic and social development'.[139] However, it was Jack Jones, who at a Fabian meeting at the 1971 Conference argued for an end to 'the stress and strain between the trade union and intellectual wings of the party'.[140] These sentiments were supported in speeches by both politicians and trade unionists, and led to the establishment in January 1972 of a new TUC–Labour Party Liaison Committee. The committee consisted of six leading M.P.s (representing the PLP), six members of the NEC and six TUC leaders.[141]

Frequent meetings of the committee provided a forum for the most influential men on both sides of the movement to exchange ideas, and during the years up to 1974 its policy statements formed the basis for future Party policy, and the presentation of a social contract to the electorate.[142] Politicians recognised the need for the goodwill of the trade unions, and although Party leaders did not ditch their commitment to an incomes policy its status was left open, realistically taking account of the fears and reservations held by the leading trade union protagonists. The politicians' concern with constitutional proprieties was also quite evident, where industrial action had political implications.

On the trade union side the social contract represented an attempt to clarify the role of the State in society. It sought the repeal of the Industrial Relations Act, thereby restoring the voluntarist framework *de jure* as well as *de facto*. But in addition it called for positive employment legislation, beneficial to workers, but especially union-organised workers, that would act as a legal support (not replacement) to voluntarism.[143] In this way it was hoped to allay fears about union autonomy and relevancy. If (and it was only if) the union role in wage determination was curtailed unions would act as a watchdog at the workplace. The call for Industrial Democracy and an independent arbitration service formed part of this package.

Although the modern Welfare State has been viewed as the successful adaptation of capitalism to the demands of modern trade unionism, trade unions still have many demands that could not be gleaned from collective bargaining alone. Political unionism in certain spheres overrides the importance of economic unionism and parts of the social contract were evidence of this.

The TUC sought controls over food prices, profits, profit margins and productivity. In housing it desired the repeal of the 1972 Housing Finance Act, the municipalisation of private rented property and greater security of tenure for tenants. This demand extended to the public ownership of building lands, and an increase in the number of houses built. The redistribution of income and wealth, increased old age pensions and improved social services also figure prominently in the TUC's plans, together with effective supervision of the investment policy of the large private corporations.[144]

The stand taken by the Heath Government illustrated that there are policy areas where Tory governments are not willing to negotiate with the trade unions, because they regard them as within their prerogative of government. But, even if they were willing to forego the constitutional principle involved, the Conservative Party must have regard to its traditional support in the country, and their ideological preferences. The implications of this have been that the positive actions that the trade unions required of the State could only be forthcoming from a Labour Government.

The basic parliamentarianism that underwrites British society, which is accepted by union leaders and members, suggests that in a system of 'competing elites', the trade unions must look to the election of a Labour Government, and once it was elected in February 1974, to its continuation in office.[145] In which case, past events suggested that a Government undertaking the positive tasks that the trade unions desired must also seek symmetry in its outlook, and hence have an interventionist role (of sorts) in the sphere of collective bargaining. First, because it is not likely to win the election otherwise; second, unless a Government is able to control inflation it is unlikely it could facilitate those reforms that the trade unions desired.

Union recognition of this, together with the fears outlined earlier about political uncertainties, explain the unanimity at the 1974 TUC for the General Council's policy of support for the social contract. They are also the key to understanding the support for respective pay norms of £6, £2.50 to £4.00, and 10 per cent in the years 1975–78. The rapprochement between the trade unions and the Party leaders was nowhere better illustrated than at the 1975 Conference when Jack Jones publicly reprimanded the old Leftist warhorse M.P. Ian Mikardo for his attacks on the Government's policies.[146]

The social contract is best understood not only as a description of substantive policy contents, it is also descriptive of a political method and procedure; a way of reconciling the voluntarism of trade unionism with the governmental objectives of the Labour Party. At its zenith it is a paradigm of the alliance between the unions and the Labour Party; but it also encapsulates the seeds of stress.

Whether, in substantive terms, either the unions or the Labour Government have delivered their share of the contract is for future historians to consider in the perspective of time. But in the four years of the contract the latent constraints on both unions and the Labour Government have resurfaced to which the 1978 Party Conference bears witness. On the union side these are the complex bargaining arrangements in British industry, neither of which readily lend themselves to central direction. This, together with the jealous sense of bargaining autonomy, which rightly or wrongly shop stewards have; and the expectation from union members, socialist and non-socialist alike, that the union is the vehicle of their desires explains the increasing disenchantment with incomes policies. The constraints on the Government side are the familiar ones facing socialist governments, fears of destabilising an inherited mixed economy, world financial opinion and a desire to retain broad electoral support.

The dilemma does not stop there; agreement by the unions to pay restraint in the period 1975–78 implied the responsible acceptance, no matter how tacit, that excessive wage demands contribute to inflation. In which case withdrawal from incomes policy means one of two things – either that unfettered collective bargaining will permit current social and economic arrangements to continue, or unfettered collective bargaining will destabilise the economy and society. The former is basically business unionism, and precludes or severely restricts political initiatives in the social sphere. The latter leads to chaos unless the object is revolution; and the role of trade unions is Marxist–Leninist.

Either way voluntarism as a tangible philosophy would be dead. A social contract without an incomes policy (albeit a voluntary and highly flexible one) must have one of these consequences. The dilemma from a Labour Government's point of view (and from a sane Tory point of view, also) is that having accepted the legitimacy and strength of the union movement in society, they must adopt economic and social policies within parameters that trade unions and their members will feel are worth the undertaking of obligations. But in addition it is the responsibility of the Party to convince the wider society and the international community that such policies are necessary for industrial stability in the UK.

The British Labour movement is steeped in ambivalence, in particular in its attitude to the role of the State in society, a tendency that is reflected in its relationship with the Labour Party. The evolution of a 'social contract' in the 1970s was an attempt to resolve the tensions which had enmeshed union–Party relations in the late 1960s; nevertheless this 'new consensus' also contains the seeds of conflict. How matters will resolve themselves is a moot point. It is possible but unlikely that 1931 will repeat itself this time as tragedy. What is more probable is that the current generation of trade unionists and politicians has learned from the lessons of the past. Despite the almost unconscious step-by-step approach of previous labour leaders, they have left a 'house that is not for Time's throwing'.

July 1978

Notes

1. E. Hobsbawm, *Labouring Men*, Weidenfeld & Nicolson (London) 1976, p. 377.
2. A. Flanders, 'The Tradition of Voluntarism', *British Journal of Industrial Relations*, Vol. XII, No. 3, November 1974.
3. A. Lozovsky, *Marx and the Trade Unions*, quoted in W. E. J. McCarthy (Ed.), *Trade Unions*, Penguin (London) 1972, p. 57.
4. See I. Richter, *Political Purpose in Trade Unions*, Allen & Unwin (London) 1973, p. 43.
5. Quoted in D. Robinson, 'Labour Market Policies', in W. Beckerman (Ed.), *The Labour Government's Economic Record 1964–70*, Duckworth (London) 1972, p. 332.
6. H. A. Clegg, A. Fox, A. F. Thompson, *A History of British Trade Unions Since 1889*, Vol. 1, OUP, 1964, p. 486.
7. Quoted in L. Minkin, 'The British Labour Party and the Trade Unions: Crisis and Compact', in *Industrial and Labour Relations Review*, Vol. 28, No. 1, October 1974, p. 19.
8. Ibid., p. 9.
9. Quoted in S. Beer, *Modern British Politics*, Faber & Faber (London) 1965, p. 113.
10. See A. Flanders, *Management and Unions* Faber & Faber (London) 1970, p. 289 and pp. 24–37; and M. Rogin, 'Voluntarism: The Political Functions of an Anti-political Doctrine', *Industrial and Labour Relations Review*, Vol. 15, No. 4, June 1962.
11. See A. Briggs, 'The Language of "Class" in Early Nineteenth Century England', in A. Briggs and J. Saville (eds), *Essays in Labour History*, Vol. 1, Macmillan (London) 1967; E. Hobsbawm, *Labouring Men*, op. cit., p. 323; C. A. R. Crosland, *The Future of Socialism*, Schocken Books (New York) 1963, pp. 62 and 133; M. Bulmer (Ed.), *Working Class Images of Society*, RKP (London) 1975, p. 5.
12. R. Blake, *Disraeli*, Eyre & Spottiswoode (London) 1967, p. 555.
13. E. Phelps Brown, *The Growth of British Industrial Relations*, Macmillan (London) 1959, p. xxi.
14. R. Moore, *The Emergence of the Labour Party 1880–1924*, Hodder and Stoughton (London) 1978, p. 24.
15. See J. Lovell, *British Trade Unions 1875–1933*, Macmillan (London) 1977, Ch. 2 passim.
16. H. A. Clegg *et al.*, op. cit., p. 297 and R. Moore, op. cit., p. 31.

17. F. Bealey and H. Pelling, *Labour and Politics 1900–1906*, Macmillan (London) 1958, pp. 12, 22–3, 74.
18. E. Hobsbawm, op. cit., p. 184; and G. Stedman Jones, *Outcast London*, Clarendon Press (Oxford) 1971, p. 348.
19. R. Moore, op. cit., p. 68.
20. Ibid., p. 68.
21. G. Stedman Jones, op. cit., p. 317 and J. Saville 'Trade Unions and Free Labour: the Background to the Taff Vale Decision', in A. Briggs and J. Saville, op. cit., passim.
22. H. A. Clegg *et al.*, op. cit., pp. 362–3.
23. F. Bealey and H. Pelling, op. cit., p. 14, and J. Saville, op. cit., p. 317.
24. F. Bealey and H. Pelling, op. cit., p. 83.
25. H. Pelling *A Short History of the Labour Party*, Macmillan (London) 1974, p. 11.
26. For a discussion of the events surrounding 'Taff Vale' see F. Bealey and H. Pelling, op. cit., Ch. IV, passim.
27. R. McKibbin, *The Evolution of the Labour Party 1910–1924*, OUP (London), 1974, p. 56.
28. Ibid., p. 86, and D. Howell, *British Social Democracy*, Croom Helm (London) 1976, p. 23.
29. Quoted in B. Simpson, *Labour: The Unions and The Party*, Allen & Unwin (London) 1973, p. 58.
30. R. Moore, op. cit., p. 85.
31. S. Beer, op. cit., p. 119–20; H. Pelling, *A Short History of the Labour Party*, op. cit., p. 21.
32. H. Pelling, ibid., p. 30; R. McKibbin, op. cit., p. 20.
33. R. McKibbin, ibid., p. 81.
34. R. Miliband, *Parliamentary Socialism*, Merlin Press (London) 1973, p. 28.
35. S. Webb to Lady Betty Balfour in N. MacKenzie (Ed.), *The Letters of Sidney and Beatrice Webb*, 3 vols., CUP, 1978, Vol. III, p. 27.
36. S. Webb to B. Webb, op. cit., p. 72.
37. H. Pelling, *A Short History of the Labour Party*, op. cit., pp. 25–6.
38. R. Miliband, op. cit., p. 35.
39. R. McKibbin, op. cit., p. 89. Also see R. Harrison, 'The War Emergency Workers' National Committee 1914–20', in A. Briggs and J. Saville (eds), *Essays in Labour History 1886–1923*, Vol. II Macmillan (London) 1971.
40. L. Birch (Ed.), *The History of the TUC 1868–1968*, TUC (London) 1968, p. 66.
41. A. Bullock, *The Life and Times of Ernest Bevin*, Heinemann (London) 1960, Vol. 1, pp. 45–6.
42. J. Lovell and B. C. Roberts, *A Short History of the TUC*, Macmillan (London) 1968, p. 50 and M. B. Hammond, *British Labour Conditions and Legislation During the War*, (New York) 1919, Ch. 5, passim.
43. J. Hinton, *The First Shop Stewards Movement*, Allen & Unwin (London) 1973, pp. 42–3.
44. A. Bullock, op. cit., p. 49.
45. For details of the above see R. Harrison, op. cit., passim; and R. McKibbin, op. cit., passim, pp. 104–5.
46. S. Beer, op. cit., p. 149.
47. R. Harrison, op. cit., p. 259.
48. J. M. Winter, 'Arthur Henderson and the Russian Revolution, and the Reconstruction of the Labour Party', *Historical Journal*, XV, 4, 1972.

49. R. McKibbin, op. cit., pp. 98–102 and 244; B. Pimlott, *Labour and the Left in the 1930s*, CUP, (Cambridge) 1977, p. 113.
50. R. McKibbin, op. cit., Ch. 7, p. 242–3.
51. R. Barker, 'Political Myth: Ramsey MacDonald and the Labour Party', *History*, Vol. 61, No. 201, Feb. 1976, p. 54.
52. S. Webb to B. Webb, 23/1/1917, N. MacKenzie, op. cit., Vol. III, p. 78; H. Pelling, *A Short History of the Labour Party*, op. cit., p. 39.
53. The establishment of the General Council of the TUC in 1921 was an attempt to come to terms with what Bevin described as 'a great shapeless mass, all the time struggling to co-ordinate its efforts, but finding itself without a head to direct'. J. Lovell and B. C. Roberts, op. cit., p. 59.
54. A. Bullock, op. cit., p. 135.
55. A. J. P. Taylor, *English History 1918–1945*, Pelican (London) 1976, p. 193.
56. V. L. Allen, *Trade Unions and the Government*, Longmans (London) 1960, pp. 149–50.
57. Ibid., p. 226; also see R. Miliband, op. cit., p. 109.
58. H. Pelling, *A History of British Trade Unionism*, Pelican (London) 1971, p. 170.
59. V. L. Allen, op. cit., p. 232.
60. H. Pelling, *A Short History of the Labour Party*, op. cit., p. 59; V. L. Allen, op. cit., p. 225; W. D. Muller, *The Kept Men*, Harvester Press (London) 1977, pp. 36–9.
61. H. Pelling, ibid., p. 49.
62. W. D. Muller, op. cit., p. 40.
63. See, for example, H. Pelling, *A Short History of the Labour Party*, op. cit., p. 61; A. Bullock, op. cit., Ch. 13, passim; B. Simpson, op. cit., p. 95; L. Daly, 'Protest and Disturbance in the Trade Union Movement', *The Political Quarterly*, Vol. 40, No. 4, Dec. 1969, p. 451.
64. A. Bevan, *In Place of Fear*, Heinemann (London) 1952, p. 25.
65. B. Webb to J. M. Keynes in MacKenzie (Ed.), *Letters*, op. cit., Vol. 2, p. 271; also see B. Webb, *Diaries 1924–1932*, Penguin (Harmondsworth) p. 92.
66. K. W. Wedderburn, *The Worker and the Law*, Pelican (London) 1971, p. 30; and S. Pollard 'Trade Union Reactions to the Economic Crisis', in S. Pollard (Ed.) *The Gold Standard and Employment Policies Between the Wars*, Methuen (London) 1970, p. 151.
67. G. D. H. Cole, *A History of the Labour Party from 1914*, Routledge & Kegan Paul (London) 1948, p. 205.
68. K. D. Muller, op. cit., p. 42.
69. S. Pollard, op. cit., passim.
70. R. Miliband, op. cit., p. 206; note that trade union membership declined from 8½ million in 1920 to 4½ million in the early 1930s, S. Pollard, op. cit., p. 159.
71. H. Pelling, *A Short History of the Labour Party*, op. cit., p. 77.
72. B. Pimlott, op. cit., p. 19.
73. H. Pelling, *A Short History of the Labour Party*, op. cit., p. 77; B. Pimlott, op. cit., p. 19; R. Eatwell and A. Wright, 'Labour and the Lessons of 1931', *History*, Vol. 63, No. 207, Feb. 1978.
74. S. Beer, op. cit., p. 162; G. D. H. Cole, op. cit., pp. 336 and 344; and for the NFRB and SSIP see G. D. H. Cole, op. cit., p. 282 and B. Pimlott, op. cit., p. 44.
75. See G. W. McDonald and H. Gospel, 'Mond-Turner Talks 1927–1933 – A

Study in Industrial Co-operation', *Historical Journal*, XVi, 4, 1973.
76. N. Branson and M. Heinemann, *Britain in the Nineteen Thirties*, Panther (London) 1971, p. 128.
77. R. Miliband, op. cit., pp. 211–12.
78. S. Pollard, op. cit., p. 160.
79. N. Branson and M. Heinemann, op. cit., p. 25.
80. V. L. Allen, op. cit., p. 32.
81. J. Lovell and B. C. Roberts, op. cit., p. 131; Branson and Heinemann, op. cit., pp. 105–6; H. Pelling, *A History of British Trade Unionism*, p. 198; C. F. Brand, *The British Labour Party – A Short History*, Stanford University Press, 1965, p. 166.
82. See B. Pimlott, op. cit., pp. 174–81, and H. Pelling, *A Short History of the Labour Party*, op. cit., p. 84.
83. M. R. Gordon, *Conflict and Consensus in Labour's Foreign Policy*, Stanford University Press, 1969, p. 74.
84. B. Pimlott, op. cit., pp. 111–40, passim.
85. R. Miliband, op. cit., p. 216.
86. S. Pollard, op. cit., passim.
87. J. Lovell and B. C. Roberts, op. cit., p. 143.
88. P. Addison, *The Road to 1945*, Quartet Books (London) 1977.
89. W. R. Townley, 'British Trade Unions and Government Regulation', *American Federationist*, 1937, p. 1197.
90. Ibid., p. 1198.
91. P. Addison, op. cit., p. 76.
92. Ibid., pp. 100–4, and A. Flanders, *Tradition of Voluntarism*, op. cit., p. 361.
93. L. Birch (Ed.), *The History of the TUC 1868–1968*, pp. 126–7.
94. P. Addison, op. cit., p. 113; H. Pelling, *A History of British Trade Unionism*, op. cit., p. 216.
95. H. Pelling, *A History of British Trade Unionism*, op. cit., p. 213.
96. Ibid., p. 216.
97. Ibid., p. 216.
98. Ibid., p. 231.
99. See L. Minkin, op. cit., p. 13; H. Pelling, *A Short History of the Labour Party*, op. cit., p. 101; S. Beer, op. cit., p. 222.
100. V. L. Allen, *Trade Union Leadership*, Longmans, Green & Co. Ltd. (London) 1957, p. 104.
101. I. Richter, op. cit., p. 43; also see V. L. Allen, ibid., p. 131.
102. S. Beer, op. cit., pp. 200–8, passim.
103. L. Panitch, *Social Democracy and Industrial Militancy*, CUP (Cambridge), 1976, p. 33 and Ch. 1, passim; R. Miliband, op. cit., p. 305.
104. H. Pelling, *A History of British Trade Unionism*, op. cit., p. 228.
105. R. Miliband, op. cit., p. 319; L. Panitch, op. cit., p. 39; H. Pelling, *A Short History of the Labour Party*, op. cit., pp. 109–10.
106. B. Simpson, op. cit., p. 102; L. Panitch, op. cit., p. 40.
107. V. L. Allen, *Trade Unions and the Government*, op. cit., pp. 23–34; P. Addison, op. cit., p. 25; R. Miliband, op. cit., p. 330.
108. R. Miliband, ibid., p. 323.
109. Ibid., pp. 328–9; H. Pelling, *A Short History of the Labour Party*, op. cit., p. 113.
110. V. L. Allen, *Trade Unions and the Government*, op. cit., pp. 109–10.
111. C. A. R. Crosland, op. cit., pp. 13–14, 62, 68 and 133–5.
112. S. Haseler, *The Gaitskellites 1951–1966*, Macmillan, (London) 1969,

pp. 145 and 165; L. Minkin, op. cit., pp. 16–17.

113. Lord Windlesham, *Communication and Political Power*, Jonathan Cape (London) 1966, p. 97.

114. V. Bogdanor, 'The Labour Party in Opposition 1951–64', in V. Bogdanor and R. Skidelsky, *The Age of Affluence 1951–1964*, Macmillan, 1970, p. 98.

115. S. Haseler, op. cit., pp. 168 and 175 and 208.

116. Ibid., p. 174.

117. Lord Windlesham, op. cit., pp. 119–20.

118. L. Panitch, op. cit., p. 52.

119. L. Minkin, op. cit., p. 19–20.

120. L. Minkin, op. cit., p. 26; L. Panitch, op. cit., p. 118.

121. L. Panitch, op. cit., p. 117.

122. Ibid., p. 111; Cousins criticised attempts to undermine, 'the authority of the voluntary system which has been erected by understanding between employers and employees on what wages should be'.

123. Ibid., pp. 138 and 155.

124. Ibid., p. 179.

125. Ibid., p. 182; E. Silver, *Vic Feather, TUC* (A biography), Gollancz (London) 1973, pp. 138–9.

126. See P. Jenkins, *The Battle of Downing Street*, Charles Knight (London) 1970; L. Panitch, op. cit., p. 202; D. Robinson, 'Labour Market Policies', in W. Beckerman (Ed.), *The Labour Government's Economic Record 1964–70*, p. 300, passim; H. Wilson, *The Labour Government*, Penguin (Harmondsworth) 1971, pp. 324–7.

127. L. Panitch, op. cit., p. 188; L. Minkin, op. cit., p. 20.

128. Ibid., p. 190.

129. Ibid., p. 150.

130. L. Minkin, op. cit., p. 24; H. Wilson, op. cit., p. 822; L. Panitch, op. cit., p. 81.

131. See J. Hughes and R. Moore (Eds), *A Special Case*, Penguin (London) 1972, especially Ch. 10, passim and H. A. Turner and F. Wilkinson 'Real net incomes and the wage explosion', *New Society*, 25.2.71.

132. L. Panitch, op. cit., p. 208.

133. See L. Minkin, op. cit., pp. 29–30.

134. For a discussion of Conservative Government policy, see A. Barrett, 'Heath, the Unions and the State', *New Left Review*, No. 77, Jan–Feb. 1973 pp. 3–42.

135. J. Griffiths, 'Reflections on the Rule of Law', *New Statesman*, 24.11.72, pp. 756–8.

136. L. Minkin, op. cit., p. 31.

137. See, for example, J. Jones' speech to TGWU Bicentennial Conference at Blackpool, 1975; *The Times*, 2.7.1975; and also see *The Observer* and *Sunday Times*, 25.6.1978 re Lord Briginshaw.

138. E. Hobsbawm, *Industry and Empire*, Penguin (Harmondsworth) 1978, p. 17.

139. Thomas Balogh, *Labour and Inflation*, Fabian Trust, 1971, p. 6; D. Basnett, *Sunday Times*, 8.4.1973.

140. J. Elliott, *Conflict or Co-operation – The Growth of Industrial Democracy*, Kogan Page, (London) 1978, p. 27.

141. Labour Party Annual Conference Report 1971, p. 8.

142. The Labour Party Manifesto 1974, p. 9; Butler and Kavanagh, *The British General Election of February, 1974*, Macmillan (London), p. 52; L. Panitch,

op. cit., p. 232, passim.
143. For example S. 27, 28, 23, 62, 58, 59 of the Employment Protection
Consolidation Act 1978 and S. 11, 16, 17 and 99 of the Employment
Protection Act support this contention.
144. See the TUC Annual Report, Appendix B and C, 1973.
145. For the commitment to Parliamentarianism, see L. Panitch, op. cit., p. 256;
and K. D. Muller, op. cit., p. 172.
146. See *The Times*, 2.10.1975. Jones interrupted Mikardo's speech to a Tribune
meeting to warn, 'I deplore this sort of attack on trade unions'.

Chapter 4

Labour's electoral base

Chris Cook

The rise of the Labour Party, from its earliest days as a weak pressure group to its towering election victory in 1945, constitutes one of the major political changes of the present century. And crucial to an understanding of this process is an analysis of the changing electoral strengths and weaknesses of the Party. Like the history of the Party itself, an analysis of its varying electoral fortunes produces a welter of paradox. Thus Labour polled a greater percentage of the popular vote in 1931 (traditionally one of the Party's worst moments) than in 1923, when it was to form its first minority Government. Labour's greatest ever number of votes polled – in 1951 – was in an election Labour lost. And Labour came to power in February 1974 with a smaller share of the national vote than at any election since 1935.

Any study of the electoral base of the Party must really begin with the 'Coupon Election' of 1918. Prior to 1918 Labour was represented in Parliament almost entirely as a result of the Gladstone–MacDonald 'pact' of 1903.[1] This was signed to ensure Liberal–Labour co-operation by avoiding conflicting candidatures at constituency level.

This pact was to be absolutely vital in securing Labour success in the 1906 election. Of the combined total of 54 Lib–Lab and Labour members elected, all except six were in constituencies where a pact operated. Only in the three English seats of Deptford, Bradford West and Chester-le-Street and in one of the two seats in Merthyr Tydfil were Labour successful against Liberal opposition. The weakness of the *independent* Labour challenge cannot be too strongly stressed. It is perhaps best illustrated in the case of Scotland, where there was no pact between Labour and the Liberals. Of the 12 Labour candidates in Scotland, only two were elected and the average vote of the Labour candidates was a meagre 2,809 votes. Neither the General Elections of January and December 1910 nor the municipal elections up to 1913 gave Labour any firmer independent electoral base.

All this changed with the important advance secured by Labour in the 1918 election. But the scale of the 1918 achievement must not be exaggerated. For the Labour Party, the results of the 1918 election produced a mixture of disappointment and real advance. With 371 candidates in the field, compared to only 56 in December 1910, the number of Labour M.P.s returned rose from 42 to 60. If this total was relatively disappointing, there was much more comfort in the total votes polled for Labour – 2,245,777 compared with 371,772 in 1910. In a wide variety of industrial seats Labour finished second, forcing the Liberals into third place – itself a distinct advance on the pre-1914 position. Yet the 60 seats won by Labour were not particularly good evidence for the supposed new-found strength of the Party. Eleven of these were unopposed, whilst a variety of other Labour M.P.s had faced only Left-wing 'Socialist' opponents. Similarly, Labour failed to make more than partial inroads even into such mining areas as South Wales, West Lancashire and Yorkshire. Such overwhelmingly industrial seats as Aberdare or Pontypridd in South Wales and the Gorbals and Bridgeton divisions of Glasgow, all returned Coalition Liberals.[2] In the whole of the Greater London area, Labour secured only four seats. In the confused politics of 1918, Labour also won a few unexpected seats which it failed to secure regularly again.

Whatever the shortcomings of Labour's forward march in 1918, its progress was resumed during the very important by-elections of the period 1918 to 1922. Much the most significant feature of the by-elections during the lifetime of the Coalition was this advance of Labour. During 1919 the party won Bothwell (16 July) and Widnes (30 August) from Coalition Conservatives and, in a closely fought contest, gained Spen Valley on 20 December. Labour also polled some extraordinarily high votes in several suburban and middle-class areas. In December 1919, in straight fights against Conservatives, Labour took 42.4 per cent of the vote in St Albans and 47.5 per cent in Bromley. Both were constituencies which Labour had not even contested in 1918. The series of Labour by-election gains continued during 1920 and 1921. In March 1921, Labour notched up three victories – at Dudley, Kirkcaldy and Penistone – within the space of three days. After March 1921 the tide of Labour's advance slackened, although the Party gained Heywood and Radcliffe on 8 June. During the winter of 1921–22 Labour's advance picked up again, with the Party capturing Southwark South-East (14 December 1921), Manchester Clayton (18 February 1922), Camberwell North (20 February) and Leicester East (30 March). Before the fall of the Coalition, Labour made a final gain at Pontypridd on 25 July 1922. In all, between 1918 and 1922 Labour had gained no less than 14 by-election victories, but all except two of these were in working-class strongholds.[3]

With the fall of the Lloyd George Coalition in 1922, Labour was to secure its most impressive advance yet made in the November 1922 election. Indeed, for the Labour Party the results were little short of a triumph. The Party returned with 142 seats, having fielded 414 candidates compared with 371 in 1918. This total of 142 was made up of four unopposed returns, 52 other seats successfully defended and 86 new seats won. Labour failed to hold 19 of the seats it was defending. No fewer than 89 of Labour's 142 seats were held with a majority of the votes cast, compared with the many Liberal seats won on minority votes. The 1922 election left Labour's seats concentrated in certain well-defined areas. Mining districts provided 39 of the 86 Labour gains, while 28 more came from Glasgow, Greater London, Tyneside and Sheffield. The Glasgow returns provided the most striking result, with Labour taking ten of the seats it contested, usually on large swings. In industrial Sheffield enormous swings to Labour of 30 per cent occurred in Attercliffe and Hillsborough. A less satisfactory result of the 1922 advance for Labour was that it was far from evenly spread. Whilst overall the Labour vote rose from 22.2 per cent in the 1918 Coupon Election to 29.4 per cent, the main areas of increase were heavily concentrated in mining areas, Glasgow and the Clyde, Sheffield and parts of London.

These areas produced 64 of the 82 Labour gains. In 85 seats, Labour actually lost ground compared to 1918.[4] The seats where Labour lost heavily in 1922 came in two main categories: agricultural seats, especially in the South Midlands, together with the textile districts of East Lancashire and West Yorkshire. In 64 seats, Labour did not contest constituencies fought in the Coupon Election. In the 83 seats fought by Labour in 1922, but not in 1918, support for the Party rarely exceeded 15 per cent. Since Labour did not contest 135 seats either in 1918 or 1922, and with withdrawals in 64 and declining support in a further 85, there were no less than 284 seats in which, even where a Labour candidate was seen, support was minimal. The Party, although on the road to becoming a truly national Party, still had far to go.

The net outcome of 1922 for the Labour Party was its growth from a relatively ineffective and insecurely-based force to the position of a vigorous and determined opposition, securely based in several major industrial regions.

The Conservative Government under Bonar Law which came to power in 1922 had a comfortable working majority. It seemed likely that another election might not come for four or even five years. Within a single year however Bonar Law had died, to be succeeded by Baldwin, and the country had seen another General Election in December 1923. It was this election – fought largely over the issue of Protection versus Free Trade – which brought about the advent of the first minority Labour Government.

For the 1923 election, Labour fought on a wider front than ever before – a testimony of the extension of at least a rudimentary organisation into more and more rural and suburban areas. With 427 candidates, Labour went on to capture a tally of 41 further seats. The overall outcome was the Conservatives with 258 seats, Labour with 191 and the Liberals with 158.

The 41 Labour gains were almost exclusively to be found in working class industrial constituencies. Labour won 11 metropolitan borough seats, making its first gain in West London, as well as making inroads into such working-class areas as St Pancras, where the Party took two seats. Otherwise, the bulk of the Labour gains were in the boroughs of northern England, with occasional exceptions such as Coventry, Ipswich and Cardiff.

Of the county seats won by Labour, only two, Norfolk South and Maldon, could be classed as rural and in neither case was Labour faced with a Liberal opponent.[5] Otherwise, the Labour gains in county constituencies were confined to such mining divisions as The Wrekin, Frome and Barnard Castle, and semi-industrial seats in the London area, such as Enfield and Gravesend.

The 1923 election marked an important advance by Labour into the remaining Liberal strongholds in the industrial areas. Liberal losses were particularly heavy in their former strongholds in the industrial Midlands. Northampton, Wellingborough, Mansfield, Lichfield and East Leicester were all lost. The Liberals also lost their few remaining strongholds in London, together with such traditional areas as Bristol and Norwich. Four more Liberal seats in Scotland fell to Labour. However, despite these losses, the Liberals had still not been dislodged from their working-class territory in the North-East, together with a variety of textile towns in Lancashire and Yorkshire. Labour's breakthrough in these areas was to come in October 1924.

Overall, the best advance for Labour in 1923 was the Greater London area. The number of members returned leapt from 16 to 37. Otherwise, the same areas contributed the bulk of the Parliamentary Party. Wales and Scotland returned 53 members, Lancashire and the North-West sent 27 and Yorkshire and the North-East 37. In all, these three areas contributed 61 per cent of the total Labour M.P.s after 1923, compared to 75 per cent after 1922.

The 1923 election which heralded the first Labour Government provides a useful point to examine Labour's electoral base from a different angle: the areas where Labour still remained a weak or even non-existent force electorally. Of these, the most obvious and most extensive remained the rural county seats.

Throughout the inter-war period, Labour failed to make any real inroads into the agricultural constituencies. In the 86 most rural seats in Britain, those in which over 30 per cent of the employed male work-force were engaged in agriculture, Labour never won more than five of these in any inter-war election, a total the Party achieved in 1923 and 1929.[6] The only constituency to return a Labour representative consistently was Norfolk North. There were many rural seats which did not see a Labour candidate until 1929 or even 1935 – whilst the potential Labour voters of Leominster (admittedly not a teeming throng) had to wait until 1945 until their first candidate was seen at a General Election.

Apart from the rural constituencies, two important areas of Labour weakness were Birmingham and Liverpool. Neither town returned a single Labour M.P. in the 1923 election. In Birmingham, working-class Conservatism stemmed from the Jo Chamberlain period, while the Protestant anti-Irish vote on Merseyside kept the Conservatives entrenched in Liverpool. Outside these areas, the Liberals also still retained several working class strongholds – not only in the textile areas and the North East. Thus in 1923 such diverse places as Bootle, Wolverhampton, Bethnal Green and Stoke returned at least one Liberal to Parliament. In several cases, Labour remained weak in these areas throughout the inter-war period.

The fact that Labour formed an administration was perhaps the most significant stimulus to the Party's electoral advance that it had ever achieved – at least in the long term. In the short term – as the by-elections of 1924 revealed – it led to frightened Liberals joining the Conservatives and previously apathetic Conservatives jerked into activity. The downfall of the Labour Government over the Campbell affair (see p. 113) brought about one of the most crucial elections in the history of the Party. For it was the election of October 1924 which finally obliterated the Liberal Party and confirmed Labour's position as the alternative to the Conservatives. Too many historians have interpreted this election as a major rebuff for Labour. In the short term, it was. Labour fell from office, with a net loss of 42 seats. But in terms of votes, Labour's absolute vote went from 4,439,780 to 5,489,087 and its share of the vote from 30.7 per cent to 33.3 per cent.

The statistics of the 1924 election require detailed analysis, for they provide a vital backcloth to Labour's electoral fortunes. Labour lost 64 seats in 1924, nine to the Liberals and 55 to the Conservatives. All nine losses to the Liberals were the result of Conservative–Liberal electoral pacts. A striking feature of the 64 Labour losses was that in only 12 cases did the Labour vote actually *decrease*. In these 64 seats, overall the Labour vote *rose* by 99,871. Of the 55 Conservative gains from Labour, 40 occurred in straight-fights, only 15 in three-cornered contests.[7]

Despite its losses, Labour secured 22 gains, several of which were quite remarkable. All these gains were in industrial constituencies. Twelve of the 22 were in constituencies that had previously been held by Labour. Of the other 10 constituencies, the most remarkable gain came in East Edinburgh, a Liberal seat not previously contested by Labour. Labour's sweetest victory was in Paisley, where Asquith was defeated in a straight fight by 2,228 votes. A succession of northern industrial seats were captured by Labour: no less than 13 gains were made in Yorkshire, the North-East and Scotland. In the North-East, Labour captured East Middlesbrough and Gateshead, both in three-cornered contests. Bradford South, Rochdale and Penistone completed these Labour victories in northern England.

The statistics of seats won and lost by Labour in fact disguised the improvement the Party had made in certain areas of the country. Thus, in the West Midlands area, the whole region actually witnessed a fractional swing to Labour. Labour did exceptionally well in Bilston, Walsall (a 5 per cent swing) and Dudley – where Oliver Baldwin secured a 17.8 per cent swing to Labour. There were good results in the Potteries (where Burslem was gained) and in such rural areas as Stone and Rugby.

had gone on to form its first administration. Six Labour M.P.s were returned unopposed in 1931, whereas none had enjoyed this luxury in 1929.

But in 1931 another aspect of the battle-lines had changed. In over 400 constituencies, Labour candidates found themselves faced with a single opponent. Only 99 Labour candidates faced both Conservative *and* Liberal opponents, compared to 447 in 1929. At no previous election in the inter-war period had there been so many straight fights or so few three-cornered contests.[9]

This coming-together of Labour's opponents greatly diminished Labour's electoral prospects. These prospects received their final bodyblow as the election campaign developed.

In the circumstances of 1931, a victory for the National Government was probably inevitable. In the event, the Conservatives were returned with no less than 471 seats. Labour secured a mere 52 seats, the Liberal Nationals returned 35, the Samuelite Liberals 33 and the Lloyd George family group numbered four. There were 12 National Labour members.

In terms of gains and losses, Labour could hardly have fared more disastrously; it had lost no less than 215 seats, with not a solitary gain to compensate for this disaster. The Conservatives, with 202 gains and not a single loss, had captured a huge haul of 182 Labour seats. Liberal Nationals had captured another 10 Labour seats, while Liberals had taken 14.

For the Labour leadership, the results were even worse: the Parliamentary Labour Party had been almost completely annihilated, and its leading figures had suffered worse than most. No fewer than 13 former Cabinet Ministers were defeated and 21 former junior ministers. Thus not only had some 215 Labour M.P.s gone crashing down to defeat, but the most experienced and able of the Party's leadership was either out of Parliament or had defected with MacDonald.

Even the most seemingly secure of the Party's strongholds had been lost: five seats in Durham alone had gone, including such working-class bastions as Blaydon, Houghton and even Jarrow. Five more seats went in Glasgow. In industrial Scotland, the Labour strongholds of Lanarkshire virtually all fell. Of the big cities, Labour was totally without representation in such towns as Birmingham, Salford, Cardiff, Wolverhampton and Plymouth. Almost incredibly, no less than 30 constituencies with a Labour majority of over 10,000 in 1929 had fallen. Not all parts of the country, however, were equally disastrous for Labour.

Many of the mining areas – especially South Wales, West Lancashire and West Yorkshire – remained unshaken in their loyalty to Labour and the Party still retained much of its strength in the slum areas of the East End of London and in Glasgow. These, however, were small consolations as Labour viewed the triumphant coalition forces.

It is these statistics of the Party's grim slaughter in 1931 that have made this election so much a part of Labour's mythology. A closer analysis of the *vote* actually polled by Labour presents a rather different verdict on the 'disaster' of 1931. The first fact that cannot be too strongly emphasised is that Labour polled more votes in 1931 than in any previous election except for 1929. Even the average vote obtained by Labour candidates in 1931 was higher than in 1918 or even 1922. The simple reason why Labour had lost four out of every five seats it was defending was that its opponents were united. Linked to this was the collapse of the Liberal vote. This Liberal collapse, not desertions from the Labour faithful, was the key factor in explaining the heavy loss of seats.[10]

In explaining many facets of political behaviour in the 1930s, this fact is of cardinal importance. For in many of its industrial heartlands, the Labour vote did *not* collapse in 1931. One such example can be seen in South Wales. In the mining areas of Glamorgan, Labour's vote, far from collapsing, actually increased. In every constituency in the county Labour's vote was up from its 1929 level. Labour's support in the mining seats of Monmouthshire was equally impressive. As far as the valleys of South Wales were concerned, 1931 was one of the best-ever electoral performances by the Labour Party.

Perhaps the most interesting display of the solidarity of the Labour vote can be seen, not in South Wales, but in Durham and the North-East, the very area where MacDonald's personal influence might be expected to be strongest. Labour's solidarity in Durham was remarkable. It was not only Durham which demonstrated the solidity of the Labour vote in 1931. Elsewhere in the North-East, Labour's support in its working-class strongholds held remarkably well, while elsewhere the railway towns held to Labour. Thus Swindon and Carlisle actually saw increased Labour votes in 1931, while two more, Crewe and York, had only a slight decline.

An important corollary of Labour's relative success in working-class strongholds was the fact that Labour was also doing well in areas of the greatest unemployment. The depressed areas had always been solidly Labour. In 1931 they retained this loyalty. In the 12 borough constituencies with the highest levels of unemployment, the Labour vote was 95 per cent of its total in 1929. In four seats its absolute vote had risen, in four more it was over 90 per cent of its 1929 level.[11]

Labour's share of the total vote was invariably worse in towns where the *middle-class* vote was largest. In none of the major provincial cities in 1931 did Labour obtain over 50 per cent of the votes cast. However, Labour's *relatively* best results were in the working-class towns, such as Stoke, Sheffield and Hull, and the worst in more middle-class areas such as Portsmouth, Nottingham and Edinburgh. Birmingham, as ever, was an exception to this rule – a working-class town with a very poor Labour performance.

In the aftermath of 1931, abject pessimism by Labour activists was only natural. It was only with Labour's rapid recovery at local level after 1931 that it became apparent even to the Party activists that the Party's basic support and vitality had not been destroyed in 1931. This recovery was soon seen in the by-elections. Labour's first by-election victory occurred on 21 April 1932, when Wakefield was recaptured from the Conservatives on a swing of 8.1 per cent. Labour went on to gain a second by-election victory at Wednesbury, on 26 July 1932. Only two further by-elections occurred during 1932, at Twickenham and Cardiganshire. However, the 17.8 per cent swing recorded to Labour in the straight fight at Twickenham was the largest swing-back to Labour yet evidenced. It was a portent of another major area of Labour revival – the municipal elections of November 1932.

The results of 1931 had been a nightmare for Labour. A mere 12 months later, however, a reversal of Labour's fortunes at municipal level had very suddenly occurred. Labour won 458 seats in 1932, one of its highest success rates to date. Although, compared with 1929, Labour only gained a net tally of 15 seats, this was a gain over one of its previous best years. The size of the Labour recovery compared to 1931 was remarkable. Only a year after the debacle of 1931, Labour was again a Party to be reckoned with in municipal politics. Any chance of a vacuum for extremist parties to exploit had gone.

In the wake of these highly successful municipal contests, Labour's record in parliamentary by-elections also improved as 1933 began. During 1933, Labour gained a variety of seats lost to the Conservatives, including the industrial Rotherham seat and a spectacular win in East Fulham, whilst 1934 saw the recapture of Hammersmith North and Upton. It was not merely in terms of seats gained, however, that Labour was doing well. It was achieving very large and consistent swings in its favour.

Labour's recovery, already marked in 1932, reached new heights in the local elections of 1933. In municipal terms, 1933 was one of the best years the Party ever enjoyed. In the urban district council elections, Labour appeared to have regained, and probably surpassed, its previous high-water mark. The following year, in 1934, for the first time ever, Labour captured control of the London County Council – the largest unit of local government in the country.

By the autumn of 1935, Labour could seem to be reasonably confident that the electoral trough of 1931 had long since been left far behind. In parliamentary by-elections, Labour had captured no less than 10 seats from the Government. A variety of urban seats had been regained for the Party. In municipal elections, the Party had recovered so fast from the debacle of 1931 that it reached targets in 1933 and again in 1934 that it had not reached in the best years of 1926 to 1929. Boroughs that had never before been controlled by Labour, such as Burnley and Greenock, were won by the Party. The reasons for the optimism of both Labour agents and the Party leadership were understandable. But their optimism was to be rudely shattered by the results of the 1935 General Election.

Labour was well prepared for the 1935 contest. Labour's total field of candidates, 552 compared to 516 in 1931, reflected the Party's renewed strength. Apart from a few very rural English county seats, Labour was challenging virtually every constituency. Thirteen of the Party's M.P.s enjoyed an unopposed return.

The overall outcome of the 1935 election was a heavy blow for the Labour Party; it secured 154 seats, but after the high hopes of the 1934 period this net gain of 94 seats came as a bitter disappointment. For though Labour achieved many pleasing results, it was the unevenness of the Party's performance that caused most worries. In Scotland, Labour had still only captured 20 of the 71 seats at stake. Wales was rather better, with 18 of the 35 constituencies returning Labour M.P.s.

In England, Labour's patchy performance was most apparent. A relatively disappointing area was industrial Lancashire. While Labour regained three seats in Manchester, in Liverpool the Party gained only the Everton division and lost the Wavertree seat won in the February by-election. Salford, failed to return a Labour member for any of its three divisions. The two-membered seats in Lancashire and Cheshire also remained extremely loyal to the National Government, with neither Bolton, Oldham, Preston nor Stockport returning a single Labour representative.[12]

Lancashire was not the only industrial area to produce Labour disappointment. In the North-East, such industrial towns as Sunderland, Stockton and the Hartlepools were held for the Government, even though the county divisions voted solidly for Labour. Among the other large industrial cities to stay loyal to the National Government were the railway towns. All the most prominent railway centres, including Derby, Swindon, Crewe, Carlisle and York, returned supporters of the Government. In all, no less than 20 large towns, returning two or more members to Parliament, failed to return a solitary Labour representative to Westminster. Not a single Labour M.P. was returned in Birmingham, Cardiff, Newcastle or Leicester. London was the scene of some of Labour's best results. Whether spurred by Morrison's organisation, or encouraged by the LCC victory in 1934, the Party went on to gain 17 seats in the General Election – returning 22 Labour members compared to five in 1931. The fact remained, however, that in many of the largest boroughs Labour's representation was still woefully thin.

Nor were the results merely the consequence of the vagaries of the electoral system. In only two of these major provincial boroughs (Stoke 53 per cent and Sheffield 51.5 per cent) had Labour obtained a majority of all votes cast. Only in eight other cities (Glasgow 43.4 per cent, Liverpool 44.3 per cent, Manchester 42.2 per cent, Leeds 44.5 per cent, Bristol 46.5 per cent, Bradford 43.5 per cent, Hull 46.3 per cent, Cardiff 41 per cent) could Labour poll over 40 per cent of the votes cast. In terms of Labour's share of the total vote, the worst three Labour towns were Portsmouth (29.4 per cent), Birmingham (33.9 per cent) and Edinburgh (34 per cent). These were figures that gave little consolation to the party.

What, in fact, lay behind Labour's poor performance? A more

detailed examination of the swing in 1935 provides at least some of the answers.

On average, in the 230 constituencies in which there was a straight fight between Labour and Conservative in 1931 and 1935, there was an average swing to Labour of approximately 10 per cent. The differences over the whole country were not very noticeable, except that London swung rather more to Labour (a 12 per cent movement) and Wales slightly less so (8 per cent). Otherwise, variations were not very marked. However, some particular areas and sub-areas showed very marked divergencies from the national pattern. In the case of the major provincial boroughs, these variations of swing were significant. The figures reveal several important trends. In two of these towns, Portsmouth and Plymouth, the rearmament question was clearly a factor keeping the pro-Labour swing at a low ebb.[13] Constituencies with a high percentage of naval or military voters showed swings very much below the average.

In addition, a variety of towns dependent on steel and susceptible to rearmament orders also showed low swings (St Helens 6.1 per cent, Warrington 5.5 per cent, Westhoughton 6.9 per cent, Widnes 6.1 per cent).

A far more interesting element to be seen in the swings in large towns concerned the West Midlands. A very distinct regional pattern of low pro-Labour swings could clearly be seen. Thus, in Wolverhampton there was an average swing of only 2.6 per cent to Labour. In the 12 Birmingham divisions (a city in which Labour failed to win a single seat) the average swing was a lowly 5.7 per cent. Even more remarkable was the brewing centre of Burton-upon-Trent which registered a mere 0.2 per cent swing to Labour. This working-class town remained solidly Conservative. This trend remained confined very much to the West Midlands.

In addition to the West Midlands, a further disappointment for Labour came in the Newcastle and Gateshead area. These results were doubly disappointing, for Newcastle and Gateshead had been among the worst Labour results in the North-East in 1931.

As a general rule, Labour's recovery was often greatest in 1935 where its vote had slipped most in 1931. Some of the towns with large swings to Labour (such as Leicester) were thus simply redressing the balance. And yet there was a curious paradox of the results in 1935. Labour was doing best in its worst areas. Suburban seats, safe rural Tory fiefs, all showed heavy swings from the National Government. One explanation lay in Labour's inability to attract the middle ground; in particular, the former Liberal vote which had gone Tory in 1931.

In its disappointment, however, Labour tended to miss the significance of several good features of the Party's performance. In 1935, Labour had become more of a national Party than ever before in its history. Its field of 552 candidates was a record. Its spread of support was far more even. In 1935 there were very few constituencies which were either not contested or in which Labour failed to save its deposit. The verdict of 1935 was never really challenged or disturbed in the last years of the Depression. From 1935 to the outbreak of war, in by-elections and in municipal contests, electoral politics maintained a fairly even keel. Between the General Election of 1935 and the outbreak of war in September 1939, the pattern of by-election results was very similar to the results of the 1931–35 period. Labour did well, with many big swings in its favour; but none of the swings was large enough to suggest an overall Labour majority. Although Labour gained 13 seats from the Government, virtually all had previously been Labour territory.

Such Labour gains as Wandsworth Central, Ipswich and Kennington (all on swings above 9.5 per cent) were undoubtedly good results. But they were exceptions. The average swing to Labour in the seats it had captured was only 7 per cent. In a variety of by-elections in late 1938 and early 1939, some very low swings to Labour were recorded. It is a sobering thought, in terms of any 1940 General Election, that in the last three contests before the outbreak of war the average swing to Labour was only 3.7 per cent.[14]

During the war, however, a profound change came over British public opinion. Despite the truce called by the parties, this change could be detected in both by-elections and opinion polls. Admittedly, the by-elections were distorted by outdated registers and the wartime factors of conscription and blackout, but the strong anti-Conservative vote in traditional Conservative seats such as Grantham, Wallasey and Eddisbury was unmistakable. In April 1945 the Conservatives lost both Chelmsford and Motherwell, yet *The Times* found 'nothing remarkable' about the result. From mid-1943, the British Institute of Public Opinion began registering a strong Leftward swing. The surveys of the research organisation *Mass Observation* reinforced these findings. By 1945 the nation's mood had not changed. A Gallup Poll published in the *News Chronicle* on 11 July gave Labour 47 per cent of the vote, the Tories 41 per cent and the Liberals 10 per cent – a forecast which proved accurate to within 1 per cent. Despite this evidence, the most extraordinary fact of the 1945 election campaign was the general expectation that the Conservatives would win. As Alan Sked has written:

Most observers appeared to assume that the Conservative Party would win. This was the view of most British politicians and journalists, and even Stalin believed it. He told Churchill at Potsdam that according to Russian and Communist sources the Tories would have a majority of eighty – a figure to which by the end of the campaign Conservative Central Office itself was looking expectantly. Labour Party stalwarts viewed the poll with apprehension and Labour Party Leaders were even accused of seeking their own defeat.[15]

When the votes were counted, the results totally confounded the prophets. Labour won with an absolute majority of a massive 154 – the first time in its history it had won an overall majority. On a swing of 12 per cent since 1935, Labour took no less than 210 seats from the

Conservatives and won 79 seats which had never before returned a
Labour M.P. Its popular vote had risen from 8,325,000 in 1935 to just
under 12 million. Armed with the largest majority yet seen in post-war
British history, the electoral landslide had seen a historic shift as
fundamental as 1906 or 1832.

In every area of the country Labour swept to success. In Scotland
Labour consolidated its strength by winning another 15 seats; in Wales
it gained six seats, among them the three Cardiff ones. It was, however,
in England that the greatest landslide had taken place. The English
boroughs, excluding London, returned 173 Labour M.P.s compared
with only 53 beforehand. In London itself, Labour representation
increased from 27 to 49 M.P.s – Herbert Morrison's majority of 15,000
at Lewisham East, a seat which never before had returned a Labour
candidate, reflecting opinion within the capital. Yet the chief sensation
were the results from the English counties. Traditionally these had been
the strongholds of Conservatism but they now returned 110 Labour
members as opposed to 112 Tories. Moreover, in terms of the popular
vote, Labour had actually come out on top with 4,606,000 votes
compared with 4,412,000 for the Conservatives. The latter had to be
content with wresting the West Country and parts of Wales from the
Liberals.

To win 394 seats, Labour had broken into territory which had never
previously been captured. Of the 209 net Labour gains, 79 were in seats
which had never before returned a Labour M.P. – a total which included
18 which had consistently voted Conservative for a century! At the same
time, Labour made a clean sweep of many of the larger towns, picking
up even the middle-class areas of these cities which had previously
eluded Labour. Thus Labour made a clean sweep at such towns as
Bradford (4) seats, Nottingham (4), Hull (4), Leicester (3), Plymouth (3),
Wolverhampton (3) and Cardiff (3). The most extraordinary large-city
result was Birmingham. In 1935, all 12 Birmingham seats were
Conservative. In 1945, with the number of seats extended to 13, Labour
made no less than 10 gains on an enormous swing of 23 per cent.

In the smaller towns, some of Labour's gains were remarkable. For
such seats as Winchester, Chislehurst, Hitchin and Buckingham to
return Labour M.P.s was a measure of the turnover in 1945.[16] Two other
statistics also reveal the nature of Labour's triumph: throughout the
country, the Party lost only two deposits – a smaller number than the
five Conservative. And whereas the Conservatives managed to achieve a
majority of over 20,000 in only one constituency, no less than 27 Labour
candidates had 20,000+ majorities, with three even topping 30,000.

The election of 1945 had thus produced the largest contingent of
Labour M.P.s ever seen at Westminster – well above even the 364 who
were to be returned in 1966. The Party had polled 48.2 per cent of the
total vote (a figure, ironically, which was exceeded in 1951, when it
polled 48.8 per cent but was defeated).

The size of the national swing to Labour was 12 per cent, but the variations were both large and important. Labour achieved only an average swing of 2.5 per cent in the 15 Glasgow seats and only 6.5 per cent in Liverpool's 11 seats. Yet in some of the most middle-class and safely-Conservative of all seats it achieved enormous swings, often as high as 20 per cent.

After the extraordinary sweeping victory of 1945, the five years up to the election of 1950 produced very little electoral excitement. In these five years, no Government seat was lost to the Conservatives – an extraordinary feat given that Labour lost 16 seats at by-elections between 1966 and 1970. However, a persistent swing to the Conservatives was evident in the by-elections: in 1947 this averaged 6.3 per cent, in 1948 8.4 per cent and in 1949 6.5 per cent. Against this background, Labour clearly went into the 1950 election on the defensive. The outcome (on an 84 per cent poll, the heaviest ever recorded in British history) was paradoxical: Labour was to poll 13,267,466 votes (more than at any previous election in its history) but throughout the country there was an average swing of 2.9 per cent to the Conservatives. As in 1945, very substantial variations in swing occurred in different areas. Kinnear has calculated that 92 mainly middle-class seats swung Conservative by over 7 per cent, while 48 seats actually swung Labour. The 48 seats to swing Labour were the 17 mining seats in South Wales (average swing of 2.3 per cent), ten Durham mining seats (0.9 per cent) and parts of rural Wales and some Scottish industrial seats. A feature of the election was Labour's setback in the middle-class London suburbs.

The cause of Labour's downfall was England – for both Scotland and Wales actually *increased* their representation. As Alan Sked commented on the difference between Labour's setback in the south and elsewhere:

Labour had frightened the middle classes in the suburbs of the home counties and the north as well, although it survived this loss of popularity because it could count on enthusiastic working-class support.[17]

The setback for Labour in 1950 thus led to a much weakened second term of office for Labour with an overall majority of only five. The Attlee Government of 1950–51, with its divisions and resignations, and with its senior Ministers clearly worn out, was an unhappy administration (see pp. 132–3). It was put out of its misery when an election was called for 25 October 1951. This election was to inaugurate a period of 13 years in the political wilderness for Labour. Rarely could an outcome have been more paradoxical. For in the 1951 election, Labour amassed the highest vote – both before and since – in the history of the Party. Its total vote was 13,948,883 and its share of the vote 48.8 per cent – higher even than the 48.0 per cent achieved in 1945 or the 48.1 per cent secured by Harold Wilson in 1966. It represented an increase of 2.7 per cent on its 1950 share. And yet Labour suffered a net loss of 19 seats – losing 21 to the Conservatives but picking up two from the Liberals – for a total tally of 295.

What then was the explanation for Labour's defeat? It could hardly be attributed to a large swing – the average swing nationally was 0.9 per cent, with the 1.2 per cent in England higher than in Scotland or Wales. Several parts of the country – notably Liverpool, Sheffield and Clydeside – barely moved to the Right at all. The real explanation for Labour's defeat lay in the fate of the Liberal vote. The Liberals fielded a mere 109 candidates for the election. Hence, in 1951, there were no less than 495 straight fights between Labour and Conservative, compared to only 113 in 1950. A mass of floating Liberal voters was thus open to capture. It is clear from the Nuffield election analysis that those who deserted their Liberal faith divided 2 to 1 in favour of the Conservatives.[18] The larger the Liberal vote had been, the more the Conservatives benefitted. It was thus the debacle of the Liberal Party which, with a nice touch of irony, enabled that erstwhile Liberal, Winston Churchill, to form his first peace-time administration.

Although Churchill's majority was only modest, his Government easily survived in Parliament. With the economy reviving, with the by-elections quiescent (the Conservatives actually *gained* Sunderland South in May 1953 on a 1.6 per cent swing to the Government), Churchill was able to hand over to his successor, Anthony Eden, in the spring of 1955. It was an opportune moment for a new Prime Minister to appeal to the country. On 26 May 1955 the Conservatives were returned to power with an increased majority.

In terms of a change in Labour's electoral base, the 1955 election was insignificant. In the General Election, including *all* parties, only 15 seats changed hands – the lowest total in any post-war General Election. Although the Conservatives gained 11 seats from Labour, the swing in different parts of the country was tiny: a mere 0.9 per cent to the Conservatives in Wales, 1.3 per cent in Scotland and 1.8 per cent in England. Within England, the Midlands (and particularly the West Midlands, with its 2.7 per cent swing) went more to the Conservatives, whilst London with a 1.8 per cent swing also drifted to the Right. The North was slower to shift. With the exception of the Midlands, the swing was uniformly within 1 per cent of the national average. As a result, there was a relatively small change in total votes – Labour falling from 48.8 per cent to 46.4 per cent, the Conservatives up from 48.0 per cent to 49.7 per cent. One universal feature of the election was a fall in turnout – significantly, the fall was highest in Labour's traditional big city strongholds. Not surprisingly, it was the 13.1 per cent fall in S.W. Islington which was the biggest in the country.[19] In 1955 – and even more in 1959 – there began the start of a trend that has continued ever since (except for 1966 and except for Scotland) in British politics: a tendency for Labour to rely ever more heavily on its traditional support in the big towns, the North, and in industrial Wales and for the Conservatives to become increasingly dominant in the South, the rural areas and the suburbs.

With Labour's second successive defeat in 1955, the most interesting electoral feature of the by-elections was the rapid Conservative recovery in the wake of Suez and the beginnings of a Liberal revival. Between 1955 and 1959 Labour captured only three seats from the Conservatives. It was a significant comment on Labour's lack of electoral appeal that in the six by-elections held in 1959 before the General Election, the swing to Labour was a mere 2 per cent.

The election of October 1959 is rightly regarded as the apogee of Conservative electoral success and a personal triumph for Harold Macmillan. For Gaitskell it was a disaster. With 35 seats changing hands in the election Labour had suffered a net loss of 23 to the Conservatives. Although a disaster for Labour, the results showed very marked regional variations. Of the 28 seats the Conservatives won from Labour, 10 were in the Midlands and nine in the Greater London area. Thus, whilst on average England swung 1.4 per cent to the Conservatives, the swing was far higher in Birmingham (3.3 per cent), the Black Country (4.0 per cent) and Leicester (3.3 per cent). Similarly there were high swings in London and the South – 2.7 per cent in Essex, 2.5 per cent in Hampshire and 4.3 per cent in Plymouth. At the opposite extreme, the Manchester and S.E. Lancashire area actually swung to Labour. The real *bête noir* of the election, however, was Scotland. The whole of Scotland swung 1.4 per cent to Labour and the Conservatives lost four Scottish seats. The swing was most marked in Glasgow and the Clyde. Post-election analysis of Labour's defeat suggested that Labour had lost ground amongst young voters and men, but gained compared to 1955 amongst the over-65s.[20]

Curiously the most significant feature of the election was not perhaps Labour's poor performance but the showing of the Liberals – whose share of the vote increased from 2.7 per cent to 5.9 per cent. This Liberal revival – which was to reach its peak in 1962–63 at Orpington – not only threatened the Conservatives' electoral ascendancy but was to be a contributory factor in Labour's narrow electoral victory in 1964.

In 1959, however, Labour was far more concerned about its loss of support in such areas as the Midlands. To some political observers, it seemed the 'affluent worker' had deserted his traditional party allegiance. With prosperous industrial towns such as Luton and Leicester returning Conservatives, it was clear that Labour would have to revitalise quickly if it were not to become relegated to a permanent state of opposition.

Or so it seemed in 1959, as the defeated Party decided to bury the hatchet in one another. But Labour was to be saved, not by its own unity or strength, but by the increasing difficulties of the Conservative Government under Macmillan. As difficulties mounted with the economy, and as scandals such as the Profumo affair rocked the Government, the by-elections witnessed a dramatic Liberal revival. But at no stage did the Liberals hurt Labour's electoral base. Liberals did best in middle-class and suburban areas, especially in the Home Counties and South-East. Even at the height of the Liberal upsurge, in the 1962 municipal elections, the Labour-controlled boroughs of the

North and Midlands (and in the South-East in such places as Acton and Watford) were hardly affected by the Liberal revival.

Hence, although the Conservatives had recovered lost ground by the time of the October 1964 election, and the Liberal revival had sunk slowly in the West, the basic factor of Labour's 1964 election victory still remained: a Conservative vote weakened by sufficient Liberal defectors to enable Labour (with its own vote stable) to gain victory. In fact, despite Wilson's skill during the campaign, Labour only won the election with the tiniest of majorities. The result was:

Party	Vote	Vote (%)	M.P.s
Conservative	12,001,396	43.4	304
Labour	12,205,814	44.1	317
Liberal	3,092,878	11.2	9
Others	347,905	1.3	–
Total	27,655,374	100.0	630

Overall, the swing to Labour since 1959 had been 2.9 per cent. A feature of the swing in 1964 was its marked variation in different parts of the country – a variation probably due to the patchiness of the Liberal revival and the degree of economic prosperity of the area concerned. Thus depressed areas such as Glasgow, Liverpool and East Lancashire, the Scottish Highlands and Central Scotland, had markedly higher swings to Labour than more prosperous areas such as Birmingham or the agricultural seats of East Anglia.[21] In Birmingham and the Black Country – epitomised by such seats as Smethwick – the immigration question also undoubtedly harmed Labour. The fact that in 1964 Labour won less agricultural seats than in 1950 (the last election when Labour had had a very small majority) can be attributed to the greater prosperity of the agricultural labourers. In contrast to the agricultural areas, almost all the large cities showed above-average swings to Labour – with the exception already mentioned of the West Midlands. The pattern of the 'two nations' was still being forged.

The extremely narrow outcome of Labour's election victory (made even more precarious by the shock by-election loss of Leyton on 21 January 1965) meant that a second General Election was likely within a short time. With Labour's rating high in the opinion polls, and with a swing in its favour of 4.5 per cent in the Hull North by-election of January 1966, an election was called for 31 March 1966. The outcome was Labour's best result since 1945. The party elected 364 M.P.s (compared to 393 in 1945), and polled 13,096,629 votes (48.1 per cent of the total vote). Its net gain of seats was 46. Compared to 1964, the 3.5 per cent swing to Labour across the country was relatively uniform, even in Conservative strongholds. In some cases where the swing was greater than average, the explanation was clearly that Labour was 'compensating' where it had done least well in 1964.[22] This was true of Birmingham, and parts of Leicestershire and London. In all, however, only 22 seats swung more than 7 per cent to Labour – mainly seats in large conurbations, with Hull a particularly good area. Once again, the trend for Labour to do best in the urban areas and worst in the rural areas was reinforced – in 146 large city seats, the average swing was 4.6 per cent; in the 92 most rural seats, the average swing was 2.9 per cent.

In Labour's hour of triumph, this two-nation division was obscured by Labour's obvious successes. Yet less than two years after the 1966 victory, Labour's seemingly secure electoral base had crumbled. With the Labour Government buffeted by successive economic crises, an unprecedented change in the electoral map of the country occurred.

After the 1966 election an almost hitherto unknown volatility began to be seen in electoral behaviour. By-elections, even in the safest of Labour seats, produced political sensations. In the 13 years the Conservatives were in power (from 1951 to 1964) the Party had lost only ten seats.[23] Yet Labour, between 1966 and 1970, lost an incredible 16 of the 31 seats it was defending – a figure even more amazing if one remembers that the Party had lost only 15 seats in the whole period from 1900 to 1964.

Labour's nightmare was at its worst in the 10 months from September 1967 to June 1968. During these months, Labour lost some of its safest strongholds in the country on swings that had not been seen in British politics for a generation. The casualties included such seats as Walthamstow West (swing 18.4 per cent), S.W. Leicester (16.5 per cent), Hamilton (a stunning gain by the SNP), Dudley (21.2 per cent), Acton and Oldham West. Nor was the humiliation confined to seats lost: in March 1967, the voters of West Rhondda, the very symbol of the Labour movement, had come within a whisker of electing a Nationalist M.P.

On all sides, Labour's electoral base seemed to be crumbling: there were massive desertions to the Conservatives in England, while in Wales and Scotland the new phenomenon of Nationalism seemed to threaten Labour's safest seats – seats vital if Labour was to form majority governments at Westminster.

Almost as remarkable as Labour's collapse in these by-elections was its rapid recovery after mid-1969. Such was the recovery – or so it seemed from the Opinion Polls – that Wilson called an early election for 18 June 1970. It was a gamble that went sadly astray.

The Conservatives swept to a comfortable and unexpected victory in June 1970, with the largest swing at an election since 1945. The result is shown opposite.

The 4.7 per cent swing was only slightly less than the 5.2 per cent swing which put Mrs Thatcher into power in May 1979. The largest swings to the Conservatives occurred in the Midlands – there were swings of 9 per cent in such Black Country seats as Dudley and Wolverhampton and in the 12 East Midland seats round Leicester and Nottingham an average swing of 7.2 per cent. A second area to swing heavily Conservative was Lancashire – where the swing in the 16 textile towns averaged 7.4 per cent. Elsewhere in the North and Scotland – as in 1979 – Labour suffered only very low swings against them. This was most noticeable in Merseyside, in Hull and on Tyne and Wear.[24]

Party	Vote	Vote (%)	M.P.s
Conservative	13,145,123	46.4	330
Labour	12,179,341	43.0	287
Liberal	2,117,035	7.5	6
Others	903,299	3.2	7
Total	28,344,798	100.0	630

Hence the 1970 election, with its divergent swings not only between city and country seats, but between North and South, confirmed the long-term trend towards Labour domination of the big cities and the Conservative stranglehold in the suburban and rural areas. The Labour Party after 1970 was more dependent than ever on its traditional areas of support. Perhaps the most striking statistics of 1970 were that Labour held only two seats of the 53 returned by the counties along the South Coast; and not a single Labour M.P. sat for an English seat which was predominantly rural.

One consolation for Labour in 1970 was the relative failure of the Scottish Nationalists, who won only one seat – the remote Western Isles constituency. However, as the by-elections of 1970–74 started to swing almost as violently against the Government as they had from 1966 to 1970, once again it was the third parties who benefitted. In England, Liberals swept to an astonishing series of victories; in Wales and Scotland, Labour's flank seemed once again dangerously exposed.

The Conservative Government, in conflict with the trade unions, went to the country in February 1974 when support for third parties had never been higher in post-war politics. The election was thus a crucial test both of Labour's and the Conservatives' electoral base.

The General Election of February 1974 was one of the most extraordinary in British history. It was held against a background of a state of emergency and a three-day week. It was a time of political crisis and the campaign was bitter. And, as if to intensify the crisis, for the first time since 1929, the election gave no party an overall majority. Labour won 301 seats (compared to 287 in 1970), while the Conservatives captured 296 (as against 330 in 1970). The other parties, with 13, held the balance. After the refusal of the Liberals to enter into a working relationship with Heath, Wilson took office again on 4 March 1974.

Labour was in power again. But it was clear that another election would be needed to resolve the deadlock. This took place in October 1974.

Despite widespread predictions that Labour would win with a comfortable majority, the result proved to be yet another cliff-hanger, as more and more Conservative-held marginal seats stubbornly defied the swing to Labour. In the event, Labour won 319 seats, the Conservatives 277, Liberals 13, the Scottish Nationalists 11 and Plaid Cymru 3. The Conservatives had polled 10,461,583 votes (35.8 per cent), Labour 11,457,079 (39.2 per cent), the Liberals slipped to 5,346,754 (18.3 per cent), while the combined Nationalist vote in Wales and Scotland passed the 1 million mark for the first time.

Labour's majority, though even smaller than the photo-finish result of 1964, was in fact in terms of practical politics considerably more comfortable than it appeared, with a majority over the Conservatives of 43, while the majority over Conservatives and Liberals combined was still 30.

In all, Labour gained 19 seats, for the loss of only one constituency (Carmarthen) to Plaid Cymru. Eighteen of these 19 gains were in England.

Over the whole country Labour achieved a swing of 2.2 per cent from Conservatives. If this swing had occurred uniformly in each constituency, Labour would have achieved an over-all majority of 25. Labour, in fact, could only achieve a small swing of 1.2 per cent in the key Conservative-held marginals that they needed to win. Seats such as Northampton South, Brentford and Norfolk North-West all stayed Conservative, though they would have fallen to Labour on a swing of less than 1 per cent. Part of the explanation seems to lie with the fact of the Liberal vote reverting to the Conservatives. Among the regional variations in swing, Scotland (3.9 per cent) and the North (2.2 per cent) swung Labour far more than the South-West (1.4 per cent) or East Anglia (1.1 per cent). For only the third time in its history (the previous occasions were 1945 and 1966) Labour won *more* seats in England than the Conservatives (251–248) – unlike 1964, when the Conservatives had 261 and Labour 246.

Apart from Labour's inability to win these key marginals, Labour also failed to achieve success in the agricultural areas. In the 50 most agricultural seats, Labour achieved a swing of only 1.6 per cent. Indeed, the result was that the Labour Government formed in October 1974 was supported by fewer M.P.s from agricultural or rural constituencies than any previous Government. Indeed, as if to highlight the point, Labour's most agricultural seat, Carmarthen, was its only loss of the election. The only Conservative marginal to swing Right was the most farming one – N.W. Norfolk – while the one Labour marginal which the Conservatives nearly gained was Labour's most agricultural seat in England – West Gloucestershire.

At the other extreme, no previous administration had been so solidly supported by the big cities. All the major cities swung heavily to Labour – led by Stoke and Hull (5.7 per cent) followed by Newcastle. Not only did Labour do well in the cities, but it polled best in its safest seats. To this extent, Labour tended to pile up its votes in those areas such as Lambeth or Liverpool where it mattered least. Ironically, Labour also did best in some of its most hopeless seats – such as Eastbourne and Hove with the abandonment of the 'tactical voting' that had been seen in February 1974.

The two elections of 1974 provide a useful point to compare the main features of the electoral map of England compared with 1950. The main constituents of Labour's electoral base had remained stable. Its traditional areas of support had stayed the same. The most important change had been Labour's increasing domination of the cities. This is perhaps best illustrated by how the *Conservatives* have declined in these areas. Dr Ramsden has calculated that in 1950 the Conservatives won 28 per cent of the seats in Inner London; in October 1974 they won a mere 17 per cent. Even more dramatic had been the decline in the 14 largest provincial cities. In 1950 the Conservatives won 24 of these seats (30 per cent); in October 1974 they won only eight (a tiny 10 per cent). Expressed differently, the percentage of seats won by Labour in London and the largest cities has risen from 71 per cent in 1950 to 87 per cent in 1974. Partly, this trend is accountable by population redistribution and partly by the breaking-down of old-established patterns of voting (as on Merseyside or in Glasgow, where Nationalism has complicated the voting pattern). Within this pattern, the West Midlands has been a maverick, showing a persistent swing to the Right (the largest swing against the Government from 1966–70 was in the West Midlands seat of Dudley!) Other more specific factors have helped Labour gain individual seats. Thus Labour has picked up seats in Chatham, Plymouth and Portsmouth due to the run-down of the Navy. In the opposite direction, Labour has weakened since 1950 in parts of Wales, the West Riding, East Midlands and East Anglia. Thus, although there is some truth that Britain had polarised in the 1960s and early 1970s into predominantly urban, industrialised Labour-voting areas on the one hand and predominantly rural or suburban Tory areas on the other, this is not as simple an explanation as it appears.

As if to ensure that the psephologists should never be allowed to generalise, the by-elections from 1974 to 1979 and the election of 3 May 1979 all served to emphasise the volatility of the British electorate.

No sooner had Labour returned to power in October 1974 than the by-elections began to show an ever-increasing disillusion with the Government. The first by-election of the new parliament, at Woolwich West on 26 June 1975, produced a Conservative gain on a swing of 7.6 per cent. By the late spring of 1976, swings of 13 per cent to the Conservatives were occurring in seats such as Rotherham. When the mining constituency of Ashfield was lost on 28 April 1977 on a swing of 20.8 per cent, it seemed as if the grim era of 1966–70 was back again. Although Labour's record at by-elections never fell to quite the disastrous levels of 1968, nonetheless no less than six seats were lost to the Conservatives. And the very day after the Government's defeat in the 'no-confidence' vote, the 'safe' Labour seat of Liverpool Edge Hill was lost to the Liberals on an incredible swing of 32.4 per cent – the largest swing to the Liberals in any post-war election.

Labour thus entered the May 1979 election against a background of poor by-election results, with the opinion polls all showing a large Conservative lead and with the knowledge that no previous government had fallen in a no-confidence vote since MacDonald's first administration in 1924. The outcome confirmed the worst of Labour's fears. On a swing of 5.2 per cent, the largest swing at an election since 1945, the Conservatives swept to power with an overall majority of 43 seats. Labour secured 268 seats, gaining 11 but losing 51 to the Conservatives. The party polled 11,509,524 votes (36.9 per cent of the total). The Conservatives polled 13,697,753 (43.9 per cent of the total). For Labour, its share of the total poll was its lowest at any election since 1931. In consolation, Mrs Thatcher formed a Conservative Government with a lower share of the total vote than any previous post-war Conservative Government – a paradox explained by the unexpected resilience in the Liberal vote (13.8 per cent of the total, with over 5.3 million votes).

The swing in 1979 varied not only from region to region but once again between town and country.[25] Scotland actually swung *to* Labour, enabling Labour to gain the Cathcart seat in Glasgow. Wales, at the other extreme, returned more Conservatives than at any election since 1874, with a 10.7 per cent swing in rural Wales. Labour's most disastrous results occurred in the South-East, notably in Greater London. In N.E. London there were enormous swings of over 13 per cent in Barking and Dagenham, with almost equally violent swings in such new towns as Basildon and Hertford and Stevenage. In general, Labour did best in the big cities of the North – such as Leeds and Manchester – and in areas of high immigration (such as Leicester, Southall and Bradford). Not all the North stayed loyal to Labour but – as the following figures show – the trend for Labour to consolidate in the North since 1955 was still marked.

Seats Won in the North of England		
	Conservative	*Labour*
1955	111	126
1979	78	151

As the *Economist* observed, only 20 per cent of the victorious Conservative M.P.s represented constituencies in the north of Britain and less than one in four came from the largest towns.[26]

But Labour's strength in its traditional areas was little consolation for its marked defeat. The first direct elections for Europe, held on 7 June

1979, reinforced this electoral map. Labour won only 17 seats, compared to the 60 won by the Conservatives. All were in areas that even Keir Hardie would have known as the Labour heartland.

In the wake of these two electoral rebuffs, as Labour devoted itself to the twin tasks of building a New Jerusalem and manoeuvring to secure an acceptable successor to Callaghan, the claim of Harold Wilson seemed strangely unreal. Labour had not become 'the natural party of government'. It seemed rather to have reverted to its more historic role as the natural – and divided – party of opposition.

Notes

1. For details of the MacDonald–Gladstone pact, see H. M. Pelling, *A Short History of the Labour Party*, 2nd edn, Macmillan (London) 1965.
2. For a further discussion of 1918, see M. Kinnear, *The British Voter*, Batsford (London) 1968.
3. The standard study of by-elections, with full details of results and swing, is C. Cook and J. Ramsden (Eds), *By-Elections in British Politics*, Macmillan (London) 1973.
4. See C. Cook, *The Age of Alignment: Electoral Politics in Britain*, Macmillan (London) 1975.
5. Ibid.
6. For a more detailed discussion of the agricultural vote, see M. Kinnear, op. cit.
7. See C. Cook, op.cit.
8. See J. Stevenson and C. Cook, *The Slump: Society and Politics During the Depression*, Jonathan Cape (London) 1977.
9. Ibid.
10. See C. Cook, *A Short History of the Liberal Party*, Macmillan (London) 1976.
11. J. Stevenson and C. Cook, op. cit.
12. Ibid.
13. Ibid.
14. C. Cook and J. Ramsden, op cit.
15. A. Sked and C. Cook, *Post-War Britain: A Political History*, Pelican (London) 1979.
16. M. Kinnear, op. cit.
17. A. Sked and C. Cook, op. cit.
18. D. Butler, *The British General Election of 1951*, Macmillan (London) 1952.
19. D. Butler, *The British General Election of 1955*, Macmillan (London) 1956.
20. D. Butler, *The British General Election of 1959*, Macmillan (London) 1960.
21. M. Kinnear, op. cit.
22. A. Sked and C. Cook, op. cit.
23. C. Cook and J. Ramsden, op. cit.
24. D. Butler and M. Pinto-Duschinsky, *The British General Election of 1970*, Macmillan (London) 1971.
25. *Guardian*, 5. 5. 1979.
26. *Economist*, 11. 5. 1979.

Chapter 5

Labour in office: 1924, 1929–31

David Roberts

British politics moved into unknown territory in January 1924. The Conservative Government of Stanley Baldwin, fighting on a protectionist platform, had lost its overall majority in the December 1923 election, although it remained in office with 259 M.P.s to face Parliament in January 1924. Labour, led by Ramsay MacDonald, had strengthened its position as the second largest Party by returning 191 M.P.s. The Liberal Party, reunited in resistance to protection, claimed 159 seats. On 10 December, the Labour leaders had announced their readiness, if called upon, to form a minority Government. Following this, on 18 December, the Liberal leader, Asquith, declared that his Party would not use its support to keep the Conservatives in office, or to deny Labour the right to govern. As the new year opened, a Labour Government was in prospect for the first time in Britain. The country suddenly seemed gripped in some sections by rabid fear, and by elation in others. According to the Tory press, red revolution was at hand: the armed forces and civil service would be corrupted; the Duke of Northumberland predicted the introduction of free love. For another section of the population, however, it seemed that after years of struggle they now stood on the threshold of great possibilities. Labour was a working-class Party, with working-class support and working-class leaders – men whose reputations were uncontaminated by political failures or by public loss of faith. Although there was a twinge of apprehension in the Labour Party, few objected to taking office. On 21 January 1924 the Conservative Government was defeated by 72 votes on a Labour amendment to the King's speech. The next day Baldwin resigned, and the first Labour Government took office. Yet, both those who prophesied doom, and those who hoped for the New Jerusalem, had miscalculated.

The prospects of revolution under the Labour Government were remote. Fears soon evaporated as the Labour leaders went out of their way to be respectable. To begin with, MacDonald's was a Ministry of many colours. The highest offices, predictably, went to the pioneers of the Labour movement: MacDonald himself took the Foreign Office as well as the Premiership, and Philip Snowden the Exchequer; Arthur Henderson, the only leading member of the Party with previous Cabinet experience, became Home Secretary. In the Cabinet of 20 were two old-guard Fabians, Sidney Webb and Lord Olivier, and seven representatives of the trade union world, including J. R. Clynes and J. H. Thomas. Stephen Walsh, John Wheatley and Vernon Hartshorn were all ex-miners. To balance these, MacDonald included Lord Parmoor (an erstwhile Conservative), Lord Haldane (a former Liberal Minister) and Lord Chelmsford (an ex-Viceroy of India), and found places for recent middle-class recruits from the Liberal Party, such as C. P. Trevelyan and Noel Buxton. Moreover, the demeanour of the first Labour Cabinet was meek and mild. They provoked no serious clashes with civil servants in the Government departments. Walsh, who had once been a private in the army, went to the War Office full of reverence for the generals now under his command.

Ramsay MacDonald's first reassuring speech as Prime Minister in the House of Commons on 12 February set the tone for his Ministry. It was a long address, covering a vast array of topics and plotting the course for the new Government: promises of a more benevolent attitude regarding old age pensions and sickness and unemployment benefit, proposals to examine the question of the National Debt, and assurances that it would work to revive trade in an effort to bring down unemployment. Of the capital levy, the most radical and controversial proposal in the Labour manifesto, there was no mention, and newspapers were already predicting that it would be put into cold storage. Indeed, few of the new Government's plans could not be found in the manifestoes of other parties. Even its bold recognition of the Soviet Union on 1 February, just over a week after Lenin's death, had been advocated by leading Liberals for some time. 'It is no new departure,' was Asquith's verdict on the Prime Minister's programme.[1]

Labour turned out to be thoroughly constitutional. It entered office when a serious rail strike was already under way, and although this was soon ended, Ernest Bevin's dockers and the London tram workers, as well as smaller unions, became embroiled in industrial action. The number of industrial disputes, whilst not increasing, did not notably decrease with the advent of a Labour Government. It was with some amazement that trade unionists heard that their own Government was prepared to have recourse to the despised Emergency Powers Act to deal with the strikes. Perhaps fortunately for Labour, it was never needed. All told, after only a matter of days in office, the Conservative press was finding more tender feelings towards the Government than it thought itself capable of, or than many Labour people felt comfortable with. 'They have come in like a lamb,' Lloyd George told his daughter in February. 'Will they go out like a lion? Who knows? For the present, "their tameness is shocking to me".'[2]

Of course, the Labour Government faced checks on its freedom of action. Its course over the next eight months reflected the disposition of the Party's leaders, but also the character of the political battle in the 1920s and the position in which Labour found itself as a result of the

1923 election. Since 1918, Labour had been the outsider struggling to break into the traditional two-Party system: now, unexpectedly, it had been presented with an opportunity to record a significant advance. It rivalled the ailing Liberal Party for the position of chief political alternative to the Conservatives. Asquith had acquiesced in the formation of a Labour Government in part out of respect for constitutional practice, and in part because he expected Labour to be shown to be utterly incompetent and the Liberals to reap the political benefit. The immediate aim of the Labour Government, therefore, was bound to be unambitious: it was to prove that it was capable of governing the country, and thereby throw the Liberals into the shade and win over many of their voters to the Labour cause. Even the most uncompromising of socialists considered this to be only sensible. If people whose minds had been closed to socialism could be made to realise that the skies would not fall if a Labour Government was formed, then at least in future they might view socialist proposals in a relatively rational manner.

In any event, this was in itself no easy task, for the Labour Government was a somewhat fragile and isolated creature. Although governments lacking an absolute parliamentary majority were not uncommon, never before in recent times had a Party taken office when it could be outnumbered even by a single rival party in the House of Commons. By modern standards, the Labour leaders of 1924 seemed curiously maladroit in handling the situation. On paper they relied on Liberal votes to survive. Yet there was no Lib–Lab pact, no parliamentary deal, or even consultations between the parties to facilitate the discharge of parliamentary business. Instead, the relationship between Liberals and Labour was persistently one of jealous antagonism. Perhaps it was only to be expected. MacDonald complained that in many instances the Liberals had fought dirtier than the Tories in the 1923 election; on a personal level, he was never on friendly terms with Asquith, and held Lloyd George beneath contempt. If anything, in 1924 Labour and the Conservatives seemed to share a common interest in the disappearance of the Liberal Party. The Liberals, meantime, grew more and more indignant that the Government had cold-shouldered them. In any case, Labour, as MacDonald made plain in his first speech, had no use for collaboration or coalition with anyone. It had come to office pledging a fresh approach to the country's problems, and aiming to succeed where the older political parties had failed. To turn to either of the older parties for help would be tantamount to an admission of defeat.

However, the Labour Ministers quickly showed that they could run the country as competently as any other party. Sir Maurice Hankey, the Cabinet secretary who had served under four Prime Ministers, thought them 'a very businesslike government' which had by April 1924 won 'a great deal of good will from the British People'.[3] Haldane, who had once held office in a Liberal Cabinet, considered that (in addition to

MacDonald) Snowden, Thomas, Wheatley and Webb were men of 'first-rate administrative ability'.[4] The Labour leaders had their troubles. Some Ministers were not entirely at ease at the Despatch Box in the Commons facing sniping from the Opposition benches; some were ruffled by disgruntled criticism from the Left-wing section of the ILP. But these were minor problems. In its first few months in office, Labour acquitted itself well. In May 1924, in Liverpool, the Government actually won a seat from the Opposition at a by-election – a feat achieved only four times in the last 60 years.

It claimed, too, some lasting achievements. The first Labour Budget in April was a master-stroke. It delighted Liberals by following their own guiding lights of free trade and lower taxes. Snowden reduced the taxes on a number of foods, and swept away the McKenna duties which had been imposed in 1915 on the import of luxury items such as cars; at the same time, he cut both indirect and direct taxes – though the reduction in direct taxation was considerably less than that of previous Chancellors. Of course the capital levy made no appearance – which doubtless relieved the City – and no start was made on the massive task of redistributing the nation's wealth by means of taxation. But for all its Liberal credentials, Snowden's Budget filled the Labour movement with admiration. The *Socialist Review* hailed him as the 'hero of the month'.[5] By August, Labour had found another hero in John Wheatley, the Minister of Health, who was promoting a working-class housing initiative. His Act, providing local authorities with subsidies to build houses for renting, presented the Government with its most solid socialist measure. During August, too, the Government was winning glory in international affairs. Labour's approach was to work through the League of Nations to encourage France to grant the equality which Germany sought. This strategy had some success, fostered by MacDonald's conciliatory manner and personal style of diplomacy. In the summer of 1924, France agreed to evacuate the Ruhr, and agreement was reached on the Dawes Plan – with its more lenient approach to Germany – for settling reparations. But the Geneva Protocol – an attempt to fortify the League policy by introducing a system of arbitration backed by sanctions to settle disputes – was never carried through. It was not approved by all in the Labour Party, and in any case the Government fell before the question was settled.

Yet, for all its youth and inexperience, its severe limitations and modest aims, the Labour Party had come to office saddled with great expectations. Many of its voters in the years of disillusion since 1918 had been drawn by the lure of promises of a new world: a world in which unemployment and poverty, injustice and oppression, would melt away. In 1924, Labour was given an opportunity to practise what it preached. In fact, it had made a rod to pickle its own back. No purposeful advance was made towards the 'new social order', and no significant contribution was made to liquidating the pressing problem of unemployment.

Unemployment had been a central issue in the 1923 election, by which time it was claiming over 1 million victims. At its root was the decline of Britain's long-established export industries, such as coal and textiles, as a result of dwindling markets overseas – a process accentuated by the First World War. Labour, fighting under a 'Work or Maintenance' banner in 1923, had pledged some public works schemes and more considerate instincts towards those out of work. Once in office, however, the Labour Government was decidedly sluggish. Fundamentally, it looked to a trade revival for the solution to the problem. It was, it is true, more sensitive to the plight of the unemployed, raising benefits and reducing the 'waiting period' before payment was made. But before long, Ministers were being arraigned by opponents and supporters alike for failing to live up to their promises. 'Men who sit and stare at their navels for months on end', thundered the Clydeside M.P. Tom Johnston, 'may be suited to Thibetan temples, but not to the control of British Departments of State.'[6] Only belatedly were a few public works schemes for electrification sanctioned by the Cabinet. On unemployment, the Labour Government fell far short of its expectations.

1924 revealed that the true nature of Britain's economic problems could not be grasped by a Labour Party which lacked a precise programme of measures to put its socialist beliefs into practice. The influential 1918 declaration, *Labour and the New Social Order*, was a collection of long-term ideals, ranging from Irish home rule to married women's income tax. It was not a plan of action. Thus when the Party came unexpectedly to office six years later, although the general direction in which it should travel was apparent, the actual route was blurred and the steps it should take vague. Most importantly, socialist economic thinking, despite a mass of writings and speeches over the years, was lamentably weak. Capitalism was the cause of the country's ills, and socialism was the cure. Yet precisely how the socialist cure was to be applied remained unclear. Was it to be by using the power of the State to create work? The idea propounded by J. M. Keynes of a major public works programme aroused only derision in the Labour ranks. Was it to be by using taxation to take from the rich and give to the poor? Was it to be by the public ownership and control of certain industries – the notion of 'planning' which was to be so beloved of progressive politicians in the 1930s? Eight months in office exposed to the Labour Party the flaws in its thinking, its preparations and its programme. Alas, they were obscured from view by the Government's limited aims, and by the confused and dramatic circumstances of its fall.

During August and September 1924, storm clouds began to gather for the Government. For some time the Liberals had been smarting under Labour's high-handed treatment: they were nothing more than 'patient oxen' who were expected continually to pull the Government through to parliamentary safety, and receive nothing in return. By the summer, they were looking to turn out the Government, and in September they saw their opportunity, and moved.

On 6 August, after several months' difficult negotiations, the Government signed two treaties with the Soviet Union. Their aim was to place Anglo-Soviet relations on a settled basis. Britain wanted repayment to its bond-holders who had incurred losses during the Bolshevik revolution; the Soviet Government wanted a financial loan. The Opposition fastened on the proposed bargain. Labour had at last taken off its respectable, moderate hat and donned its revolutionary cap: it was prepared to lend money to a communist ally which had declared its interest in revolution in Britain; all the fears expressed in January 1924 had not been groundless after all. The charges may have been preposterous, but the Government certainly came out of the affair in a poor light. Only a day before Arthur Ponsonby, the Under-Secretary announced the completion of the treaties, it had been proclaimed that after five months the negotiations had broken down; and the eleventh-hour intervention of six backbench Labour M.P.s, which contributed to the agreement, looked suspiciously like Left-wing pressure. Viewed from another angle, the treaties were something of a non-event. They consisted of a commercial treaty to improve trade between the two countries, and an agreement which merely provided for further negotiations over British claims leading to a third treaty. Only when this was completed would Britain guarantee a loan. Conservative objection in Parliament was inevitable. What was significant was that during August and September the Liberals, led by Lloyd George and, more cautiously, by Asquith, began to mount a formidable attack. MacDonald and his Government stood their ground and resolved to fight it out. On 1 October, the Liberal Party tabled a resolution in the House rejecting the treaties and refusing to endorse them. The life of the Labour Government was now practically over.

The end, though, came more dramatically. MacDonald's slip in Parliament over the 'Campbell Case' on 30 September provided his opponents with bullets, and the occasion to fire them. After the appearance of an article in the communist *Workers' Weekly* urging soldiers not to use guns against fellow workers if ordered to do so, the Government had begun, and then withdrawn, a prosecution of the acting editor, J. R. Campbell, for incitement to mutiny. The Attorney-General's original action had been remarkably feckless: before the war, MacDonald himself had protested against a similar prosecution of Tom Mann; moreover it roused considerable Left-wing ire. But it was primarily Campbell's apparent willingness to supply what would be more or less an apology that persuaded the Cabinet to call off the prosecution.[7] Both Tories and Liberals were alive to the political advantage for them in all this: the episode merely intensified the opinion that the Labour Government was partial to communists. On 30 September, under fire in the House of Commons, the Prime Minister wrongly – but accidentally, it would seem – gave the impression that he had not been consulted over the withdrawal. The next day the Conservatives registered a motion of censure on the Government, and the Liberals followed with an amendment – a possible way out for the Government – calling only for a select committee inquiry. The Cabinet, however, resolved to make both motions a matter of confidence, on which it would resign if defeated. On 8 October, the Conservatives shrewdly abandoned their own motion and voted for the Liberal amendment. In a flurry of manoeuvre and counter-manoeuvre, the Government was brought down on a trivial issue by 364 votes to 198. The next morning the King granted MacDonald a dissolution of Parliament, and a General Election was announced.

The Government could not have lasted much longer anyway. Its frailty, the sour criticism of a section of the ILP, and the joining of Liberal and Conservative hands in opposition, made its position almost impossible. By the end, MacDonald and his colleagues were relieved to be able to appeal to the country on their record in office. Yet given that record, and the aura of the first Labour Government, the course which the 1924 election campaign took must have been considerably frustrating. For Labour was cleverly driven by its opponents into the communist corner – defending the Russian treaties, defending the dropping of the communist prosecution. A *Punch* cartoon depicted an unsavoury Bolshevik character carrying the placard 'Vote for Mac-Donald and ME'. On 25 October, four days before polling, the famous 'Zinoviev letter' was published by the *Daily Mail*. No one knew then – least of all MacDonald – that it was a forgery, and his initial silence and then the Foreign Office's official protest demoralised the Labour campaign. Even had it been genuine, the letter should not have caused such a furore: Zinoviev had in fact been writing such letters regularly for six years. Its impact merely highlights the febrile atmosphere in which the election was fought.

In the event, the Conservative Party won a huge majority, returning 413 M.P.s, with Labour slipping to 151 and the Liberals, even more disastrously, to a mere 40. The 'red bogey' coloured Labour's exit from office as it had coloured its entry. It apparently spurred many voters who had not voted in 1923, and probably many who had supported the Liberals, to opt for Conservatism. Even so, the Labour Party took comfort: despite the anti-Bolshevik battle-cry, it actually increased its total vote by over 1 million, and its working-class support, especially in the industrial North and in the West Midlands, was unshaken. Labour reaped the fruit of its efforts to overtake the Liberals: whereas in 1923 the Labour Party had polled only 100,000 more votes than the Liberal Party, in 1924 the gap between their totals had widened to $2\frac{1}{2}$ million. Further, Labour had ready excuses – the Zinoviev letter, the leadership's blunders, the Liberals' chicanery – to mask its real weaknesses in office. What mattered was not what the Labour Government had done, but the mere fact that it had existed. It was enough that a detached observer of the Government would note, as R. H. Tawney put it, that 'the savage animal, before whose approach he had trembled, has not bitten him even once'.[8]

Angry post-mortems followed the defeat, all the same. The whole idea of taking office in a minority, the outlook and methods of the administration, and more than anything the leadership of Ramsay MacDonald came into question. In the ILP there was a mood of discontentment. The Labour Ministers and the Clydesiders had glowered at each other throughout the period of the Government. Now, guided by James Maxton and John Wheatley, the Clydeside M.P.s launched into a demand for a more full-blooded socialist policy, and at the 1925 ILP conference disowned their Government's actions and virulently attacked MacDonald. They represented a minority. Despite their criticisms, the conference passed a resolution applauding the Government's work. But the militant men from the Clyde were rapidly acquiring a firm grip on the ILP. Here was the beginning of a tussle between the Labour leadership and the ILP that was to end in a permanent breach in 1932. In addition, even amongst the Party leaders, there was much bitterness. Personal rivalries and antagonisms bedevilled the first two Labour Governments, and no doubt Mac-Donald's often remote and introspective behaviour contributed to the situation. After the 1924 election, rumours began to spread of a move to depose him. One of MacDonald's chief rivals and fiercest critics was his former Chancellor of the Exchequer, Philip Snowden. The two men had never been friends, and clearly, Snowden had different ideas on how to run the Party. Following the defeat, he accused MacDonald privately of 'the most incompetent leadership which ever brought a Government to ruin'.[9] Yet MacDonald survived it all. His rallying speech at the Party Conference at Liverpool in 1925 restored his reputation, and showed the enthusiasm he could still inspire in the Party rank and file. The fact was that Labour had no one capable of taking his place, and by September 1926 Beatrice Webb was observing that he was 'the inevitable leader of the PLP'.[10] For the rest of the 1920s MacDonald exerted a dominant hold over his Party.

What might have been a more salutary reaction did not come. The lessons of 1924 went unheeded, and during its period in opposition in the 1920s the Labour Party made no determined effort to translate its socialist ideas into a practical policy which would confront the nation's economic problems. The Party probably lacked the tools for the task. Its research department at the Party's headquarters was a paltry affair, the original Labour Research Department having been disbanded in the early 1920s because of communist infiltration. A number of Advisory Committees had been set up in 1917, but even the most lasting of these contributed little. The Fabian Society, which was to become a fertile source of ideas and policies in the 1930s, fell into quiescence in the 1920s and offered no constructive thinking on the unemployment problem.

There were intellectual stirrings in some quarters in the 1920s. Sir Oswald Mosley, a former Tory M.P. who had joined the Labour Party in March 1924, and who had narrowly failed to secure election for a Birmingham constituency in November, was one of the first to look at

Britain's problems along fresh lines. Mosley was a glamorous, wealthy, aristocratic young man with a searching mind, who was already being talked of as a future leader of the Labour Party. Drawing ideas from Keynes and from the radical economist J. A. Hobson, Mosley began working out measures to combat unemployment. In May 1925 he outlined his 'Birmingham proposals', which attracted considerable support inside the Birmingham Labour Party. They argued for pumping money into the economy, largely by the Government control of credit and banking, thus being able to increase demand by placing money in the hands of the less well-off. Close behind was the ILP. In September 1926, it brought out its 'Living Wage' report, the result of a committee of inquiry set up after 1924. It, too, was based upon Hobson's 'underconsumptionist' thesis: unemployment was caused by a lack of consumption of goods produced; if consumption was increased, more goods would be needed, and more people would be employed. So the ILP advocated the establishment of a national minimum wage as one means of expanding purchasing power and stimulating demand. Outside the Labour Party altogether, even the Liberals, decrepit as they often seemed, were promoting fresh thinking on the economy. The 1926 Liberal Summer School, a forum for pooling ideas, had set up an industrial inquiry, whose report – the famous Liberal 'Yellow Book' – appeared in February 1928. The 'Yellow Book', too, was really the inspiration of Keynes, the first detailed airing of his economic ideas. Its main proposal was a vast programme of public works to provide work for the unemployed. Though they differed on various details, these were all pointers to the planned economy which was to be the norm 20 years later. Yet they were radical challenges to orthodox economic opinion in the 1920s.

All this made little impression on the Labour Party. Mosley's ideas had a poor reception. The advance of the rich aristocrat in the Labour world was not welcomed by everyone in the Party. In any case, his proposals were widely regarded as impractical or undesirable. Hugh Dalton, one of the trained economists among Labour's younger politicians, thought Mosley 'very uninstructed'.[11] The ILP's policies might have been slightly more influential had they not been used as an implement to attack the Labour leadership. MacDonald was a friend of Hobson, and thought well of many of the 'Living Wage' proposals. Once they became a focal point for criticism of his leadership, he had no use for them. Early in 1926, under the chairmanship of Maxton, the ILP had opened a campaign for 'Socialism in Our Time', and the fight with the Labour leadership had begun in earnest. In March 1927, the ILP decided to end its practice of nominating MacDonald for the Party treasurership. The publication of the Cook–Maxton manifesto in June 1928 merely carried the ILP's campaign a stage further. Snowden resigned from the ILP in 1927, and although MacDonald could not bring himself to do so, its attitude deeply disturbed him. However, the challenge to the leadership in the 1920s lacked weight. Numerically, the

ILP was already a declining force from the mid-1920s, and at Party conferences its dissenting voice was easily stifled. Maxton and his colleagues could be dismissed as a small minority of perpetual grumblers. Moreover, there was no unity between the challengers: Mosley thought the 'Living Wage', as he wrote later, merely 'a dummy to knock down'.[12] Thus the conservative approach to the economy that Snowden had shown in 1924, and in his acceptance of the return to the gold standard since, easily held the loyalty of the vast majority of the Labour movement. By the end of the 1920s, the supremacy of MacDonald and Snowden was virtually unquestioned.

The Labour Party did at least revise its programme. The Party's National Executive Committee, elected by the Annual Conference and responsible for framing policy, set about the task after the 1927 Conference, in preparation for the next election. Several drafts of a new programme were produced, not without dissension. Mosley, who had been elected to the Executive in 1927, along with Ellen Wilkinson and Charles Trevelyan, wrote a brief, incisive statement of measures to be carried out by a Labour Government. MacDonald had other ideas. He drafted a longer general statement of socialist aims, which would be fulfilled in time, but would not tie Labour's hands when it came to office. After some haggling, it was decided that R. H. Tawney should compose the new programme, based on MacDonald's draft, but that a shorter statement would be prepared for the election. Thus *Labour and the Nation* emerged in 1928 to supersede *Labour and the New Social Order*, but in fact to reaffirm the Party's belief in the gradualist road to socialism. Public ownership of certain selected industries was to be pursued 'without haste and without rest'; some public works schemes, the establishment of a national economic committee and an increase in the purchasing power of workers were all advocated. But these were only a few proposals among many: even a four-page summary of the programme listed over 70 proposals, and no order of priorities was suggested. *Labour and the Nation* was a guide-book to general socialist principles. Palpably it was not a blueprint for action. 'It was obvious that nothing short of a miracle,' wrote Clement Attlee a decade later, 'could have enabled the Party, even with an overwhelming majority, to get all these measures passed into law within the life of one parliament....'[13]

Yet at the time *Labour and the Nation* was a powerful spur to the Labour movement. The 1928 conference at Birmingham disposed of the ILP's criticisms and approved the new programme without a vote. No one of any stature in the Party dissented. Sidney Webb, the author of the 1918 programme, had thought that MacDonald's draft programme had been 'properly vague and comprehensive'.[14] MacDonald's strategy rested on the belief that the speed at which socialism could be realised depended on the number of socialists in the country. The object, therefore, must be to make more socialists. This was where MacDonald was at his best: as propagandists for socialism over the years, both he and Snowden had been second to none. It is hard, too, to deny that the strategy was a success. The programme formed the basis of the Party's manifesto in the General Election of May 1929, when Labour gained nearly 3 million votes and over 130 seats to become the largest Party in the House of Commons. Mrs M. A. Hamilton, a successful candidate in 1929, wrote later that *Labour and the Nation* had been 'a sword of strength in the hands of candidates, organisers and propagandists'.[15]

After 1926, the Conservative Government's popularity had flagged, though the extension of the franchise in 1928 to include women over 21 made the outcome of an election uncertain. When it drew near in 1929, it was the Liberals who surged forward. Asquith had died in 1928, and although old wounds did not suddenly heal, the Liberal Party appeared united under Lloyd George. On 1 March 1929 Lloyd George brandished before the electors 'We Can Conquer Unemployment' – a plan for a massive public works programme, financed by a loan, which would in one year reduce unemployment to 'normal proportions'. It was a challenging enterprise, and the Conservative and Labour campaigns in May were defined by their reaction to it. The Conservative Party fell back on the slogan of 'Safety First' – 'we will not promise more than we can perform. We therefore promise nothing. . . .', as Keynes and Hubert Henderson bitingly characterised it.[16] The Labour Party was distinctly unsettled: it accused the Liberals of stealing Labour ideas, and then dismissed their programme as an old Lloyd George gimmick. In 1929 Labour's hold on the position of major progressive Party in British politics was still precarious: it still aimed to trounce the Liberals as much as the Tories. At the finish, the Liberal campaign fell flat. The result of the General Election in May 1929 was a virtual stalemate. Although Labour polled 8,370,417 votes to the Conservatives' 8,656,225, it returned 27 more M.P.s: 287 to 260. The Liberals trailed far behind with 59. On 5 June Labour formed a Government for the second time.

The men of 1924, with a few exceptions, again ran the administration. Ramsay MacDonald's career had been a remarkable series of ups and downs. Now, Prime Minister for the second time at the age of 62, he had reached the pinnacle of his career. On a personal level, his relations with his senior Party colleagues were distant. But in the Labour Party as a whole, and in the country generally, he commanded a loyal following. Philip Snowden again assumed the Chancellorship; Arthur Henderson, after a quarrel, this time claimed the Foreign Office, and quickly acquired a reputation as a peacemaker. The ILP faction, not surprisingly, did not find their way into the Government, although George Lansbury (whose paper, *Lansbury's Labour Weekly*, had been critical of the leadership) did. The new Government had daunting problems. As in 1924, it lacked a parliamentary majority; but, also as in 1924, no alliance between Labour and the Liberals, who held the balance in the House, was in sight. Personal enmities and political rivalries ran too deep. Moreover, the unemployment cloud hung over the Labour Government from the start. This time MacDonald set up a loose-knit 'ministry of employment', headed by J. H. Thomas, the Lord Privy Seal, and helped by a team of Ministers consisting of Lansbury, Mosley and Tom Johnston. Thomas was an astute man, and he began moderately well. When the Government took office, unemployment seemed to be falling slightly (though it was still over 1 million), exports were rising modestly and the country had a balance of payments surplus. The King's speech in July proclaimed certain relief works, such as a five-year road-building scheme, and the desire to survey industry and devise means of making it more efficient. But the scourge of the 'intractible million' remained, and this was a small effort to grapple with it. Basically, Labour, like the Conservatives, pinned its hopes on a world trade revival.

The second Labour Government would not anyway have survived what was to come. In every democratic country, the Great Depression swept away the Government of the day. The Wall Street crash of October 1929 set off a disastrous trail of falling commodity prices and sharply curtailed trade around the world. By April 1930 the effects were well and truly being felt in Britain. The number of people unemployed was lifted from 1,533,000 in January 1930 to 2,725,000 by the end of the year, relentlessly lowering living standards and bringing hardship to millions.

It is fashionable to decry the second Labour Government for ignoring the solution to the crisis that was at hand – an expansionist programme of government spending on public works on Keynesian lines, a British 'New Deal' – either from ignorance, from a commitment to an airy socialist solution, from weak-kneed subservience to economic ortho-doxy, or from all three.[17] Certainly, Labour rejected a sweeping public works programme as the key to the unemployment problem. Public works schemes in themselves were not worthless, but they were merely temporary repairs to the economy, not a lasting restoration. The fact that Lloyd George had taken them up in 1929 only served to make them less appealing. There were, in addition, powerful practical barriers to such a pioneering solution to the crisis. Keynesian economic thinking was still at the experimental stage. Practically everywhere in the world the Depression was met by policies of deflation; indeed the Labour Government was somewhat unconventional in not following suit. The Keynesian alternative to deflation was not fully understood or coherently argued, even by those who claimed to be its advocates. Moreover, great changes would have been needed in Britain if such a new and untried course was to have been embarked upon. It took the onset of a world war nearly a decade later to convert political and public opinion to the kind of State control of the economy necessary for an expansionist programme to be effective. Finally, radical policies had not captured popular support. The Liberals, for all their verve and imagination in 1929, returned only 59 M.P.s – and not all of them endorsed Lloyd George's bold initiative. Thus the Labour Government of 1929–31 trod nervously between the tried orthodoxy of the Treasury and international practice, and the adventurous promptings of the new economic thinkers. It may be that no Government could have done better; in view of the fact that Labour had no developed economic policy of its own, little else could be expected of it.

The story of the second Labour Government was thus one of growing gloom and helplessness. Nevertheless, as the crisis engulfed it, the Government did vainly search for a life-line. David Marquand's biography of MacDonald reveals him as a man more receptive to new ideas than is often thought, but politically and intellectually unable to counter Snowden's commitment to economies, balanced budgets and free trade. MacDonald enlisted Hubert Henderson, a pupil of Keynes, as his personal economic adviser. In January 1930 he assembled the Economic Advisory Council, a think-tank of economic specialists – including Keynes and Tawney – to advise the Government. It was an imaginative idea, and one taken up by later governments. But the experts could not agree – a telling comment on the economic crisis – and came forward with no fruitful contribution.

In January 1930, too, Oswald Mosley, restless at the Government's seeming inertia, rebelled. Over Christmas 1929 Mosley had been putting together a set of proposals based on his own economic thinking, keeping in touch with his colleagues Lansbury and Johnston, and with Keynes. On 23 January he sent a memorandum direct to the Prime Minister. It argued in the long term for an end to Britain's dependence on exports and for the development of the home market, aided by the restriction of imports; and in the short term for a public works programme, financed by a loan, to swallow up the unemployed. It was a lucid and lively document ('an injudicious mixture of Karl Marx and Lord Rothermere', in Lloyd George's words)[18] and an attempt to drive the Labour Government into action. On 8 May a Cabinet committee in which Snowden had a decisive hand rejected the proposals. MacDonald, who was much less hostile to Mosley, then referred the memorandum to a committee of Ministers: again they stalled on the question of expensive public works schemes. It was not just Snowden's influence that killed off the proposals: neither MacDonald, nor the Party as a whole, were great believers in public works. In addition, Mosley seemed like a rash, idealistic young man, asking for too much. He resigned from the Government on 20 May. In a fighting mood, he appealed to the Parliamentary Labour Party, and was defeated by 210 votes to 29. He took his case to the Party Conference in October, and after receiving a great ovation was narrowly voted down. Within months, Mosley had formed the New Party.

The Government was on the retreat throughout 1930. MacDonald now took over the direction of unemployment policy, leading a 'panel of Ministers' including Vernon Hartshorn, who replaced J. H. Thomas. By the autumn, a plot to overthrow the Prime Minister was evidently in the air. It came to nothing, but, together with the Mosley episode and a series of disappointing by-election results, it was an indicator of dissatisfaction in the Party and the country. Ministers seemed helpless to prevent the unemployment figures climbing over the 2 million mark. Between February and September 1930 the Government doubled the amount of money being spent on public works; but public works alone were fast becoming irrelevant. Much more to the point was the growing movement of opinion in favour of protecting the home market. The Conservatives did not need much persuading to take up the banner; suffering industries pleaded for protection; in 1930–31 Keynes was converted to it, and Ramsay MacDonald was slowly coming to favour it. Protection, however, had never had much appeal for Labour. Besides, Philip Snowden was an implacable free trader, and under his guidance the Cabinet in September 1930 resolved to stand by its traditional trading policies.

The effects of the Depression even thawed much of the iciness between the Labour and Liberal Parties. In May 1930 MacDonald appealed for the co-operation of the Opposition leaders in a concerted attack on an economic crisis that was not of Labour's making. Only Lloyd George, who had long hoped for such an invitation, accepted. Labour, after much soul-searching, promised the Liberals electoral reform; the Liberals, in turn, promised to sustain the Government in office, and strengthen its hand in the struggle against the 'economic blizzard'. By December 1930 the deal seems to have been struck. The Electoral Reform Bill was passed in February 1931, though it never became law. In April, Lloyd George and 30 Liberals voted with the Government against a Conservative censure motion. No Lib–Lab pact was ever signed, and it was not a formal coalition. Yet, undeniably, it was a parliamentary alliance that lasted until the end of the Government's life. By mid-1931 rumours were rife that Lloyd George and other leading Liberals would actually enter the Government. This suggestion is not entirely fanciful. Even George Lansbury, who by the Cabinet's standards stood on the Labour Left, urged Lloyd George in February 1931 to join Labour, and there is tantalising, though not conclusive, evidence that MacDonald was seriously contemplating having Liberals in his Government in the summer of 1931.[19] Other events, however, intervened.

Although the 1929–31 Government was weighed down by economic problems from the start, in other fields it had mixed results. It suffered frustrations and scored some successes. Trevelyan's Bill to raise the school-leaving age was killed by the House of Lords in March 1931; the repeal of the Trade Disputes Act of 1927 had to be dropped because of Liberal opposition. The Coal Mines Act of 1930, however, an unskilful compromise between miners and mine-owners, was pushed through with Liberal help. Arthur Greenwood's 1930 Housing Act began a process of slum clearance, while Christopher Addison's Land Utilisation Act – giving the Minister of Agriculture powers to acquire land for use by rural unemployed – and Herbert Morrison's London Passenger Transport Bill, which a later Government enacted, were perhaps

Labour's most daring measures. In foreign affairs, Arthur Henderson won acclaim for his work for peace. The Government endorsed the evacuation of allied troops from the Rhineland, and the reduction of Germany's reparations obligations. The London Naval Conference of 1930 showed Labour willing to give a lead on disarmament, and helped to create a climate of opinion in which the League of Nations Council resolved in January 1931 to open the long-awaited World Disarmament Conference the following year.

By the spring of 1931 the Labour Government's prospects had somehow picked up. Its problems had not suddenly dissolved, though unemployment figures levelled off for a period at around 2,700,000. Two Government Ministers died in March, Snowden fell seriously ill, and MacDonald himself was under considerable strain. In March, too, Trevelyan resigned as President of the Board of Education, and attacked the Government. In the main, however, Labour M.P.s rallied behind their leaders. They responded to prodding by ILP critics, in Jennie Lee's phrase, 'like a load of damp cement'.[20] The final act of the tragedy was played in the summer of 1931, when Britain's particular economic problems reached a peak, and coincided with the impact in London of an international financial crisis.

The increasing difficulty of breaking the Depression's hold on the country had hardened the deflationary outlook of Snowden and the Treasury. They believed that a budget deficit, the traditional sign of bad housekeeping, as was expected in 1931, would bring nothing but harm, destroying confidence in the pound and in the British economy. In January, Snowden told the Cabinet that tough measures would be needed to balance the budget. The following month, under Liberal pressure, he appointed a committee under Sir George May, formerly of the Prudential Assurance Company, to investigate possible savings to be made in Government expenditure. From the opposite side, Keynes in March came out strongly in favour of a revenue tariff, to be harnessed to an expansionist economic policy. His arguments were lost on Snowden. In April, the Chancellor presented a delicately balanced Budget; it was no more than a holding operation, and he anticipated a further Budget in the autumn when the May Committee had completed its findings. The May report was published at the end of July 1931, preceded by the report of the Macmillan Committee on Finance and Industry. Macmillan's conclusions underlined the failures of orthodox economic policies, but its impact was slight. The May report, on the contrary, was momentous. It announced a colossal budget deficit of £120 million, and recommended cuts of £97 million in Government expenditure – £67 million of which were to come from cuts in unemployment benefit. Asked by MacDonald for his views on the report, Keynes replied that they were not fit for publication.

Britain had already been caught up in the swirl of an international financial crisis. From the collapse of the Kreditanstalt bank in Vienna in May 1931, it had spread through central Europe and Germany to

Britain, the banker of the world. Faced with foreigners wanting to withdraw their money, the Bank of England, which had been engaged in long-term lending and only short-term borrowing, and with much of its money trapped in Germany by the Hoover moratorium on international debts, had to pay out from its gold reserves. On 26 July the Government borrowed £50 million from Paris and New York. The appearance of the May report on Britain's economy only heightened the sense of panic: it led to a run on the pound and sinking confidence in sterling. On 7 August Snowden warned MacDonald that unless drastic action was taken the point of exhaustion would soon be reached. Probably the only way the Labour Government could have saved itself by this time was by going off the gold standard – the basis for international currencies and exchange rates. This was Keynes's advice to MacDonald on 5 August. Yet it was an exceedingly difficult thing to do. The weight of economic opinion was against it. To the Bank of England, the Treasury, the leading economists and to Snowden, stringent cuts and a balanced budget were the only alternatives. The gold standard was a central plank in classical economic thinking, and the Labour Party had never hidden its dim view of the decision to return to gold in 1925; but very few Labour men believed that they could now abandon it. Even G. D. H. Cole, who supported Keynes, admitted that it would have provoked a tremendous outcry from financial interests. In September the National Government was forced off the gold standard – but that was a different matter. In August 1931 the Labour Government chose the path of safety: it decided not to devalue, but to balance the budget.

Days of deep crisis followed with three weeks of complex, harrying negotiations between bankers, politicians and trade unionists. From day to day, from hour to hour, the situation changed as MacDonald and his colleagues wrestled with the problem, and all the time gold drained away from London. In August, the economic–financial crisis turned also into a political crisis. The Labour Cabinet was at one in its decision to balance the budget; it foundered on the rock of a cut in unemployment insurance in order to secure it. Britain paid out more in social services than any country in the world, and as unemployment had risen steeply, so too had the cost of providing benefit. To remote minds in Whitehall, the City and abroad, it was clear that if economies had to be made, then the unemployment payments would be a prime target. No pill, however, could have been more bitter for the Labour Party, and in the end it refused to swallow it. By 20 August the Labour Cabinet had drifted into a trap from which there seemed no honest escape. The Cabinet economy committee, set up to consider the May Report and consisting of MacDonald, Snowden, Henderson, Thomas and Graham, suggested economies in unemployment insurance amounting to £43.5 millions – much less than the May recommendations; on 19 August the Cabinet lowered this figure to around £22 millions. The chorus of bankers, Opposition leaders and most newspapers, who were calling for drastic cuts, considered this not enough. On 20 August came the meeting that in effect sealed the Government's fate: the TUC General Council announced its total opposition to any cuts in unemployment insurance. 'The General Council are pigs,' Lord Passfield informed his wife.[21]

By 21 August a decision had become urgent. According to the Bank of England, gold reserves would last only a matter of days, a loan was needed immediately from New York and a bigger economy programme was required to secure it. The Cabinet could raise the savings in unemployment insurance by the necessary £20 millions only by including in the list of economies a 10 per cent cut in the actual rate of unemployment benefit. This would satisfy bankers, opposition parties and the like, but not the Labour Party and trade unionists. On 22 August in a straggling, confused fashion, without taking a final decision, the Cabinet authorised MacDonald to approach the bankers J. P. Morgan of New York for a loan on the basis of this new programme of cuts. But a number of Ministers, including Henderson, clearly would resign if this was put into effect. The Prime Minister explained the situation to the King, who seems vaguely to have floated the idea of a National Government under MacDonald – which the Labour leader dismissed. On 23 August came the reply from New York: a loan would be forthcoming if the economy programme was approved by the Bank and the City. The Cabinet had now to decide finally on the 10 per cent unemployment benefit cut: 11 were in favour; nine, led by Henderson, were against. It was the end of the road for the Labour Government, and MacDonald left for Buckingham Palace with its resignation in his pocket. By the next morning, the King's persuasions had succeeded. After a further meeting with the King and the Opposition leaders, MacDonald returned to tell the Cabinet that he was remaining on as Prime Minister and head of a National Government which would include Conservatives and Liberals.

24 August 1931 passed into Labour mythology as the day of the 'great betrayal'. The memory of it still haunts the Labour Party some 50 years later. The members of the Cabinet had realised that they could not continue in office, and they expected to resign as a Government. Instead, MacDonald, accompanied by Snowden, Thomas and Lord Sankey, joined the Conservative and Liberal leaders (except Lloyd George, who was ill) in a new coalition government. Arthur Henderson led the mass of the Labour Party into opposition. On 28 September MacDonald was expelled from the Party he had done much to build, and was ostracised for the rest of his days by people who had previously idolised him. By October MacDonald and Snowden were facing their old colleagues in a bitter election struggle. They accused Labour of running away from the crisis; the Labour leaders accused MacDonald and Snowden of deserting the unemployed and their own Party. Labour went down to the most calamitous electoral defeat in history. It lost 2 million votes, and the number of its M.P.s slumped to 52 – just a handful more than Labour's 1910 figure. After gaining so much so quickly, Labour now lost political influence for a decade.

In the years that followed, disputes raged, and 1931 continued to be seen in highly impassioned terms: violently anti-MacDonald accounts came from the pens of his former colleagues, provoking a few exaggerated defences from loyal friends. Yet the true picture of 1931 was never quite as clear-cut as Labour mythology painted it. First, MacDonald's motives were the highest. Earlier suggestions that the formation of the National Government was a deep-laid plot on MacDonald's part are now largely discredited. Although the thought of a coalition had crossed his mind at various times during the economic troubles of the previous two years, he strove to the last to keep Labour in office. There is ample evidence that when this became impossible, his intention was to resign and go into opposition. Late on 23 August Baldwin expected to become Prime Minister the next day. After talking with MacDonald, Baldwin wrote to his wife: 'The P.M. said he couldn't join me'.[22] Only forceful pressure from the King changed MacDonald's mind. He may have been wrong to have yielded, but it was from a high sense of duty. Second, there was more immediate good will towards MacDonald in the Labour Party than is often realised. There were hints of approval from the Party rank and file, while Margaret Bondfield and Stafford Cripps were among prominent members of the Party who wrote to express admiration for MacDonald's action. MacDonald wrote personally to every Labour M.P., and although only about a dozen backbenchers actually supported him, nearly every reply he received showed respect for what he had done. MacDonald did not attend the meeting of the Parliamentary Labour Party on 28 August, though more than one observer believed that, had he done so, he might still have swayed M.P.s[23] Finally, both MacDonald and Henderson, and others, believed at first that the estrangement would be temporary. The coalition was a 'government of individuals', formed for the duration of the crisis only. As soon as this was over, normal party politics would be resumed. This was not to be, and the strongest evidence suggests that MacDonald regretted this: the expulsion, the breaking of old ties and the savage reaction within the Labour Party deeply distressed him.

The tragedy was that MacDonald and the Government had fallen fighting unnecessary battles: defending the gold standard, resisting protection. The formation of the National Government secured the loan from America, and the Economy Bill was pushed through Parliament. But the crisis did not subside. The loss of gold continued, and on 21 September Britain was finally driven off the gold standard, without bringing economic ruin. Tariffs were introduced in 1932 and free trade similarly sank into oblivion. Furthermore, the new Government's policies did little to lift the country out of the Depression. Unemployment remained at defiantly high levels until the outbreak of war in 1939. It may be that the Labour Party would anyway have met with defeat after being in office between 1929 and 1931; but much of the ignominy might have been spared.

So ended the first two Labour Governments. In 1931, as in 1924, there

were scapegoats: the bankers, the King, above all MacDonald and
Snowden. But it was the Labour Party as a whole that had faltered. It
had been thrust into office without any prepared programme of
economic measures with which to put its ideas into effect, or with which
to shield itself from the effects of the severest trade depression of the
century. The verdict on the death of the Labour Government was, as
Tawney recorded, 'neither murder, nor misadventure, but pernicious
anaemia producing general futility'.[24] In terms purely of the Party
political race, Labour had made a striking advance since 1924. In spite
of its political weakness in the 1930s, it presented the only credible
alternative to the Conservative Party; by 1931 the Liberals had almost
ceased to count. Yet much groundwork remained to be done: the Party
had still to prove itself. Labour in office had neither confirmed fears of
wholesale revolution, nor fulfilled hopes of a better society. 'I tell you
frankly,' remarked the French historian Élie Halévy in 1934, 'that I
shudder at the thought of the Labour Party ever having a real majority,
not for the sake of capitalism, but for the sake of socialism.'[25]

Notes

1. 169 H. C., *Parl. Deb.*, 5th ser., 858.
2. K. O. Morgan (Ed.), *Lloyd George Family Letters, 1885-1936*, University of Wales Press (Cardiff) 1973, p. 202.
3. S. Roskill, *Hankey: Man of Secrets, II, 1919-31*, Collins (London) 1972, p. 366.
4. R. B. Haldane, *An Autobiography*, Hodder & Stoughton (London) 1929, p. 330.
5. R. W. Lyman, *The First Labour Government, 1924*, Chapman & Hall (London) 1957, p. 148.
6. Robert E. Dowse, 'The left-wing opposition during the first two Labour Governments', *Parliamentary Affairs*, XIV 1960-1, p. 85.
7. See D. Marquand, *Ramsay MacDonald*, Cape (London) 1977, p. 368.
8. R. H. Tawney, *The British Labor Movement* (New Haven), 1925, p. 4.
9. Quoted Fenner Brockway, *Socialism over Sixty Years: Life of Jowett of Bradford*, Allen & Unwin (London) 1946, p. 222.
10. M. Cole (Ed.), *Beatrice Webb Diaries, 1924-32*, Longmans (London) 1956, p. 118.
11. R. Skidelsky, *Oswald Mosley*, Macmillan (London) 1975, p. 151.
12. Oswald Mosley, *My Life*, Nelson (London) 1968, p. 221.
13. C. R. Attlee, *The Labour Party in Perspective*, Gollancz (London) 1937, p. 53.
14. N. MacKenzie (Ed.), *Letters of Sidney and Beatrice Webb, iii, 1912-47*, CUP (Cambridge) 1978, pp. 296-7.
15. M. A. Hamilton, *The Labour Party Today*, (London) 1939, p. 31.
16. J. Campbell, *Lloyd George: The Goat in the Wilderness*, Cape (London) 1977, p. 233.
17. See R. Skidelsky, *Politicians and the Slump*, Macmillan (London) 1967; for an alternative viewpoint, see R. McKibbin, 'The Economic Policy of the

Second Labour Government, 1929–31', *Past and Present*, Vol. 68, August 1975, pp. 95–123.
18. J. Campbell, op. cit., p. 265.
19. D. Marquand, '1924–1932', in D. Butler (Ed.), *Coalitions in British Politics*, Macmillan (London) 1978, p. 58.
20. Jennie Lee, *This Great Journey*, MacGibbon & Kee (London) 1963, p. 112.
21. Quoted R. Skidelsky, op. cit., p. 414.
22. K. Middlemas and J. Barnes, *Baldwin*, Weidenfeld & Nicolson (London) 1969, p. 628.
23. D. Marquand, *Ramsay MacDonald*, p. 650.
24. R. H. Tawney, 'The Choice before the Labour Party', *Political Quarterly*, July–Sept. 1932.
25. Élie Halévy, *The Era of Tyrannies*, Allen Lane (London) 1965, p. 255.

Chapter 6

Labour in office: the post-war experience

David Steel

At the time of the General Election of May 1979 the Labour Party had been in office for just over half of the post-war period. Its three spells in government, each lasting for five or six years, cannot be fully assessed in a single chapter. The focus here therefore will be on just two questions. Labour's victory in four out of the six most recent General Elections and its tenure of office for almost 11 of the last 15 years has led many to claim that it has supplanted the Conservatives as the natural party of government in the United Kingdom. How, then, have Labour Ministers reacted to a system of government, the main features of which were established before the Party's birth? After 17 years in office it is also germane to assess the use that Labour has made of its opportunities to change the social and economic life of the country. A comprehensive analysis of its achievements would be a difficult task and certainly lies beyond the scope of this chapter. But it is possible to examine how far Labour Ministers have succeeded in realising the aspirations of their own supporters. First, however, the record of each of the post-war Labour governments must be outlined, paying particular attention to the measures they took and to the constraints upon their freedom of action.

Outline of Labour's record

1945-51

The result of the General Election of July 1945 came as a great surprise to most people, not least to many of the Labour Party's leaders. Far from according Mr Churchill and the Conservatives a vote of confidence in the still-continuing war effort, the electorate gave them their most crushing defeat since 1906. The Conservatives and their allies lost about 200 seats; Labour gained 227 and had an overall majority in the House of Commons of 146. For the first time, Labour was not only in office but also in power.

Labour had been in an enviable position in the election. It was free of any blame for the problems of the 1930s but, unlike most oppositions, its leaders had become known to the public and had proved their competence in government through their membership of the war-time coalition. These well-known figures dominated the Cabinet. The Prime Minister, Clement Attlee, had been Deputy Prime Minister since 1942 and had effectively been in charge of domestic affairs. Ernest Bevin and Herbert Morrison, who were appointed Foreign Secretary and Lord President of the Council (responsible for co-ordinating the Government's legislative programme) respectively, had both been members of the War Cabinet; and Hugh Dalton, the Chancellor of the Exchequer, had been an economics Minister throughout the war. Generally the Cabinet must have provided a degree of reassurance to those who feared that the 1945 election heralded a political revolution. Its average age was about 60, most of its members were stalwarts of the 1935 Parliament, and the only adventurous step was the appointment to the Ministry of Health of Aneurin Bevan, who had been vocal in his opposition to the coalition government and a frequent critic of Labour's leadership.

Nevertheless the early days of the new administration were full of excitement and anticipation of the new era that was beginning. But they were overshadowed by international events. Within a fortnight of the election, Attlee had to return to the Potsdam peace conference which he had attended previously only at the invitation of Churchill; and the formation of the new Government had literally been overshadowed by the dropping of the atomic bomb on Hiroshima. The war with Japan ended, however, a few weeks later, and the Government's energies could be devoted singlemindedly to the daunting task of achieving a smooth transition to peace. The war had severely damaged the British economy. External liabilities had increased by £3,000 million, overseas investments of £1,000 million had been sold and exports had fallen by two-thirds. Enemy action had destroyed or damaged a substantial part of the nation's physical assets – houses, factories, ships, port facilities – and most of what remained was in desperate need of repair. To make things worse, Lend-Lease (the arrangement under which the Americans had effectively financed the war effort since 1941) was abruptly and unexpectedly ended immediately after the Japanese surrender. To avert immediate bankruptcy, a new loan agreement had urgently to be negotiated with both the Americans and the Canadians, to which stringent conditions were attached. It was also intended that this sort of assistance should be short-lived. Inevitably therefore the Government's first priority was the battle for economic solvency and the need to increase production and exports.

Despite these problems, the first few months of the Government's life were characterised by great optimism. An immediate start was made on the implementation of the Party programme that had been developed during the inter-war years. This task was facilitated by the large amount of preparatory work that had been undertaken during the war both within departments and by committees such as the Beveridge Committee on Social Insurance. Between January and April 1946 Bills were introduced to nationalise the mines, to repeal the anti-union legislation that had been enacted in the aftermath of the General Strike, to set up a national insurance scheme and to establish a National Health Service. Even in the economic sphere, there were encouraging signs. The Government's initial strategy for managing the economy placed more emphasis upon physical controls than on fiscal or monetary policy. The war-time planning machinery was retained under the supervision of Herbert Morrison, the Lord President of the Council; investment was controlled by building licences and raw material allocations; the balance of payments was protected by import controls; and consumer spending was restrained by rationing which was even extended in 1946 to include bread, which had not been rationed during the war. Meanwhile interest rates were lowered still further than in wartime to keep down the burden of war debt and in an attempt to assist borrowers rather than lenders of money.

For a short time this strategy appeared to be having some success. Demobilisation proceeded without the great tensions that had occurred after the First World War and industrial production and exports were beginning to increase. However, these hopes were rudely shattered by the events of 1947. Even during 1946 there had been some signs of food and fuel shortages. Both occurred early in 1947, the latter made much more serious by extremely severe weather. This had a serious effect upon industry, which was partially shut down for several weeks, and was reflected in a temporary increase in unemployment to over 2 million and in a dramatic reduction in exports. To make things worse, the Government was committed under the terms of its American loan agreement to restore the convertibility of the pound in July 1947. This produced an immediate foreign exchange crisis. Convertibility lasted only five weeks and the Government was compelled to seek further assistance from the United States in order to finance the balance of payments deficit. This came eventually in the form of the European Recovery Programme, generally known as Marshall Aid, which provided four years of American assistance for Britain and other European countries. The convertibility crisis, coming so soon after the fuel crisis, provoked widespread concern about the Government's handling of the economy. In an attempt to allay these fears, Sir Stafford Cripps was appointed to a new post of Minister for Economic Affairs with responsibility for directing the programme of economic recovery. Two months later, following an indiscretion by Dalton over the details of his autumn Budget, Cripps also became Chancellor of the Exchequer.

Cripps's three years as Chancellor saw the abandonment of both of the pillars of Dalton's economic policy – physical controls and cheap money. A start had been made in this direction by Dalton himself but it was Cripps who was primarily responsible for the shift in emphasis and whose name has become synonymous with the austerity measures of 1948–50. In peacetime physical controls had been found to be ineffective and unpopular and under Cripps's overall direction his successor at the Board of Trade, Harold Wilson, began to dismantle many controls and eased most of those that had to remain. Cripps did not however abandon altogether the attempt to plan the economy but his efforts were based more upon persuasion, backed up by fiscal measures, than on compulsion. (Although interest rates were allowed to rise, monetary policy was not used as a weapon of economic management.) Consumer spending was restrained by taxation policy; investment was encouraged by tax allowances on new plant and machinery; and strict controls were maintained over public expenditure. But much of Cripps's energy was devoted to securing voluntary co-operation with his programme for economic recovery. The export drive was assisted by a system of export targets agreed in considerable detail with all the main industries, working parties were established to study the problems of particular industries and the TUC's support was secured for a policy of wage restraint between 1948 and 1950 which succeeded in keeping the rise in wage rates below the increase in retail prices. Doubts were expressed within the trade union movement about the equity and usefulness of such restraint and their concurrence was largely a reflection of the depth of their loyalty to the Government. A major factor in accounting for this was their trust in Ernest Bevin. His standing in the Labour movement guaranteed the Government the support of the major unions, most of whose leaders saw their role as that of protecting Ministers against attacks from the Left wing of the Party.

On domestic matters, however, the Government came under little criticism from within the Party. This reflected the fact that during its first three years in office it was highly successful in implementing the Party's programme. The Bank of England, coal, electricity, gas and most of the inland transport industry were nationalised. Almost all of the Beveridge Committee's proposals were implemented, thus establishing a comprehensive system of insurance for sickness, unemployment, retirement and widowhood, a new insurance scheme for industrial injuries, family allowances paid for each child other than the first, and a more generous system of means-tested national assistance for those not covered by insurance or with special needs. In July 1948, following difficult negotiations with the medical profession, Labour's jewel – the National Health Service – came into existence, providing a comprehensive and free service for all. The provisions of the 1944 Education Act were implemented and in 1947 the minimum school-leaving age was raised to 15. A new system of town and country planning was introduced to extend the powers of central and local government to plan and control development. A programme of house-building, based primarily upon council housing, was quickly started, although the initial targets had to be scaled down in the wake of the 1947 crisis. Moreover, despite the scale of the country's economic problems, full employment was maintained and both production and the balance of payments were showing signs of recovery.

The most contentious areas of policy within the Party were foreign affairs and defence. In 1945 there had been considerable support for what was loosely thought of as a 'socialist foreign policy'. However, the pressures of economic dependence upon the United States and the growing intransigence of the USSR led Bevin to seek close collaboration with the United States. He played a major part in the creation of the Marshall Plan and was a prime mover in the establishment of the North Atlantic Treaty Organisation. This policy was opposed by a group of M.P.s in the Parliamentary Labour Party (PLP) who advocated the creation of a 'third force' between Russia and America in which Britain would play a prominent role. Their only success, however, was in persuading the Government in 1947 to cut the length of enforced military service from 18 months to 12. Also a source of controversy within the Party was Bevin's handling of the situation in Palestine where the withdrawal of British troops in 1948 was followed by a period of conflict between the Jews and Arabs. It stood in marked contrast to the smooth transition to independence of four of Britain's Asian colonies, India, Pakistan, Burma and Ceylon.

By the beginning of 1949, Britain's balance of payments position seemed healthier than at any time since the war. However, a slight recession in the United States largely wiped out the progress that had been made since the crisis of 1947. After talks in Washington had failed to produce any alternative solution, Cripps devalued the pound in September 1949 by 30 per cent from $4.03 to $2.80. For some time it had widely been thought that the pound was overvalued but the extent of the change, intended to give British exports to the dollar area an extra competitive margin, was larger than expected. Devaluation was followed by further measures to cut home demand, including cuts in government spending and in capital expenditure programmes. It succeeded, however, in restoring the balance of payments which was in surplus on current account throughout 1950.

Politically however the effect of devaluation was to underline the fragility of the recovery of the economy. This had important implications for the General Election which had to occur by July 1950. Although the Government had not lost a single by-election during its life, its performance in municipal elections provided some indication of the unpopularity of its austerity programme. Moreover, it was confronted by a revitalised Conservative Party both in terms of policy and organisation. The result of the election called by Attlee in February 1950, therefore, did not come as a great surprise. Although Labour increased its vote and polled 750,000 more votes than the Conservatives, its share of the poll fell and, once this had been translated into seats, its overall majority in the House of Commons was reduced to only six.

Such a small majority made another election inevitable in the near future. Compared with the situation in 1977-79, the opposition was much less fragmented (the Government's majority over the Conservatives was only 16). In addition, both the Government and its most senior members were showing signs of strain. The Party had failed to come up with a new programme to replace that of 1945, which had largely been implemented by 1948, and a period in opposition was needed to chart the way forward. Moreover, most of the senior members of the Government who had been in office continuously since 1940 – were physically and mentally exhausted. Ill-health caused the resignation of Cripps in 1950 and Bevin in 1951 and both died shortly afterwards. To replace Cripps as Chancellor, Attlee promoted Hugh Gaitskell, who had a good reputation as a Minister but who lacked stature in the Party. Morrison, at his own insistence, was Bevin's successor at the Foreign Office but his inexperience of foreign affairs and lack of flair for diplomacy were soon apparent, for instance in his handling of a dispute with Persia in 1951 which resulted in the nationalisation of the Anglo-Iranian Oil Company and the expulsion of its staff by the Persian Government.

The main issue of domestic controversy during the 1950 Parliament arose over the Government's decision to proceed with the nationalis-ation of iron and steel. The Iron and Steel Act had been passed in 1949 but the House of Lords' assent had been obtained only by a promise that it would not be put into effect until after the General Election. The Government's decision to proceed was approved by the Commons against bitter opposition from the Conservatives. On this and other issues their policy was to harry a Government that was clearly tired and demoralised, making use of every parliamentary tactic open to them.

Meanwhile the Government was attempting to cope with a deteriorating international and domestic economic situation. The outbreak of hostilities in Korea in 1950 led to a major escalation in rearmament throughout the world. The resulting increase in raw material prices had a serious effect upon the balance of payments and the level of inflation. This would have been serious in any case but it was exacerbated by the expansion of Britain's own defence programme. To pay for this and to ease the pressure on the balance of payments, Gaitskell introduced a deflationary budget which increased taxation and imposed charges for false teeth and spectacles, which since 1948 had been supplied free under the National Health Service. This decision, taken in the absence of Attlee who was in hospital, provoked the resignation of two members of the Cabinet, Aneurin Bevan and Harold Wilson, who argued both that this step was objectionable in itself and that the rearmament programme was imposing too great a strain on the economy.

In spite of these divisions, Attlee decided to call a new election in October 1951. In one sense the result was surprisingly good for Labour for it secured the largest number of votes ever recorded for a single party and it had a small majority of votes over the Conservatives. But the quirks of the electoral system gave the Conservatives an overall majority in the House of Commons of 17 seats. So, only six years after many people had thought that Labour was in power for good, the Party was back in opposition.

1964–70

The Labour Party was not returned to office until October 1964, and then only with a majority of five in the House of Commons. After 13 years in opposition, there was little previous experience upon which the new Prime Minister, Harold Wilson, could draw. Apart from Wilson himself, who had been President of the Board of Trade between 1947 and 1951, only two other members of the 1964 Cabinet had sat in Cabinet before. The deputy leader of the Party, George Brown, was appointed to head a new Department of Economic Affairs (DEA) which took over responsibility for economic planning and co-ordination from the Treasury, where James Callaghan became Chancellor. Wilson appointed Patrick Gordon-Walker as Foreign Secretary, even though he had been defeated in the election. His tenure of office was, however, short-lived for he failed to return to the Commons in a by-election at the beginning of 1965 and was replaced by Michael Stewart. This defeat also reduced the Government's overall majority to three.

Despite its precarious position in Parliament, the Government decided that it would proceed with the implementation of the programme on which it had been elected. In any case, in various fields urgent decisions had to be taken. On the day of the election, news had come through of the first Chinese nuclear test and of the overthrow of Khrushchev in the Soviet Union. The most pressing problem facing the Government, however, was the economic situation. It had been greeted by Treasury estimates that the balance of payments deficit in 1964 was likely to be £800 million, considerably larger than had previously been forecast. Action to deal with this crisis had been delayed by the election campaign but could not be further postponed.

Over their first weekend in office, therefore, Ministers took a vital decision that was to have a major effect upon everything else that they did. On both economic and political grounds, they decided not to devalue the pound and instead agreed on a package of measures to defend its existing parity. A 15 per cent surcharge was immediately imposed on all imports, except food and basic raw materials, and a tax rebate offered on exports. A month later the Chancellor introduced a tough deflationary Budget, which increased taxation and interest rates, and announced his intention of reviewing public expenditure, with special attention being paid to prestige projects. The Budget did, however, contain some brighter elements, such as increases in old-age pensions and the abolition of NHS prescription charges, thus fulfilling the first of Labour's election promises.

At the same time the Government made a start in working out longer-term measures to strengthen the economy. These centred upon George Brown and the mixed staff of civil servants, academics, industrialists and trade unionists that he had recruited to the DEA. Within two months of gaining office, he had secured the agreement of both sides of industry to a Joint Declaration of Interest on Productivity, Prices and Incomes, one provision of which was the setting-up of a National Board for Prices and Incomes to examine price increases and wage claims that were referred to it. Wider in scope was the work that went into the launching of the National Plan in September 1965 which set out a strategy designed to achieve 25 per cent growth of the economy by 1970.

In other areas too the Government did not allow its small majority to prevent it from taking action. During the 1964–66 Parliament a large number of statutes were enacted, including some that were fiercely contested by the Conservatives. On the other hand, it was clear that Harold Wilson would seek to strengthen the Government's position at the earliest favourable opportunity. This occurred in March 1966 and Labour was rewarded with a decisive victory, obtaining an overall majority of nearly 100 seats in the House of Commons.

Much of the euphoria of this result was soon dispelled, however, by a deterioration in the economic situation. Following a May Budget that had been neutral in its effect upon the economy, the fragile recovery of the pound was undermined by a seven-week seamen's strike. At the beginning of July there was a dramatic collapse in its value, and in an attempt to reassure foreign banking opinion, the Cabinet decided to introduce a very severe deflationary package, including a six-month freeze on all wage, salary and dividend increases to be followed by six months' 'severe restraint', tax increases, tighter hire-purchase controls and a £50 ceiling on overseas holiday expenditure. This package effectively destroyed the Government's long-term economic strategy and almost provoked the resignation of George Brown, who a month later left the DEA to become Foreign Secretary. It also undermined the harmony that had existed within the Labour movement since 1964. Earlier there had been some disquiet among Labour backbenchers and some trade unionists about Government policy but this had mainly been confined to defence and foreign affairs. Now, however, it extended to include the main pillars of economic policy and was to continue, often in a highly public manner, for most of the remainder of the Government's life.

At the beginning of 1967 the July measures appeared to be restoring the strength of the pound but only at the cost of relatively high unemployment. There was also an improvement in the balance of payments but this was adversely affected during 1967 by the six-day war in the Middle East in June 1967 and a two-month dock strike over the summer. This led to renewed pressure on the pound and in November 1967 the Cabinet eventually decided it had no option other than to devalue from $2.80 to $2.40. But, far from avoiding the need for further deflation, such action was essential if devaluation was to be effective in boosting British exports. After long and agonised debate within the Cabinet, drastic cuts in public expenditure were announced in January 1968 by Roy Jenkins, who had succeeded James Callaghan as Chancellor shortly after devaluation.

At home these cuts included the reimposition of NHS prescription charges and the postponement of the raising of the school-leaving age from 1971 to 1973, both of which were bitterly opposed within the Labour Party. The Government's critics were happier about its decision to cut defence spending abroad by withdrawing British troops from stations east of Suez and by cancelling a large order for American military aircraft. Indeed such a move had been advocated earlier but had then been rejected by the Government. As a result of this decision British defence policy in the 1970s became firmly European-based. This fitted in well with another of the Cabinet's changes in direction – its decision, again influenced by the economic situation, to apply for membership of the EEC. Negotiations on this application were vetoed by France but it remained on the table and talks were about to begin, following the retirement of President de Gaulle, at the time of the election in 1970. The other main foreign policy issue was Rhodesia. In November 1965 the white minority government in Rhodesia, led by Ian Smith, declared independence unilaterally. The Government responded immediately by imposing economic sanctions against the rebel regime and, when these failed to bring it down, it persuaded the United Nations to invoke mandatory sanctions. Two abortive attempts were made by Harold Wilson to reach a settlement with Ian Smith in 1966 and 1968.

Although the deflationary measures of 1966 and 1967 destroyed the Government's overall plans for the economy, some parts of its strategy were maintained and were given greater prominence in an attempt to plug the holes that had been opened up by the recurrent sterling crises. Of particular importance was selective intervention in private industry designed to improve its efficiency and export performance. This policy had replaced nationalisation as the principal element in Labour's industrial policy. The only instance of traditional nationalisation in this period was the renationalisation of iron and steel in 1967. In contrast, there was a major extension in State involvement in private industry, mainly through the provision of grants and loans. Initially this programme centred upon the DEA but it was gradually taken over by another of Wilson's departmental creations, the Ministry of Technology, and by a new agency – the Industrial Reorganisation Corporation – which was created in 1966 as a kind of government-sponsored merchant bank to encourage and assist the restructuring of industry.

Within the Labour Party this new industrial policy was generally welcomed as a pragmatic response to the problems of British industry. This cannot be said, however, of the other economic initiative of the post-devaluation period: the attempt to introduce legal sanctions into the framework of industrial relations. In 1966 the Government had appointed a Royal Commission to investigate the trade unions and its report, which ruled out legal sanctions, was published in 1968. Nonetheless, the Government decided, in the belief that strikes, and especially unofficial strikes, were a major cause of the country's economic problems, that Ministers should be given powers to impose a conciliation period before a strike could take place and to order a strike ballot. These proposals, published in January 1969, provoked a bitter response from the TUC and from most of the Labour Party. They were rejected overwhelmingly by a special conference of the TUC and the Chief Whip warned the Cabinet that, if it proceeded with its proposals, it would be opposed not only by those on the Left wing but also by many M.P.s who were normally its loyal supporters. After six months of internal turmoil within the Labour movement, the Cabinet agreed to drop its proposals in return for a TUC undertaking that it would itself do what it could to prevent unofficial strikes.

This row marked the nadir in the Government's relations with the trade unions and many of its own backbenchers. However, it was by no means the only source of tension. Its statutory incomes policy was decisively rejected by the TUC; the same view was taken by the Party Conference in 1968 which between 1966 and 1969 also opposed various other aspects of Government economic policy and its support for American action in Vietnam; and in Parliament there were frequent rebellions, mainly but not exclusively by Left-wing M.P.s. Generally morale in the Party was at a low ebb and it was not improved by a series of humiliating by-election defeats, the most dramatic of which was at Dudley in March 1968 where there was a swing of over 20 per cent to the Conservatives.

The Government's difficulties with the economy also limited its ability to achieve many of its other objectives, especially insofar as they involved additional public expenditure. However, although a number of the Government's plans had had to be postponed or curtailed, spending in real terms on the social services increased significantly between 1964 and 1970 and, in 1968–69, for the first time, the proportion of the gross national product spent on education exceeded that spent on defence. Similarly, although the target of building 500,000 new houses a year by 1970 had to be abandoned, the number of houses completed between 1964 and 1969 rose by more than a third in comparison with the previous five years.

In addition to increasing public spending on the social services, the Government made a number of changes in their organisation. In the field of education steady progress was made in securing the introduction of comprehensive secondary schools throughout the country. This was achieved not by legislation but by a policy of exhortation and pressure upon local education authorities such that by 1970, only a few had failed to submit reorganisation schemes and about a third of secondary-age children were being educated in comprehensive schools. Other steps were also taken to widen educational opportunities. In 1967 a policy of positive discrimination was adopted in favour of schools in areas of acute social and economic stress, known as educational priority areas. The university expansion that had been started by the Conservatives in the early 1960s was accelerated and two new kinds of institution were created at this level: first, the non-university sector was up-graded through the creation of 30 polytechnics which were to offer courses at degree and sub-degree level especially in fields relating to commerce and technology; and second, the Open University was founded, making use of television and radio, to provide university education for those who could only study at home.

Important changes were also made in the fields of housing and social security. Owner-occupiers were assisted by an option mortgage scheme designed for those who were unable to find the deposit needed for a mortgage, and by a Leasehold Reform Act which gave about 1 million leaseholders the right to buy the freehold of their houses. Controls were introduced over increases in council house rents and, in the private sector, a new Rent Act froze the rent for most unfurnished accommodation and provided a system under which fair rents could be fixed by independent arbitrators. It also gave tenants greater security of tenure and protection against harassment. The only group not directly affected by the Government's housing policy were tenants in furnished accommodation. Those who were poor were, however, assisted by general changes made in the social security system. In 1966 the National Assistance Scheme was replaced by a new Supplementary Benefits Scheme which, although in large part only a change of name, had some effect upon attitudes and was one factor in producing an increase in the number of people claiming benefits to which they were entitled. The same objective was achieved by the introduction of the 'clawback' under which an increase in family allowances was paid to all women with more than one child but was taken back in taxation from all those paying the standard rate of income tax. In addition, various new benefits were introduced, including redundancy payments, rate rebates and new allowances for the long-term sick and disabled, and the real value of most existing benefits was increased.

Two other areas of activity merit special attention: first, immigration and race relations; and second, institutional reform. Although the Labour Party had strongly opposed the tighter system of immigration control introduced by the Conservatives in 1962, it did not repeal the Act and, after an abortive attempt to secure the co-operation of Commonwealth countries in a voluntary scheme, it strengthened its provisions. This decision was bitterly criticised by many within the Party but reflected electoral pressure in areas of high immigration that manifested itself on a number of occasions during the 1960s. On the other hand the Government took important steps to try to improve the position of the coloured population already in the UK, passing two laws outlawing racial discrimination in various fields and establishing two official bodies to promote better community relations. These bodies were only two of the large number of such organisations set up by the Government to undertake specific tasks on behalf of Ministers, reflecting not only its growing involvement in social and economic affairs but also its faith in the efficacy of institutional change as a means of altering attitudes and behaviour. Such a view was also evident in relation to other aspects of the machinery of government. In 1964

Harold Wilson set up no fewer than five new departments and over the next five years there were frequent changes in the structure of departments and in the distribution of functions between them. The Government also instigated inquiries into a large number of public institutions: the Civil Service, local government, the National Health Service and both houses of Parliament; and by the time it left office it had either implemented many of their recommendations or had drawn up plans to do so.

At the beginning of 1970 there was still more than a year before a General Election had to be held. The Government was also in the process of implementing a number of major proposals, including the introduction of a new earnings-related pensions scheme, the reform of local government in England and Wales and the nationalisation of the ports. However, speculation began to mount about the possibility of an early election largely as a result of a marked improvement in the economic situation. Devaluation had not worked as quickly as Ministers had hoped; indeed, towards the end of 1968 further measures had had to be taken to protect the pound at its new parity. But gradually the trade figures began to improve and the balance of payments moved into surplus in 1969. There was also a mood of greater prosperity as wage restraint was relaxed and the Chancellor was able to make a few minor tax concessions. This was reflected in a recovery of the Government's ratings in the opinion polls and in a number of better by-election results. When this trend was confirmed in the municipal elections in May 1970, Wilson decided that an early election offered a good prospect of securing the return of the Government to power for a further five years. Until polling day itself (18 June) it looked as if he was right, but when the votes were counted the electorate was discovered to have given the Conservatives a majority of 31 seats in the House of Commons.

1974–79

The return of Labour to office following the February 1974 election was as unexpected as it had been in 1945. On this occasion, however, it was a much more close-run 'victory'. The election had been held in the middle of a state of emergency, imposed as a result of an Arab embargo on Western oil supplies and the Conservative Government's confrontation with the miners over Stage Three of its pay policy. At the beginning of the campaign success seemed assured for the Conservatives, who were calling for the return of a strong Government that was capable of dealing with Britain's economic problems and of overcoming any group of workers who used their industrial strength to frustrate it. However, as the campaign progressed, the Government's overall record came increasingly under critical scrutiny and when the votes were counted the Conservatives had lost 33 seats and Labour emerged as the largest party in the House of Commons. For a short time it looked as if the

Conservatives might succeed in staying in office with Liberal support. But, when talks on the formation of such a coalition broke down, Labour took office on its own even though it was more than 30 seats short of an overall majority in the Commons.

As in 1945, there was a large amount of ministerial experience upon which the Prime Minister, Harold Wilson, could draw. With men such as Denis Healey as Chancellor, Jim Callaghan as Foreign Secretary and Roy Jenkins as Home Secretary, Wilson himself was content to play a less prominent role than he had done throughout his first administration. Less than half of the members of the 1974 Cabinet were newcomers, and only one of them, Michael Foot, had had no previous ministerial experience. His entry into the Cabinet, particularly as Secretary of State for Employment, symbolised the changes that had occurred in the Labour Party since its electoral defeat in 1970. As a prominent member of the Tribune Group, he had been a leading campaigner for many of the new directions in Labour policy, notably on the EEC, and had played a major part in healing the breach with the trade unions.

The immediate task confronting the Government was the settlement of the miners' dispute and the ending of the emergency measures that the Conservatives had taken to deal with it. But, underlying the emergency, were more serious problems which the incoming Government could not hope to solve overnight. At the heart of these difficulties was the threefold increase in the price of oil that had occurred in 1973. This increase and a general rise in raw material prices had had a very serious effect upon the balance of payments. It also contributed to inflationary pressures that already existed within the economy. Moreover, the restrictive measures all governments had had to take to combat inflation and to correct their balance of payments deficits, were producing the most serious recession of the post-war period, reflected in high levels of unemployment.

To cope with this situation, the Government placed reliance upon a package of measures known as the Social Contract, which it had agreed with the TUC while in opposition. In return for an undertaking from the unions to keep wage settlements in line with rises in the cost of living, the Government agreed to repeal Conservative legislation on wage restraint and industrial relations, to strengthen price controls, to increase subsidies and social benefits and to extend public ownership.

Despite its minority position in the Commons, the Government was able to make a start with implementing these policies, making full use of the fact that the other parties were reluctant to force another election immediately. Over the summer of 1974 a large number of policy statements were published, for instance on devolution, industrial policy and the public ownership of development land. They formed the basis of the Government's appeal to the electorate for a clear majority in October. The result of the election was never really in doubt but the margin of Labour's victory was smaller than all the opinion polls had predicted. In the new Parliament, Labour had a majority of only three over all other parties but its position was in fact considerably stronger than this because of the fragmented nature of the opposition (its majority over the Conservatives being 43).

The next two and a half years saw the implementation of most of the specific commitments contained in Labour's 1974 election manifestos. New legislation was introduced on industrial relations, strengthening the powers of the trade unions, conferring new rights upon employees and establishing a new conciliation agency, the Advisory Conciliation and Arbitration Service. The Industry Act of 1975 established a State holding company, the National Enterprise Board, and extended the Government's powers to assist private industry. A British National Oil Corporation was created to manage and extend the State's interests in North Sea oil development and a new tax was imposed on the North Sea profits of the private oil companies. In the field of social policy, a new earnings-related and inflation-proofed State pension scheme was introduced, a Health Services Act provided for the progressive withdrawal of private medicine from National Health Service hospitals and an Education Act required local education authorities to submit proposals to abolish selection in secondary education. Most of this heavy programme of legislation was opposed vehemently by the Conservatives in the Commons, where the Government's small majority was frequently threatened but only rarely overturned, and in the House of Lords. The Lords attempted to make major changes in various Government Bills but the conflict eventually centred around two: one that sought to extend the area around the docks in which work was reserved for registered dockworkers; the other that provided for the nationalisation of the aerospace and shipbuilding industries. In the case of the former, the defection of two of its own backbenchers prevented the Government restoring its original proposals; the latter eventually became law 15 months after it had first been introduced and only after the Government had made substantial concessions.

Overseas, the Government's energies were devoted primarily to two areas: Europe and Rhodesia. In the 1974 elections Labour had undertaken to renegotiate the terms under which Britain had entered the EEC in 1973 and to consult the British people, either by referendum or through another election, as to whether the new terms should be accepted. After concluding negotiations on various issues, such as Britain's contribution to the Community Budget and the safeguarding of the interests of the Commonwealth and developing countries, a majority of the Cabinet voted to recommend continued membership. Their decision was opposed, however, by seven of their colleagues, who were allowed by the Prime Minister to voice their dissent in public without first resigning, by a majority of the backbench members of the PLP and by a special conference of the Labour Party. Nonetheless it was confirmed by a majority of more than two to one in the referendum that was held in June 1975. Although this settled the issue of Britain's membership, it did not dispel many of the doubts, by no means confined to the Labour Party, expressed about many aspects of the Community. Between 1975 and 1979, backed by popular opinion, Ministers took an increasingly tough line in negotiations on matters such as food prices, fishing and Britain's contribution to the Community Budget, and Britain was alone in 1979 in declining to take part in new arrangements for monetary harmonisation.

The other main foreign policy issue in this period was the continuing search for a settlement of the Rhodesian dispute. As internal security in Rhodesia deteriorated, efforts were made to promote discussions between the rebel regime and the various black nationalist leaders. In the autumn of 1976 a conference was held in Geneva, under the chairmanship of the Foreign Secretary, but it made no progress. The Government then worked unsuccessfully to achieve a settlement involving all the parties on the basis of a set of joint Anglo-American proposals which were published in 1977. Meanwhile, in Rhodesia, Ian Smith succeeded in reaching agreement with three moderate African leaders on the formation of a transitional government to prepare for elections and majority rule.

Any feelings of complacency that may have been induced by the Government's record of legislative achievement between 1974 and 1977 were, however, moderated by the persistence of economic difficulties, notably unemployment and inflation. During 1974 retail prices rose by more than 19 per cent and wage settlements were running 8–9 per cent ahead of prices. To deal with this situation, Denis Healey introduced a tough Budget in April 1975, increasing taxes by £1,250 million in a full year and cutting public spending. Once the EEC referendum was out of the way, this was followed by the announcement in July 1975 of a limit of £6 a week on pay settlements during the next 12 months for those earning up to £8,500 a year with no increase for those earning more. This policy was voluntary in the sense that there were no legal sanctions against trade unions but the Government announced that employers who exceeded the limit would have not only the excess but the whole of the increase disallowed for the approval of price rises.

Although this represented a major turnaround for the Government, which earlier had argued against any kind of formal pay policy, it succeeded in obtaining the agreement of the TUC which also undertook to persuade its members to comply. In part this reflected the seriousness of the situation. Trade unionists were not only alarmed as consumers by the prospect of escalating inflation; they were also concerned about its implications for the level of unemployment. Many firms were in difficulties and, in the Government's view, the only alternative to greater pay restraint was further deflationary action. The Government had already been compelled to bale out a number of companies that had run into trouble, of which British Leyland, which was nationalised in May 1975, was only the most spectacular example. Despite this and other measures designed to hold down the level of unemployment, more than a million people were out of work by mid-1975. In addition, the loyalty of the unions was won by the willingness of the Government to pursue policies on industrial relations and in other areas that had been advocated by the TUC.

During this first phase of incomes policy, British politics was taken completely by surprise by the announcement by Harold Wilson of his retirement at the relatively young age of 60. In a three-ballot contest, James Callaghan was elected by Labour M.P.s as his successor. He made a number of changes in the Cabinet, including the appointment of Michael Foot, who was runner-up in the leadership election, as Deputy Prime Minister and Leader of the House of Commons, and of Anthony Crosland as Foreign Secretary. Denis Healey, however, remained as Chancellor of the Exchequer. Further changes were made in September 1976. Combined with the resignation of Roy Jenkins at the end of 1976 on his appointment as President of the European Commission, and the death of Anthony Crosland early in 1977, who was replaced by David Owen, these changes gave the Cabinet a very different look from that of the Wilson era.

Although the £6 limit was generally observed and had some effect on the rate of inflation, the Government decided that a further period of wage restraint was needed. In April 1976 the Chancellor offered various tax cuts conditional upon the unions' agreement to a new pay limit. Such an agreement was reached the following month with a limit curbing average wage increases to 4.5 per cent in the year starting in August 1976. However, the announcement of Phase Two was overshadowed by a sharp fall in the value of the pound. One of the major causes of its weakness was a belief that the Government was borrowing excessively to finance public expenditure. In March the pound fell for the first time below the $2 mark and when confidence continued to ebb, despite some international support, the Chancellor was compelled to announce spending curbs of £1,000 million in July. These measures were not sufficient, however, to prevent a further dramatic slide in the pound during the autumn, fuelled in part by the decision of the Party Conference to press for more nationalisation and to wage a public campaign against the Government's spending cuts. To restore confidence in the pound, the Government decided to seek a $3,900 million loan from the International Monetary Fund. As a condition of such a loan, the Government was required to make further cuts in public expenditure, amounting to £3,000 million over the next two years, and to increase taxation.

These deflationary measures were strongly opposed by many of the Government's supporters, in Parliament and outside. In Parliament, their votes were crucial as the Government's majority had been whittled away by a number of by-election defeats and finally disappeared in the spring of 1977. The 1976–77 session was dominated by the Government's plans to set up elected assemblies in Scotland and Wales. Such a commitment had been included in Labour's election manifestos and a series of white papers setting out its detailed proposals had been produced since 1974. In December 1976 a Scotland and Wales Bill received a second reading with a majority of 45. However, although the Government was backed by the Nationalist M.P.s it failed to pass a 'guillotine' motion in February 1977 as a result of the defection of a number of its own backbenchers. Unable to make further progress with the devolution Bill, the Government could no longer count on the support of the Nationalists and, when the Conservatives put down a motion of no confidence in March 1977, it looked as if the Government would be defeated. However, defeat was averted by an agreement it entered into with the Liberal Party. Both parties retained their independence for electoral purposes and in the House of Commons, but in return for formal consultation on Government policy and some specific undertakings on subjects such as progress on the holding of direct elections to the European Assembly and on revision of the devolution proposals, the Liberals agreed to support the Government, initially until the end of the parliamentary session.

One of the reasons behind Liberal support for the Government was their belief that a Labour Government was most likely to be able to negotiate a further period of pay restraint with the unions. However, the TUC refused to agree to a new limit on wage settlements, believing that there should be an immediate return to free collective bargaining subject only to an undertaking that settlements should last for 12 months. In part this reflected growing union dissatisfaction with the general direction of the Government's economic policies. The deflationary measures of 1976, introduced in the middle of a serious world-wide recession, had led to a marked deterioration in the level of unemployment which was at its highest since the war. The Government had introduced various schemes to offset some of this increase, but short of general reflationary measures which it ruled out, there was little that it could do.

Despite union opposition, the Government decided to proceed unilaterally with a third phase of pay restraint, announcing a new guideline designed to keep the rise in earnings throughout the economy during 1977–78 down to 10 per cent. This policy was sufficient to secure the renewal of the Lib/Lab agreement for a further year. In any case, the Government's parliamentary position had been strengthened by the reintroduction of the devolution proposals, this time as separate Bills for Scotland and Wales. These Bills, supported now by both the Liberals and the Nationalists, reached the Statute Book in July 1978. In the face of determined opposition from the Conservatives, from a group of Labour backbenchers and from members of the House of Lords, they had a stormy passage and a number of amendments were carried against the wishes of the Government. Of these, the most important was the stipulation that the legislation would only come into force if it was endorsed by 40 per cent of the Scottish and Welsh electorates in the referendums which the Government had earlier been forced to concede in order to secure the support of some of the doubters in its own ranks. Although the average increase in earnings during Stage Three was 5 per cent higher than the Government's norm, this was much better than had been expected in view of the TUC's opposition and was one factor in the fall of the rate of inflation to about 8 per cent. Encouraged by its success, the Government announced a 5 per cent norm for 1978–79 with a number of exceptions to permit greater flexibility than in the earlier phases of its pay policy. However few people expected that Stage Four would be seriously tested in advance of a General Election. A general improvement in the economic situation, in which the Government's policies and the advent of North Sea oil had played a part along with a recovery in international trade, produced an up-turn in the Government's electoral popularity during 1978. It was widely expected therefore that a General Election would be held in the autumn, particularly once it was known that the Liberals did not intend to renew their agreement with the Government at the end of the 1977–78 session. However, the Prime Minister confounded all these expectations by announcing in September 1978 that the Government intended to continue in office until 1979 unless it was defeated in the Commons.

As the winter wore on, his decision appeared increasingly rash. Trade union opposition to the pay policy proved to be much more determined than in the previous year and was little constrained by fear of damaging Labour's electoral prospects. The first major confrontation occurred at Ford's and it was followed by a succession of disputes, involving lorry and petrol tanker drivers and public service manual workers among others, the effects of which were aggravated by severe weather conditions. These disputes were settled only by offers significantly in excess of the Government's norm and this was soon reflected in a rising rate of inflation. They also undermined one of the electoral assets which the Government had cultivated since 1974: that it was able to govern with the co-operation of the trade unions. In addition, the behaviour of some of those involved in strike action brought to the surface public concern about the power of the unions and raised doubts about some of the steps taken by the Government to strengthen their legal position.

During this assault on its pay policy, the Government was sustained in the House of Commons by the support on different occasions of Ulster Unionist and Nationalist M.P.s. The former were won over by legislation to increase the number of parliamentary constituencies in Northern Ireland, the latter by the decision to hold the devolution referendums in March 1979. These referendums, however, delivered a second body-blow to the Government's already tattered reputation. In Wales 80 per cent of those who voted rejected the Government's proposals; and in Scotland, where it had been expected that there would be a substantial majority in favour of the proposals, they were endorsed by the barest of majorities and by only a third of those entitled to vote. This outcome placed the Government in a serious dilemma. It was pressed by the Nationalists to proceed with the establishment of a

Scottish Assembly by seeking to overturn the requirement that the legislation be endorsed by 40 per cent of the Scottish electorate. However, fearing a major rebellion by its own backbenchers, it was unwilling to do this and called only for all-party talks. In these circumstances the Scottish Nationalists indicated that they would no longer support the Government and in a vote of confidence at the end of March the Government was defeated by one vote, thus precipitating an immediate dissolution of Parliament. Throughout the ensuing election campaign Labour trailed behind the Conservatives in the opinion polls, largely as a result of the winter's industrial troubles, and on polling-day at the beginning of May the Conservatives won a decisive victory, obtaining an overall majority of 44 in the House of Commons. Although Labour's vote was almost exactly the same as in October 1974 its share of the poll fell to its lowest post-war level and it lost 39 seats. For the third time since 1945 electoral defeat followed a period of just five or six years in office.

Assessment of Labour's record

The major differences in the problems facing each of the post-war Labour Governments and in the way in which they attempted to deal with them mean that for the most part their records need to be discussed separately. On the other hand, there are a number of similarities which make it possible to draw some general conclusions. Most obviously, each of the Governments inherited severe economic problems and its life was dominated by the struggle to overcome them. Partly for this reason but also because of the Party's commitment to social and economic reform, each period of Labour Government was characterised by great, and sometimes frenzied, activity. A very heavy legislative burden was imposed upon Parliament, frequently placing its procedures under strain, and its effect was greatly to extend the powers of ministerial intervention. In addition, these economic difficulties and the measures taken to deal with them were one of the principal causes of the tensions that developed within the Labour movement, especially towards the end of each period of office, and which contributed to the Party's electoral defeat on each occasion after only five or six years. Each of these features is important in explaining and understanding the two questions that will be discussed in the remainder of this chapter: first, Labour's attitude towards the institutions and processes of British government; and second, its record over 17 years of office in realising the goals of its supporters.

Labour Ministers and the governmental process

Given the Labour Party's commitment to social and economic reform it might reasonably be expected that it would seek also to make changes in a system of government, the main features of which were laid down before the Party came into existence. Indeed, at every election since Labour became a major force in British politics fears have been expressed not just that the return of a Labour Government with a large majority would lead to political change but that it would undermine the British constitution. To some extent these fears have been fuelled by the Party's use of socialist rhetoric which in certain quarters has rendered it guilty 'by association'. More important, however, have been those parts of the Party's constitution that accord supreme policy-making powers to the Party Conference, thus posing the threat that a Labour Government would be subject to direction by forces outside Parliament. Concern has also been expressed that the Party's formal links with the trade unions would impair its ability to act in the national interest.

The record of Labour in office, however, provides little justification for these fears, especially those of the more extreme kind. The position of the monarchy has not been altered and those Labour backbenchers who have sought even to limit the growth in the Royal Purse have gained little support within the Party let alone from members of the Government. Nor has there been any question of Labour refusing to accept the verdict of the electorate. In 1951 Labour polled a quarter of a million more votes than the Conservatives but failed, through the quirks of the system, to win a majority of seats in the House of Commons. Equally the independent position of the judiciary has not been eroded. Accusations have on occasion been made that Labour Ministers have been guilty of unconstitutional action, for instance in deferring the implementation of constituency boundary changes in 1969, but such charges contain a strong element of party point-scoring and have not in any case involved fundamental elements in the constitution.

None of this is very surprising given the background and composition of the Labour Party. More significant is the way in which Labour Governments have been content to operate within the conventions of Cabinet and parliamentary government. In 1945 Attlee ignored the resolution of the 1933 Party Conference which laid down that a potential Labour Prime Minister should consult the PLP prior to accepting office and this precedent was followed by Wilson in 1964 and 1974.[1] Similarly the traditions that accord to the Prime Minister the right to select the members of his Government and to seek a dissolution of Parliament have been upheld. Moreover, despite pressure from the extra-parliamentary party, each Labour Prime Minister has made it clear that the Cabinet's responsibility lies solely to the House of Commons. During the 1945 election campaign Attlee had to stress this point, following a suggestion by Harold Laski, the Party Chairman, that he was subject to direction by the National Executive Committee (NEC).[2] It has also been reflected in the scant regard paid to the views of the Party Conference and the NEC, for instance by both Wilson and Callaghan on the subject of incomes policy. Groups within the Party have attempted to alter this situation by requiring sitting M.P.s to face reselection procedures before being readopted as Labour candidates and by removing the PLP's exclusive right to select the Party leader, but neither of these proposals had been accepted at the time of the 1979 General Election. Were they to be adopted in the future the relationship between a Labour Cabinet and its extra-parliamentary supporters would be significantly changed; up to the present, however, Labour Ministers have not formally been any more constrained in this respect than their Conservative counterparts.

More controversial, especially since the mid-1960s, has been the role of the trade unions. There can be no doubt that the unions have been an influential force in post-war British politics, both in achieving their own aims and in frustrating governments that have sought to take action against their interests. Moreover this influence has generally been greater when Labour has been in office which is hardly surprising in view of the close links, historically and organisationally, between the political and industrial wings of the Labour movement. This may give rise to political doubts about the freedom of action of Labour in office, but it cannot be said to raise constitutional questions unless it can be shown that the unions have formally assumed a role in government which threatens the position of Parliament. However, even in the 1970s when this question was widely discussed, the evidence to support it was fairly flimsy and those changes that had occurred were by no means exclusively associated with the Labour Party.

Two developments have most frequently been mentioned as marking a step in the direction of corporatism. First, in 1971 a Labour Party/TUC Liaison Committee was established in an attempt to prevent a recurrence of the breach that had occurred in the later years of the Wilson Government. This committee had a major policy-making role, not only when Labour was in opposition, but during the first few years in office after 1974. However, it represented no more than a formalisation of the contacts that normally have existed between the leadership of the Party and the trade union movement and in any case its influence waned after 1976 when the TUC's call for economic expansion, higher public expenditure and import controls produced no response from the Cabinet. The other development concerned the trade unions' greater direct involvement in government through their participation in various non-departmental agencies that were established on a tripartite basis in the 1970s.[3] To a limited extent these agencies did pose a threat to the authority of Parliament, but their importance in relation to the whole field of government was not very great. In any case, although Labour played some part, most of these agencies were established or planned by the Conservatives before 1974.

As regards the running of government, Labour Ministers have also generally operated within the traditional conventions. Except for a short period during 1975, the principle of collective responsibility has been upheld and both Wilson and Callaghan extended its scope to include not only junior Ministers but also Parliamentary Private Secretaries, who neither receive official salaries nor are appointed by the Prime Minister.[4] The exception was the period running up to the EEC referendum during which Harold Wilson permitted those Ministers who opposed the Cabinet's decision to recommend continued membership to express their views publicly in the country but not in Parliament. This 'agreement to differ', however, applied only during the campaign and, particularly in view of the problems it caused for the dissenting Ministers and even more for their civil servants, it is unlikely that it will have set a precedent for the future even when a Cabinet is deeply divided.[5]

On the other hand the convention was interpreted by Wilson and Callaghan more flexibly than had been the custom in the past. Disagreements that occurred in their Cabinets and the views of individual Ministers on contemporary issues were regularly aired in public as a result of leaks, and press accounts of the Wilson Government were supplemented by a mountain of memoirs written very shortly after 1970. This greater 'openness' reflects the style of Labour Party politics but it does not amount to a formal abandonment of the convention. Indeed, both Wilson and Callaghan were frequently at pains to remind their colleagues of the obligations of the convention and sought to promulgate new rules concerning Cabinet proceedings and the publication of ministerial memoirs.

One special problem has been the position of Cabinet Ministers who were also elected members of the NEC. During the 1960s it was suggested that those appointed to the Government should resign from the NEC because the convention of collective responsibility prevented them from taking part effectively in NEC discussions as representatives of those who had elected them. This suggestion was not accepted, however, because it was generally felt that overlapping membership facilitated the maintenance of good relations between the Government and the Party. This has led to a number of apparent breaches of the convention, notably by Jim Callaghan in 1968–69 when he spoke against the Cabinet's plans for industrial relations reform and by Tony Benn during the 1974–79 period when he regularly voiced doubts about many aspects of Government policy both in the NEC and in its Home Policy Committee, which he chaired. In neither case was the offending Minister dismissed, reflecting the strength of their following in the Party at the time, but the Prime Minister publicly took steps to remind them of their obligations as members of the Government. Moreover, their indiscretions were generally sufficiently hedged so as not to provoke direct retaliation from the Prime Minister. As long as dual membership continues these problems will recur, but so far they do not amount to a formal repudiation of the convention and can be accommodated within the flexibility such unwritten rules are intended to promote.

Similarly, the years of Labour Government have not resulted in any formal change in the convention of individual ministerial responsibility.

Changes in the scale of government and in the coherence of the party system since this convention was first established have of course altered the way in which it operates, notably in respect of ministerial resignations, but the principles of the system have received firm support from Labour Ministers, most recently in 1978.[6] On the other hand the Wilson and Callaghan Governments were responsible for a number of developments that did alter the relationship between Ministers and civil servants. The establishment dùring the 1960s of new parliamentary committees of investigation, before which civil servants regularly give evidence, has given more publicity to their views on policy questions. Their work generally has also become more visible through the enquiries of the Parliamentary Commissioner for Adminstration set up in 1967 to investigate complaints of maladministration. In addition, as a result of difficulties that some Ministers have experienced in their dealings with officials, the practice has grown of Ministers bringing in their own advisers. This was first done on a significant scale in 1964, when various economic advisers who were sympathetic to the Labour Party were recruited into government as temporary civil servants, and was taken much further in 1974 with the appointment of 23 special advisers with varying backgrounds. Five of them worked in a new unit advising the Prime Minister and the others were distributed among ten other departments.[7] However, not every Minister had such an adviser and their numbers were sufficiently small not to make more than a marginal change in the Minister's traditional dependence upon his permanent officials. Nor has their relationship been altered fundamentally by the investigations of select committees and the Parliamentary Commissioner.

This makes it all the more surprising that so little action has been taken by Labour Ministers to reform the Civil Service. The only serious attempt to do this occurred in the 1960s when, as part of its general programme of institutional reform, the Wilson Government appointed a committee of enquiry into the Civil Service. Its report was severely critical of the outdatedness of the service's recruitment and training policies and of its internal organisation and management.[8] Most of its recommendations were accepted by the Government in 1968 but, ten years later, a further enquiry by a parliamentary select committee revealed that little had changed, particularly in respect of the sort of people recruited into the service and the career patterns of those occupying the most senior posts.[9] Most of the Labour members of this committee sought radical changes in the service but their views were not supported by the Government. Similarly, although the Government had for ten years been committed to eliminate unnecessary secrecy and a promise to repeal the Official Secrets Acts had been included in the October 1974 manifesto, no progress had been made by 1979 and the Government had waged a war of attrition against a backbench Bill that sought to achieve this objective. Thus, in 1979 Labour Ministers appeared as strong defenders of the traditional closed system of government in which decisions were taken behind closed doors by small groups of Ministers and civil servants, most of whom were drawn from a very narrow background, socially, educationally and geographically. In this context it does not matter whether this stance was adopted through conviction or through weakness in the face of a determined Civil Service; the fact is that 17 years of Labour Government had produced almost no significant change in the direction of opening up the processes of government.

This cautious approach can also be seen in Labour's attitude towards parliamentary reform. In terms of its procedures and working arrangements, the Parliament of 1979 resembled very closely that of 1945. During all the years Labour has been in office there has only been one short period of significant parliamentary reform: the two years between 1966 and 1968, when Richard Crossman was Leader of the House of Commons, during which an attempt was made to improve the effectiveness of parliamentary control over the executive through the creation of various new select committees of investigation and the creation of the Parliamentary Commissioner for Administration. In addition a number of other changes in procedure were made, such as the holding of morning sittings of the House of Commons.

However, all these initiatives were undertaken in a cautious manner and the Government's commitment to them proved to be rather half-hearted. Morning sittings, which in any case were held on only two days a week and during which no votes could be taken, proved unpopular and were abandoned after only one year. Select committees were appointed to deal only with questions that were relatively safe to the Government and were thus excluded from the main issues of the day such as the economy or foreign affairs. Moreover, when one of the committees – the Select Committee on Agriculture – threatened to move into sensitive areas, obstacles were thrown up in its path. On the other hand, the experiment was not abandoned and such select committees have become an accepted feature of Parliament in the 1970s. However, between 1974 and 1979 there were a number of rows between Ministers and these committees and when in 1978 the Select Committee on Procedure proposed that the investigatory role of Parliament should be further strengthened, the Government's reaction was distinctly lukewarm. Equally, the powers of the Parliamentary Commissioner were very much more limited than those of his counterparts in other countries. In deference to the views of backbenchers he was not permitted to receive complaints direct from members of the public but only via M.P.s; and in deference to the convention of ministerial responsibility his findings were not to be binding on departments.

Not only has the House of Commons been little changed by Labour. Even more surprisingly, the House of Lords remains substantially intact. In 1949 its power to delay the passage of legislation was reduced from two years to one but, despite a number of threats, no further action has been taken. In 1968 a complex scheme of reform was drawn up, again by Richard Crossman acting in conjunction with the leaders of the other parties, but it foundered on the floor of the Commons in the face of determined opposition from a group of Labour and Conservative backbenchers. The major post-war innovation affecting the House of Lords, the creation of life peers, was the result of Conservative initiative, and it was eagerly adopted by both Wilson and Callaghan as an additional form of Prime Ministerial patronage.

In two respects, however, the 1974–79 Government did initiate constitutional changes that potentially were of far-reaching significance. First, it secured the passage through Parliament of legislation to establish elected assemblies in Scotland and Wales. Second, it introduced the referendum into British politics, using this means of consulting popular opinion on continued membership of the EEC in 1975 and on devolution in 1979. The importance of these developments should not, however, be exaggerated. Both referendums were adopted largely for internal party reasons: the first to overcome divisions at all levels within the Party on the EEC; the second to win over a number of backbenchers who were unhappy about devolution. The devolution proposals were also drawn up very cautiously in an attempt to stem the Nationalist advance while disturbing existing arrangements as little as possible as regards the supremacy of Westminister and the centralisation of financial control. In any case they were effectively buried by the verdict of the electorate both in the referendum and in the ensuing General Election. This outcome and the difficulties encountered in gauging the electorate's wishes on a complex issue from simple voting figures also make it unlikely that governments will be very keen in the future to resort to use of the referendum.[10]

Thus neither of these developments really alters the picture of Labour Ministers as guardians of the traditional system of government. Indeed, during the 1970s they were considerably more committed to the status quo than their Conservative counterparts who were advocating the strengthening of parliamentary controls over the executive and were toying with the idea of a bill of rights to protect individual freedom. Coupled with the clear liking most Ministers had for the corridors of power, this institutional conservatism was one of the grounds for the widely-held view that Labour had supplanted the Conservatives as the natural party of government in Britain.

On the other hand, despite 17 years of experience, the Labour Party as a whole remained rather ill at ease in office. This was not, as we have seen, primarily a result of the Party's constitution, although that occasionally did make life more difficult for Labour Ministers. Rather it was the attitude of most of the Party's activists that was the Achilles heel of Labour as a party of government. During each period of office a gulf appeared between those actually in government and those outside, with the backbenchers in Parliament dividing between the two groups. During the 1970s this gulf was especially marked. The extra-parliamentary Party was committed to radical changes in Parliament (including the abolition of the House of Lords), in the Civil Service and in the control of the executive by the legislature. Among the constituency activists there was also strong support for changes in the Party's constitution that would strengthen their control over the parliamentary leadership. All these changes were, however, vehemently opposed by most Ministers. In part of course, this division of opinion reflected disappointment over the Government's achievements and differences on policy. But it was also a result of differing views on the attractions of holding office. These were particularly apparent in the period of minority government after 1977. Deprived of the ability to implement the Party's programme, many of its supporters would have preferred to return to the relative comfort of opposition. Ministers, on the other hand, determined to pay almost any price to remain in office. Their task was made more difficult by the lukewarm support they received from those within the Party who were unsympathetic to the compromises any government, and particularly one without a parliamentary majority, has to make.

Labour's achievements in office

At the end of each period of office, and particularly in 1970 and 1979, disappointment was voiced in much of the Labour movement about the Government's achievements. In one sense this appears to be rather a harsh judgement. Each of the post-war Labour governments has succeeded in implementing a very high proportion of the specific promises contained in the manifesto on which it was elected. But it does not follow from this achievement that Ministers have been successful in bringing about the sort of changes in society that are sought by the Labour Party. Election manifestos are only abridged versions of the Party's full programme and they are drafted with the aim of attracting as wide electoral support as possible. Moreover, the taking of a decision in London or the passage of legislation through Parliament has often not had the effects that were intended because of problems of implementation. Much of the activity of each government has also been undermined by the need to take many decisions which not only were not foreseen in its manifesto but which hindered the fulfilment of its promises. To assess Labour's record properly it is thus necessary to look at patterns of public spending as well as ministerial decisions and to try to gauge their impact upon the social and economic condition of the country.

The task of assessing Labour's success in achieving its objectives is made still more difficult by the range of opinion found within the Party. From its inception, Labour has been a coalition of groups with differing goals who have forged their unity on the basis of various shared values and adherence to the proposals contained in a particular programme. This in part explains the upsurge in internal tension towards the end of each period of office. As a government has completed the programme on which it was elected, so the debate has opened not just on the specific components of a replacement but also on more fundamental questions about its success in office and about its future course. This was most evident in the later years of the Attlee Government. For 30 years the Party had been committed to the implementation of a programme that had been drawn up after the First World War. But was that programme, largely put into effect by 1948, an end in itself or was it the first step towards a more distant goal? Similar questions were raised towards the end of both the later periods of office. However, on each occasion the imminence of the General Election prevented their full resolution and the Party was forced to adopt a low-key electoral strategy, based upon the personality of its leader and upon its competence and trustworthiness in office.

In order to assess Labour's success in achieving its goals, it is necessary therefore to apply more than one criterion. Doctrinally, the debate within the Party can very loosely be characterised as having two principal elements.[11] The first places emphasis on the need for public ownership of the 'means of production, distribution and exchange' as an important step towards a new economic order. The other downplays the importance of public ownership and places greater emphasis upon the achievement of equality in social as much as in economic life. Labour's achievements need to be assessed against both these standards. But it is important not to overlook the fact that many supporters of the Labour Party are little interested in doctrines such as these but look to a Labour Government to protect their interests, both collectively and individually, and to produce improvements in their standard of living. The record of Labour in office must also therefore be judged by this standard.

Applying the test of public ownership, it is clear that little progress has been made by Labour in office. The major part of the economy remains in private hands. The nationalisation programme of 1945–51 affected less than a quarter of the economy and, with the exception of coal and steel, it was confined to the public utility sector. Moreover, the form of organisation adopted for the nationalised industries and the appointments made to their boards minimised the changes that occurred in the power structure within each industry. The record of the later Governments in this area was even more limited. The 1964–70 Government eschewed nationalisation almost entirely and, although the 1974–79 period did see some extension of the public sector of industry, it was much more limited than had been envisaged in the Party programme drawn up in 1973. In particular, the National Enterprise Board, which had been conceived as the instrument of State participation in major and profitable manufacturing industry, was transformed into a 'casualty clearing-station' for problem companies, such as British Leyland and Rolls-Royce, and a provider of risk capital to small and medium-sized firms in the field of advanced technology. Nor has the public sector been used in the way that many of the proponents of nationalisation advocated. They believed that public ownership of the 'commanding heights of the economy' would provide an indispensable weapon of economic planning. It is true that on many occasions Labour Ministers have used the nationalised industries as tools of economic management, for instance cutting their investment programmes and restraining their wage and price increases, but this has not been undertaken as part of a planned economic strategy. When it came into office in 1945 the Attlee Government inherited an array of war-time controls over the economy but, after 1947, these were largely abandoned in favour of fiscal methods of economic management. In 1964–65 there was renewed talk of planning but the National Plan of September 1965 was a very weak document and in any case it was buried quickly by the crisis deflationary measures of July 1966. In the early 1970s Labour once again became committed to the introduction of a more planned economy. On this occasion, a State holding company, the National Enterprise Board, was to spearhead a strategy designed to increase investment in manufacturing industry and the plans of individual private companies were to be related to national needs and objectives by means of planning agreements they signed with the Government. However, neither of these proposals was implemented: the NEB assumed a different role and, in the face of industrial opposition, the Government allowed the idea of planning agreements to wither away. Instead, Denis Healey clothed himself in the garments of economic orthodoxy showing all the fervour of a recent convert to the gospel of monetarism with its emphasis upon the inflationary effects of an excessive public sector borrowing requirement. In this respect he was following firmly in the tradition of his predecessors. Between 1947 and 1950 Cripps abandoned most of the new initiatives of his predecessor and became a model Keynesian; and in the 1960s both Callaghan and Jenkins worshipped at the altar of fixed exchange rates and financial respectability.

The record of Labour in office does not therefore provide much encouragement to those of its supporters who attach importance to public ownership and a planned economy. To what extent does it give greater cheer to those who equate socialism with equality? In the 1950s it was widely believed that the Attlee Government had, through the creation of the Welfare State and by progressive taxation, taken great strides in the direction of a more egalitarian society. This belief was based on various studies that revealed a significant decrease in poverty and a marked redistribution of incomes since before the war. However, later research has tended to discredit these studies and the statistics on which they were based.[12] Moreover it has demonstrated the great difficulties involved in measuring inequalities both at any particular point in time and between different periods. Nevertheless it is possible to build up a general picture of Labour's record of egalitarian progress.[13]

Figures produced in 1975 by the Royal Commission on the Distribution of Income and Wealth show that the distribution of income did change sharply in the direction of greater equality between 1938 and 1949, and that subsequently this trend has continued but at a very much slower rate. Thus whereas in 1938 the top 10 per cent of the population earned just over a third of after-tax personal income, it earned only a quarter in 1949 and just over a fifth in the mid-1970s. While this has been a general post-war trend, caused by a variety of factors, there is evidence that the policies of the three Labour governments have made some contribution. On the other hand, the figures also reveal that it is those in the middle and upper-middle ranges of income who have benefited most from this redistribution rather than those towards the bottom.

Labour has also taken steps to redistribute wealth, which is generally regarded as a more important source of inequality than income. In this case, however, its efforts appear to have had less effect. Wealth is both less equally distributed and there has been less change since the war. Thus in the 1970s the richest 5 per cent of the adult population still owned half of total personal wealth. Concern about this situation led the 1974–79 Government to introduce a new Capital Transfer Tax, designed to close many of the loopholes of the former estate duty, the effects of which it is too soon to gauge. On the other hand, despite long-standing pressure from within the Party for a wealth tax and its inclusion in both the 1974 election manifestos, no action had been taken when the Government left office in 1979.

Progressive taxation is not the only means of reducing inequality. Action has also been taken to improve the position of the less well-off both by ensuring that they are paid more and through the provision of social security and other benefits. Improvement in the relative position of the low paid was a declared objective of the incomes policies of both the 1964–70 and 1974–79 Governments but the statistics do not reveal much evidence of progress in this direction. More significant has been the growth of the Welfare State. Quantitative assessment of the impact of social security benefits, combined with the incidence of taxation, is extremely complex. It is possible, however to make a number of general comments. The achievements of the Attlee Government in setting up both the National Insurance Scheme and the National Health Service are the most tangible products of Labour action. But its successors have built upon these foundations, adding further benefits and increasing their real value. Major improvements have also been made in the nation's social capital, such as houses and education facilities.

Nevertheless, significant inequalities remain. Standards of provision vary widely: at its best the Welfare State is very good but in parts of each service and in certain areas of the country the picture is much less rosy. Moreover, studies have shown that middle-class people benefit disproportionately from the Welfare State and, of course, when they are not satisfied, they are still able to purchase better facilities in the private sector.[14] There also remain pockets of severe poverty. In 1976 more than 1 million people, including over 200,000 children, were living below 90 per cent of the Supplementary Benefit level (a level which is generally regarded as barely adequate to meet a family's needs). On the other hand, according to one estimate, this number would have been nearly 8 million but for welfare benefits.[15]

The largest group among the poor is still the elderly, but the worst poverty in the 1970s is found in families with children. Moreover, the Child Poverty Action Group has drawn attention to a 'cycle of inequality' which causes inequalities that are inherited at birth generally to persist throughout a person's lifetime.[16] This punctured one of the Labour Party's articles of faith – that the provision of better social services, and especially improved educational opportunities, would enable people to break out of this cycle. The failure of the 1945–51 Government in this respect accounts in part for the importance attached subsequently to the abolition of selection at the age of 11, which was shown in the 1950s to discriminate against working-class children. The commitment of Labour Ministers to educational equality has, however, been somewhat ambivalent. The two Education Ministers of the 1945–51 period were strong believers in the merits of selection and in a tripartite system of secondary education consisting of grammar, technical and 'modern' schools. Their successors accepted the case for comprehensive reorganisation but moved slowly to implement it, largely but not exclusively for practical reasons. And, by the time that the majority of children were being educated in comprehensive schools (more than 80 per cent in 1979), increasing doubts were being expressed about the contribution that reorganisation could make to widening educational opportunities.

In any case the fact remains that, despite 17 years of effort by Labour to establish and nurture the Welfare State, significant inequalities remain in access to good education, health and housing. The same is true in other fields as well. For instance, in industry Labour has done much to provide greater security of employment, to enhance the welfare of employees and to make universal such benefits as earnings-related pensions that once were the preserve of the few. The power of the trade unions to protect their members' interests has also been strengthened. But ultimately the power of decision-making within industry remains firmly in the hands of small groups of directors and managers. Public ownership has made little difference to the distribution of power within those industries that were nationalised; and in the private sector Labour has made only very tentative steps in the direction of industrial democracy. Moreover, in terms of working conditions and attitudes, British industry provides a vivid illustration of the persistence of class divisions in British society. In 1979 class distinctions may be less sharply drawn and they may count for less than they did before the Second World War but, as most foreign commentators observe, they are still clearly apparent in many areas of national life.

Labour's record thus provides more encouragement for those within the Party who seek greater equality but its progress has been much more limited than they would have liked. Many of the steps in this direction have, however, been welcomed by those of its supporters who are not particularly interested in the ideal of social equality but who look to a Labour Government to protect and improve their standard of living. One of the principal reasons for the formation of the Labour Party was that it should further the interests of the working-class. A third question to be asked therefore is how far Labour has succeeded in meeting this aspiration.

There can be no doubt that each of the post-war Labour Governments has made great efforts, by means of taxation, the Welfare State and the strengthening of employees' bargaining powers, to improve the position of those whom Labour Ministers frequently call 'our people'. In addition, Labour has taken specific action to benefit particular groups, such as council house tenants and old-age pensioners, that traditionally have supported it electorally. But the actual impact of its efforts is very difficult to measure. Since the war there has been a steady increase in the standard of living of the average family. So many factors are involved, however, that it is very difficult to gauge Labour's contribution to this trend or to the changes that have occurred in the relative position of particular sections of the community. Equally, the fact that there was a slight fall in average living standards in 1976–77 is not in itself an indictment of Labour's record, for the Government could claim with some justification that it had protected many people from the full force of the economic storm. For instance, pensioners' real incomes were maintained during this period (and rose by 20 per cent between 1974 and 1979) and, but for such measures as food and transport subsidies and rent controls, the deterioration in the incomes of other groups would have been worse. On the other hand, Labour's record has not satisfied many of its supporters: as the by-election results of 1964–70 and 1974–79 testify they have expected more and have felt that many of the tough economic measures, notably pay restraint and cuts in public spending, have hit their interests particularly severely.

Still more important in this respect than increased prosperity has been the provision of greater security of employment and thus of income. Perhaps the greatest achievement of the 1945–51 Government was the virtual elimination of unemployment. Except for a few weeks during the fuel crisis of early 1947, the number of unemployed fell to less than 300,000 (compared with over 2 million for most of the 1930s), most of whom were out of work for only very short periods. Its successors, however, were less successful. Between 1967 and 1970 more than 500,000 were unemployed and for most of the life of the 1974–79 Government the figures stuck around 1.5 million (between 5 and 6 per cent of the working population). Moreover, in certain parts of the country the rate was significantly higher. In their defence, both Governments again could claim that the position would have been much worse but for their efforts. Vast sums of public money were spent to avert closures and to provide new employment. By 1977–78 it was estimated that as much as £2.5 billion was provided annually in assistance to industry and employment in the public and private sectors. In addition, action was taken to mitigate the effects of unemployment, for instance through the provision of redundancy payments and other social security benefits. Nevertheless the persistence of high levels of unemployment was a source of great distress to many within the Labour Party.

Overall therefore the success of post-war Labour Ministers in achieving the Party's goals can be summed up as follows; first, its record in improving the material wellbeing of working people has generally been a sound one, especially against a background of severe economic difficulties, but it has not lived up fully to the aspirations of its supporters; second, it has made some progress in eliminating inequalities in society but much remains to be done; and third, it has made only marginal changes in the ownership of industry or in the way in which the economy is managed.

To explain why this has happened would require a book rather than a short section of one chapter but a few general points can be made. First, the record of Labour in office reflects the nature of the Labour Party. There has never been agreement throughout the Party on the sort of society it seeks to create. Thus the record is most easily understood if one remembers that the advocates of extensive nationalisation have always been in a minority in the Party; that those who espouse equality have always been matched by those who believe in the promotion of merit; that the interests of the poor and the unemployed have had to be balanced against those of the better-paid who are in work; and that the aims of Party activists have frequently diverged from the aspirations of most Labour voters. Throughout its lifetime the Labour Party has been a broad coalition of diverse interests and its record in office testifies to that diversity.

However, this is not to deny that more could not have been achieved. Ministers have generally defended themselves by pointing to the constraints within which they had to operate. The most obvious of these has been the economic weakness of the country. It has been the misfortune of each Labour Government to be in office at a time of severe economic difficulty. Faced with near-bankruptcy, their options have been limited and inevitably they have had to dance the piper's tunes, all the more so because of Britain's dependence upon trade and upon international confidence for economic survival. The result has been the postponement, curtailment and abandonment of many projects Ministers would like to have undertaken and the necessity of taking agonising decisions about priorities in public spending. In other ways too Ministers have found their freedom of action constrained. Contrary to much of the folklore in the Labour Party, Ministers are not in possession of a set of powerful levers that produce immediate changes. Rather government is a complex and often tortuous process of persuading and cajoling other groups to co-operate, whether they are industrialists, financiers, trade union officials or those on the shop-floor. Labour has learnt by experience that there are great obstacles in the path of economic and social reform in a pluralist democracy, particularly when progress is dependent upon changes in people's attitudes.

On the other hand, Labour's disappointments cannot be laid entirely at other's doors. There is no doubt that more could have been achieved if certain key decisions had been taken differently or if the general level of ministerial competence had been higher. Others have argued that flaws have been revealed in Labour's blueprint. This is not the place to consider the views of those outside the Party, on both the Left and the Right, who claim that Labour's record in office is proof of the bankruptcy of democratic socialism.[17] What is important here is the internal debate that has taken place at the end of each period of office. Those on the Left have argued that the Government's troubles have arisen in large part because Ministers were unwilling to put their ideas into practice; those on the Right reject this interpretation but acknowledge that their own ideas need to be reformulated. In the 1950s this process of reappraisal gave birth to the social democratic doctrines associated particularly with Anthony Crosland.[18] In 1970 he recognised that the means – but not the ends – of social democracy needed to be reconsidered because of a failure to achieve the basic premise upon which this doctrine had been based, that of sustained economic growth.[19] Such a reappraisal had begun in the early 1970s, but it was brought to an abrupt halt by the sudden return to office after the crisis election of February 1974. The experience of the 1974–79 Government, however, made it all the more necessary as the problems of achieving social democratic goals within the existing economic and political system appeared still more intractable.

In 1979, therefore, all the signs point in the direction of a major and far-reaching debate on the aims and structure of the Party. If Labour is to remain a major force in British politics a difficult balance has to be struck not only between the different groups within the Party but also between all of them and the much larger number who support the Party only with their votes. The record of the 1974–79 Government and the growing strength of the Left within the extra-parliamentary party in the 1970s might suggest that the prospects of a successful conclusion to this debate look bleak. But political parties are not only the product of rational argument and the Labour Party is bound together by very strong ties of tradition and sentiment. These ties, coupled with the unifying force of opposition to a Conservative Government, should secure its survival and even its prosperity in the 1980s.

Notes

1. Contrary to popular view, the 1933 Conference did not require the Party leader to submit himself for re-election before accepting appointment as

Prime Minister but only that the PLP should meet, having first consulted the NEC and the TUC, to decide whether to form a Government.

2. This controversy arose following Churchill's invitation to Attlee to attend the Potsdam Conference between the UK, USA and USSR shortly before the 1945 election. Laski issued a statement asserting that Attlee would attend only as an observer and that the Labour Party would not be committed to any decisions reached. Despite Attlee's repudiation of Laski's statement, Churchill attempted to exploit it during the election campaign. For a full discussion, see H. Morrison, *Government and Parliament* (3rd edn), Oxford University Press (London), 1964, pp. 152–6.

3. For example, the Manpower Services Commission and the Health and Safety Commission.

4. Some Parliamentary Private Secretaries were warned when they abstained during the 1945–51 Government, but no further action was taken.

5. The problems are discussed in A. Silkin, 'The "Agreement to Differ" of 1975 and its Effect on Ministerial Responsibility', *Political Quarterly* Vol. 48, No. 1, 1977.

6. *The Civil Service, Government Observations on the Eleventh Report of the Expenditure Committee 1976–77*, Cmnd. 7117, 1978.

7. The role of special advisers is outlined by Harold Wilson in *The Governance of Britain*, Weidenfeld & Nicolson (London), 1976, pp. 202–5.

8. *Report of the Committee on the Civil Service 1966–68*, (Fulton Report) Cmnd. 3638, 1968.

9. *Eleventh Report from the Expenditure Committee 1976–77*, H. C. 535. The 'minority' views of most of the Labour M.P.s on the Committee are set out in Vol. I, pp. lxxviii–lxxxiv.

10. The main problem was how to interpret abstentions. Normally they would be seen as the result of apathy but, on this occasion, the Government had warned voters that, because of the 40 per cent requirement, an abstention amounted to a 'no' vote. After the referendum it was argued that many voters had followed this 'advice' and had voted no by staying at home.

11. The role of doctrine in the Labour Party and its influence upon Labour in office is discussed in H. M. Drucker, *Doctrine and Ethos in the Labour Party*, Allen & Unwin (London), 1979.

12. H. M. Drucker, op. cit., pp. 54–9.

13. Useful sources on this question include: the reports of the Royal Commission on the Distribution of Income and Wealth (especially Cmnd. 6171, 1975 and Cmnd. 7175, 1978); P. Townsend and N. Bosanquet (Eds.) *Labour and Inequality*, Fabian Society (London), 1972; F. Field (Ed.), *The Wealth Report*, Routledge (London), 1979; and A. B. Atkinson, 'Inequality Under Labour', *New Society*, Vol. 48, No. 864, 1979.

14. See, for example, J. Le Grand, 'Who Gains by Public Spending?', *New Society*, Vol. 45, No. 833, 1978.

15. The distribution and extent of poverty in the 1970s is discussed in D. Piachaud, 'Who Are the Poor, and What is the Best Way to Help Them?', *New Society*, Vol. 47, No. 858, 1979.

16. F. Field, *Unequal Britain*, Arrow Books (London), 1973.

17. See, for example, R. Miliband, *Parliamentary Socialism*, (2nd edn), Merlin Press (London), 1972 and D. Coates, *The Labour Party and the Struggle for Socialism*, CUP (Cambridge), 1975, on the Left; and R. E. Tyrell (Ed.), *The Future That Doesn't Work: Social Democracy's Failures in Britain*,

Doubleday (London), 1977 and Sir Ian Gilmour, *Inside Right*, Hutchinson (London), 1977, on the Right.
18. A. Crosland, *The Future of Socialism*, Cape (London), 1956.
19. A. Crosland, *Socialism Now and Other Essays*, Cape (London), 1974. See also J. P. Mackintosh, 'Has Social Democracy Failed in Britain?', *Political Quarterly*, Vol. 49, No. 3, 1978.

Chapter 7

The Labour Left

Ben Pimlott

The Labour Left is both a faction and a mood. It is defined by association and custom as well as by ideology: a Labour politician is placed on the spectrum less by his beliefs than by the company he keeps. Nevertheless, ideas have been central to the Left. There have been a variety of overlapping strands – libertarian, pacifist, internationalist and humanitarian. The most important and consistent theme has been socialism, and the Left may be said to have included those in the Labour Party 'who believed in socialism or those who wanted a more rapid approach to socialism'.[1] As such it has existed with one label or another since the inception of the Party – a generation longer than the term 'Left' has been used in a political sense in Britain.[2]

There is no Continental equivalent. Abroad, some of the same forces and passions are contained with structured, disciplined, homogeneous and exclusive communist Parties; in Britain the Labour Left has been a loose association of individuals and tendencies, often shifting in its composition from issue to issue. Communists in other Western countries have kept their independence by cultivating large and reliable electoral followings, relatively immune from the allures of rival parties; the cost has been an almost total exclusion from central government affairs. In Britain, the Labour Left has accepted or been forced to accept the necessity of links with, and dependence on, a trade-union based, 'voter-orientated' Labour Party. The consolation has been occasional periods of access to state power.

The direct effect of the Labour Left on government policy has been small. The Left has been important in indirect ways: it has aroused passions, increased commitment, won recruits, provided the agenda for debate and acted as a constraint on Labour in office – setting the limits of the possible. There have certainly been many Labour leaders whose attitudes have been coloured by an early socialist training. However, in Labour's nine administrations since 1924 there have been very few fundamental decisions or major policies for which the Left has been mainly responsible.

Why should this be so? Most explanations have been based on assumptions about the practicality of socialist ideas. Within the Labour Party, supporters of the reformist wing have regarded the schemes of the

Labour Left as unrealistic, proposing the dream of 'a revolution without blood – a nice, quiet, decent libertarian little revolution, with kindness to all'.[3] According to this view the Left is faced by an insoluble contradiction: Left-wing proposals could only be implemented through violence and dictatorship; but the Labour Left could not cope with these and in any case rejects them.[4]

On the other side, those who regard socialism as in principle workable explain the failure of the Left to bring it about in terms of the strength of its enemies. They point to the resistance of capitalist interests and institutions, and they blame traditional leadership in the Labour movement for an eagerness to compromise and for an obsession with electoral success.[5] Writers who are Marxist often find fault with the Labour Left itself, arguing that it has concentrated exclusively on personalities and parliamentary politics,[6] instead of adopting a policy of 'building connections with, and offering leadership to, the working class in struggle at the point of production itself' in order to radicalise the masses.[7]

Both reformists and socialists have tended to judge the Labour Left by much the same revolutionary yardstick: by its ability or inability to bring about a fundamental socialist change. But this may be to set an inappropriate standard. If the question is why the Labour Left has failed to produce a socialist transformation, there is perhaps little enough to discuss. On the one hand, what is or is not genuinely socialist is a matter for metaphysical not historical debate; on the other, there is no reason in a competitive world to expect one set of values to achieve a smashing victory over others.

All the same, a problem does exist. The Labour Left displays a continuity of attitudes and causes which no other group with a major parliamentary backing in Britain has ever matched. It is reasonable to ask why an assumption of exclusion and defeat should be part of the heritage: why the Left has been so marginal to the great political and social changes of the twentieth century. This essay will look at the record and (in the last section) consider whether the Labour Left has primarily been concerned with changing society, or with changing men.

Genesis

If the Labour Left is defined as the 'socialist' element in the Party then all the socialists in the Labour Representation Committee constituted the first Labour Left – often disagreeing passionately with the 'loyal but disheartened Gladstonians'[8] in affiliated trade unions. However, the socialists were never united, and some of the issues which later divided the Labour Party into Left and Right can be traced to differences of interest and approach inside and among the pre-1914 socialist societies.

The main ancestor of the modern Labour Left was the Independent Labour Party. The Social Democratic Federation, 'captained by poets, artists, Anglican clergymen and ex-army officers',[9] also left its mark. Bernard Shaw wrote that the Fabians 'should certainly not have done so well if the SDF had not pick-axed the ground for us',[10] an encomium which the Marxist and sectarian SDF would certainly have resented. The SDF abandoned the LRC in disgust in 1901, but continued to have an influence, and may be said to have established a Marxist tradition which has occasionally shaped Labour Left policies and has always been a siren call. The Fabians, intellectual, aloof and riven with feud, took little interest in the Labour movement and even less in the Party which they had helped to found. Thus from the earliest days the ILP was the most vocal, powerful and ambitious socialist influence, and the source of many of the traditions and attitudes later regarded as Left wing.

The ILP itself contained contradictory elements. On the one hand, the leadership of Keir Hardie and Ramsay MacDonald was proselytising and eclectic, rejecting 'all sectional dogmas'.[11] It was also parliamentarist, refusing to countenance violence or attempts to turn strikes into local campaigns for workers' control: Hardie was concerned with class discipline, not class war.[12] On the other hand the ILP contained its own radical wing, which objected to what it saw as an excessive preoccupation with Westminster and to an alleged eagerness to trade principles for votes. 'We decline to be respectable, and politic, and conciliatory, while men are dying on doorsteps and women have no clothing to keep their babies alive',[13] declared Robert Blatchford in 1907, launching a bitter attack on the very notion of leadership, and on any departure from 'real Socialism . . . without dilution, or compromise or apology'.[14] Part of the attack was personal to Hardie ('I cannot mix with Hardie,' Blatchford once wrote. ' He makes my flesh creep.')[15] Yet the strict constitutionalism of Hardie and the populist rhetoric of Blatchford have co-existed on the Labour Left ever since.

ILP horror of violent industrial confrontations reflected a strong pacifist strain, non-conformist in origin, which was given full expression after 1914. The ILP majority opposed British participation in the First World War partly for reasons of morality (against all war), partly on rationalist or foreign policy grounds (the folly of this war in particular). It was a difficult and unpopular line at a time when many trade unionists were unashamedly nationalistic and when the Labour movement as a whole was backing the war so that 'the world may henceforth be made safe for democracy'.[16] The ILP and E. D. Morel's Union for Democratic Control became rallying points for Liberals and others who sought a negotiated peace, and the Labour Left acquired an internationalist dimension superimposed upon its socialism. Meanwhile a semi-revolutionary Left representing quite different strands of syndicalism and Guild Socialism was gaining an influence within the trade unions and the ILP, greatly encouraged by the Bolshevik Revolution. By the time that Labour emerged as a major national party at the election of 1918, the essential attitudes of later years were well established.

The socialist constitution

Was the inclusion in the 1918 Party Constitution of Clause Four, which called for nationalisation, as much equality as possible, and 'the best obtainable system of popular administration and control of each industry or service', a triumph for the Labour Left? Clause Four gave the Labour Party an officially socialist colouring which had been rejected in 1900. The aim of 'popular administration' in industry contained enough of an echo of Guild Socialist or syndicalist demands to suggest at least a placatory motive. But, as McKibbin has shown, Clause Four was adopted with little controversy, partly as an electoral ploy, partly as a consolation prize to socialists in a package of reform which actually reduced socialist influence in the higher Party echelons.[17]

Tawney has often been quoted. 'In 1918 the Labour Party finally declared itself to be a Socialist Party. It supposed and supposes, that it thereby became one. It is mistaken. It recorded a wish, that is all; the wish has not been fulfilled.'[18] Clause Four became an issue after the 1959 General Election, when it was felt by Gaitskell to harm Labour's image in the eyes of a growing middle class. Ironically, the middle class was precisely the group that it was originally intended to attract.[19] Whether Labour's outlook and policies would have been different without the inclusion of an aspiration of such elegant vagueness is a moot point.

In one sense the 1918 Constitution was certainly a defeat for the Left. In 1918 there were some 657 local ILP branches, with 35,000 members.[20] But it was local Labour representation committees and trades councils which Henderson made the basis of the Party's new organisation, and not the myriad branches of the ILP. For the first time it became possible to be a direct member of the Labour Party without being a member of an affiliated society or union. This soon destroyed the traditional role of the ILP as the main body responsible for political activity in the constituencies. But in addition, in order to sell the reforms to a suspicious trade union movement, the five socialist society places on the National Executive were abolished. For the next 19 years local Party activists – whether in the ILP, or members of the new constituency organisations – had no representation on the Executive at all.

This helped to radicalise the ILP, which could no longer act as a catch-all body for Labour activists and became instead a faction placed uncomfortably in competition with the new individual members' sections that grew fast in size and importance. At the same time, the socialist wing of the movement was deeply affected by a period of unparalleled industrial unrest, and by the philosophy of 'Direct Action', probably the strongest anti-constitutional campaign this country has ever known. Rejecting existing governmental institutions as the product of capitalism, regarding compromise as immoral and urging the use of the general strike for political ends, Direct Action had strong trade union backing, but little support in Parliament. It created a style of politics 'which no Labour leader could ignore',[21] but which almost all rejected. It was in these bitter, strife-torn years in the aftermath of the First World War and before the General Strike, that a deep and lasting hostility developed between an electorally orientated parliamentary leadership and a revolutionary or semi-revolutionary outer fringe, which found increasing inspiration in the newly formed Communist Party.

Communism and Clydesiders

From the start, communists regarded the Labour Party with circumspection. On the one hand, they rejected its reformism; on the other, they were forced to acknowledge the extent and strength of its working class support. Hence debates about what should be the correct attitude towards Labour dominated early communist agenda. Founded in 1920, the Communist Party of Great Britain was refused affiliation to Labour, but until 1924 there was nothing to stop communists participating to the full in Labour Party affairs. Two communists were elected to Parliament in 1922, one as an official Labour candidate, the other without Labour opposition. However, communist activities in trade unions and attacks on Labour leaders ('I would take them by the hand as a preliminary to taking them by the throat,' one theoretician declared in 1922)[22], brought about a proscription of communists in the Labour Party at all levels in 1924 and 1925. Thereafter, communists ceased to be a section of the Labour Left, and became an external force.

Yet the British Communist Party continued to be a constant source of alarm, irritation and embarrassment to the Labour leadership, and of sympathy among sections of the rank and file. The allegation that the Labour Left was controlled, infiltrated, led or duped by the communists was often made. Only in the last decade has Trotskyism replaced communism as the main enemy for those attracted to conspiratorial explanations of Left-wing attitudes and behaviour.

The influence of King Street was real enough for a time: a product of communist organisational skills and dedication, and of a widespread admiration in the Labour movement for real or imagined Soviet achievements. Between the wars, the communists sought to develop their strength in the Labour Party by burrowing from below – a method which aroused great anxiety and anger. With individual membership sections still in their infancy, communists could often take control of a local Labour Party very easily, and the only way of shifting them was by disbanding the organisation. This the Labour Executive often did; 23 local Labour Parties were disaffiliated in 1926 and 1927 for failing to expel communists.[23] The policy of building up a 'whole solar system' of organisations which were in fact, but not in name, communist controlled ended in 1928 when the Comintern line shifted to 'Class against Class' and all co-operation with the Labour Party ceased, causing a temporary setback to communist influence. By this time, however, an identification between the extreme left of Labour and the communists was strong. The removal of the ILP, which contained important anti-Stalinist elements, made it stronger still.

The drift of the ILP towards a factionalist role had been hastened by the arrival in Parliament in 1922 of the 'Clydesider' group of revolutionaries, led by John Wheatley and James Maxton. These brought the passion and bitterness of Glasgow industrial strife to Westminster, and took the ILP by storm. Having secured the Labour leadership for MacDonald, they became his most implacable enemies. Only Wheatley among the Scottish group obtained major office in 1924, and the Labour administration's pursuit of respectability in domestic affairs helped to bring the Left together, setting a pattern of backbench dissidence that was to be followed in 1929, and after the Second World War. Maxton and the Clydesiders, George Lansbury, H. N. Brailsford, Bob Smillie, E. F. Wise and Fenner Brockway, attacked the Prime Minister for failing to implement socialism. The government 'should deal drastically and fundamentally with [some] of the great social evils', argued Smillie. If defeated, it should have an election from which it 'would be returned to real power as well as office'.[24] These were to become familiar cries.

Maxton completed the Clydesider takeover of the ILP in 1925 when he replaced Clifford Allen as Chairman, after a battle over land nationalisation. Allen favoured nationalisation with compensation. Maxton demanded confiscation, and won.[25] With the Maxton–Wheatley group in charge, less radical people in the ILP became inactive or resigned, and the Clydesiders tightened their control. In 1928 Maxton and the miners' leader, Arthur Cook, issued a manifesto which attacked the 'Mond–Turner' proposals that aimed at greater co-operation between unions and employers, a product of the TUC's more conciliatory attitude following the General Strike. The Cook–Maxton Manifesto accused Labour of deserting fundamental principles. 'The failure of capitalism makes it more necessary than ever that we should press forward our Socialist alternative to capitalism . . .', it declared; 'the practice of the British Labour movement shows the gradual abandonment of Socialist activity.'[26] Demands included the rapid nationalisation of industry without compensation, dissolution of the Empire, preparation of the working-class for mass resistance against war, and that the General Council should 'take up the question of unity with Russian, Norwegian and Finnish trade-union movements for the purpose of inaugurating a world-wide campaign for the establishment of international trade union unity'.[27] The ILP Administrative Committee adopted the manifesto by one vote, but both the TUC and Labour Party rejected or ignored it – along with the more serious ILP 'Socialism in Our Time' and 'Living Wage' proposals, dismissed by MacDonald as 'flashy futilities' which would ensure a Labour defeat.[28]

The return of Labour to office in 1929 made the ILP even more uncompromising. The 1930 ILP Conference reacted fiercely to attempts to force rebellious MPs into line through Standing Orders, and demanded a reconstruction of the parliamentary ILP. ILP candidates were henceforth required to obey the policy of ILP Annual Conference and 'be prepared to give effect to it in the House of Commons'.[29] Only 18 out of 37 ILP-sponsored MPs accepted the new conditions. The Clydesiders, providing the most vociferous opposition in an increasingly dispirited Parliament, were set on a course which was rapidly isolating them from the Labour Party majority.

Maxton's group was not, however, the only radical opposition to MacDonald's second government. Early in 1930 Sir Oswald Mosley, one of a committee of three Ministers set up to consider the unemployment problem, presented the Cabinet with a Memorandum calling for the expansion of credit, planning in industry and the control of imports. When this was rejected, Mosley resigned from the Government. In the autumn, he narrowly failed to get Conference backing for his demands, but sympathy for his proposals was reflected in his election to the National Executive. In December, Mosley published a Manifesto, restating his aims – with the backing of 17 other MPs (including John Strachey and Aneurin Bevan). Shortly afterwards, he left the Labour Party, and founded the 'New Party'. This defection weakened still further Labour Left opposition to the Government's deflationary policies.

The successive traumas of the formation of the National Government and the electoral holocaust in 1931 removed many of the old Labour pioneers, and with them some of the old illusions. Trade union involvement in the Party increased. For the Labour Left, the humiliations of 1931 were a vindication, indicating that the crisis of capitalism was at hand. It was in this mood that the ILP disaffiliated from the Labour Party in July 1932, taking with it five MPs and most of a local membership estimated at 16,700. Three months later, Mosley's New Party, transforming extreme Left into ultra Right, became the British Union of Fascists, the symbolic enemy of the Left for the rest of the decade. It was the end of an era. Three breakaways from Labour within 18 months demonstrated the firmness of working-class support for a trade union-backed Labour Party. No major secessions were ever to occur again. For the Left, the lesson of 1931–32 was that in electoral or parliamentary terms, no serious future existed outside the Labour fold.

The new Labour Party leadership was slimmer in numbers, younger, more cohesive than before, and ready to exercise a harsher discipline. It contained a new breed of professional politician 'rather like a Praetorian Guard, whose career keeps careful watch over his conscience'.[30] The party was also more socialist, in the sense of contemplating immediate sweeping reforms. 1932 was a year of political conversion for Labour, far more than 1918. But this was a result of the crisis and the nemesis, rather than a consequence of pressures exerted by a much depleted Left wing.

The red decade

Not all the Labour Left went out of the Party with Maxton. Indeed one
effect of his departure was to liberate Left-wing activity from the ILP
ghetto, and inject it into the constituency parties. As the ILP withered in
isolation, some members moved to the communists or dropped out of
politics altogether. But many reverted to Labour, whose local
organisations continued a rapid expansion. In 1930 there were 277,000
individual members; by 1939 the official total had reached 447,000.
Among this number were now included almost all who sought a
parliamentary road to socialism.

One vehicle for Left-wing feelings in the 1930s was the short-lived
Socialist League, founded by the ILP minority opposed to disaffiliation,
and incorporating most of G. D. H. Cole's Society for Socialist Inquiry
and Propaganda, which helped to give the new League an intellectual
tinge. The League had some influence on the tiny PLP of 1931–35, but it
was 'all leaders and no followers',[31] and even on paper its membership
never exceeded 3,000. Led by the brilliant lawyer and recent socialist
recruit, Sir Stafford Cripps, and by its 'granite-like socialist conscience'[32]
William Mellor, the League disintegrated in 1937 in a war of words and
public meetings midst the excitement created by the Spanish Civil War,
the central event of the decade for British radical opinion.

Much has been written about the 1930s intellectuals, for whom
politics 'were almost exclusively on the left'.[33] Why the 1930s? There had
been an underlying Left-wing orthodoxy among writers since the First
World War. It is odd that more than a dozen years should have elapsed
before the anger of 1918 became an explosive force, despite the far
greater turmoil and political transformation that preceded the General
Strike. Certainly, if the 1930s was the 'Red Decade' it was not Labour or
the Labour Left that made it so. Far more important among the
intelligentsia was the Communist Party.

But it was not only among intellectuals and the radically minded
middle class that communism proved such an inspirational force in the
1930s. At all levels of the movement communist influence was pervasive,
and at times the Labour Left appeared to be dominated by it. This was
partly because of the Slump, the failure of the official Labour or trade
union leadership to take a bold lead in the Distressed Areas, and the
energy and effectiveness of communists in organising the unemployed.
After 1936 it was because of Spain, and the central importance given by
Soviet foreign policy to the Spanish conflict.

Two campaigns weakened the Left in the late 1930s. Both grew out of
the 1935 Comintern decision to seek co-operation with social
democratic and Labour parties, and communist attempts to gain support
for the Republican government in Madrid. The united front or 'unity'
campaign in 1937 was intended in theory to bring together Labour,
communists and the disaffiliated ILP in a battle 'against Fascism and
against War'.[34] The popular front campaign of 1938–39 aimed at a much

broader (and more realistic) alliance of all opponents of Chamberlain and his foreign policy. In practice both campaigns were tainted by their association with the Communist Party. The unity campaign destroyed the Socialist League, and the popular front resulted in the expulsion from the Labour Party of Sir Stafford Cripps, Aneurin Bevan, Sir Charles Trevelyan, G. R. Strauss and other Left-wingers. The irony that Left-wing influence on the actual conduct of affairs was never so slight as at a time of great socialist passion and activity owed much to the infatuation with Moscow.

The Russo-German pact in August 1939 shook many British socialists from an assumption of Soviet infallibility. Within the Labour Party only a handful (D. N. Pritt, a fellow traveller on the NEC, was one) were unrepentant. A number of local Labour Parties, declaring their communist sympathies, were expelled. Yet 1939 was different from 1914, and there was little opposition to the war, except on pacifist grounds. In November 1939 20 Labour M.P.s signed a memorandum calling for a conference to secure a negotiated peace. The Scottish Socialist Party, equivalent to the former Socialist League north of the border, came out against the war. So did the dwindling ILP. But pacifism was apologetic in the Second War, unlike the First. Pacifists hoped that the war would fade away, or be ended by the people. Sir Charles Trevelyan (now out of the Party) wrote privately of 'a deep-seated feeling that none of the people want to fight and that the war will collapse'.[35] But a pacifist motion at the May 1940 Labour Conference received no support, and only 170,000 votes were cast against the Executive's decision to join Churchill's Government.

Towards a Socialist Commonwealth?

The old battle-lines of Labour Left and Right were confused when Labour entered the Coalition. Churchill picked Ministers for their patriotism, ability and political weight, and the Labour Left were not excluded. There was little reluctance to take office. Only Shinwell rejected it. He and Bevan (to whom no offer was made) became the most prominent Government critics in Parliament. By the end of 1941 Bevan had become '"snarler" in chief',[36] complaining about limitations on the freedom of the press. There were also demands for a Second Front, and attempts to use the opportunity presented by the leadership's preoccupation with the war to create a more radical programme. Harold Laski, ablest of Left wingers on the NEC, argued as early as August 1940 that the Bank of England and the land should be nationalised to raise public morale. The Labour and trade union leadership was not impressed, sending him away (as Dalton unkindly put it) 'with his little tail between his little legs'.[37]

One group outside the Labour Party which tried to channel radical opinion – Common Wealth – is interesting because in style and

172 The Labour Party

philosophy it had more in common with the propagandist Bevanites of the 1950s than the *marxisant* Crippsites of the 1930s, and also because it reflected the new egalitarianism and mood for change created by the war. Common Wealth was founded in July 1942 by J. B. Priestley and Sir Richard Acland. It offered a moral rearmament of the Left, based on three principles: Common Ownership, Vital Democracy and Morality in Politics. Common Wealth was about people, not policies. Acland believed that his movement could lead to 'the emergence of a new kind of man, with a new kind of mind, new values, a new outlook on life, and perhaps most important of all, new motives'.[38] Many supporters saw it as a Left-wing stand-in for Labour, in the conditions of the major party truce. Common Wealth won three by-elections, had 15,000 members at its peak and put up 23 candidates in 1945. Only one was successful, at Chelmsford, where no Labour candidate stood. Acland thereupon joined the Labour Party.

Did Left wingers matter during the Attlee administration of 1945–50? 'It is likely that without the consistent pressure of the Labour Left the government would have taken even fewer steps towards socialism than it did,' one historian has argued.[39] 'But there were very few cases in which the government was found to change its policy because of parliamentary pressures, and these few successes were due to the fact that the Left was able to draw support from elsewhere in the party.'[40] Apart from the nationalisation of steel and a reduction in the planned term of conscription, Left-wing pressure counted for little. There is a paradox here. The Attlee administration achieved more social reform than any other peace-time Government of the twentieth century (apart, perhaps, from 1906 to 1910). Yet no other Labour Government has been dominated so completely and intolerantly by the Right. There were former Left wingers in the government – Bevan, Cripps, Wilkinson, Shinwell, Strachey – but all (including Bevan) accepted or even helped to enforce the rules imposed by a caucus that bound together Cabinet, executive, unions and Conference.

The PLP was largely an amateur body. Two-thirds of its members were new. Lawyers, journalists, teachers, ex-servicemen – many had little background in the movement and only the flimsiest of ideological formations. Hence the Labour Left, never cohesive, was a particularly shifting and disparate band. One factor which weakened and divided it was the onset of the Cold War. 'There are some of our own people who still think that the communists are the left-wing of the socialist movement. They are not. The socialist movement was always a movement for freedom,' Attlee wrote in 1949.[41] By then most Left wingers had come to agree. Yet a lingering sympathy for the Soviet Union remained, placing the Left in an uneasy and unfashionable position when tension between the super-powers entered its most pathological phase.

Foreign policy, rather than domestic socialism, soon became the central Left-wing concern. In the autumn of 1946 a major backbench revolt supported the demand for a 'genuine middle way between the extremes of American free enterprise economics and Russian totalitarian socio-political life'.[42] The idea of a 'Third Alternative' policy was to preoccupy the Labour Left for the next 15 years. This did not mean actual support for Russia. Nevertheless a suspicion that pro-Soviet sentiments were not far submerged undoubtedly damaged the Left. Partly for this reason, Left-wing groupings that emerged while Labour was still in office were shadowy and insubstantial. In April 1947 Richard Crossman, Michael Foot and Ian Mikardo published a pamphlet called *Keep Left*, demanding the revolution which voters had allegedly asked for in 1945. Members of the group of M.P.s supporting this document also helped to produce a second statement called *Keeping Left* before the 1950 election. But by the time of Bevan's resignation in 1951, the 'loose agglomeration' which had come together on the basis of these publications had almost ceased to exist.[43] Keep Left was parliamentary, with no outside organisation. Another group, Socialist Fellowship, started by Ellis Smith in 1949, aimed to recreate the comradeship of the old ILP among the rank and file. But initial enthusiasm did not last, and the Fellowship collapsed after the 1950 election.[44]

Yet among the Party rank and file real progress was being made. Individual membership, which began to grow fast towards the end of the war, expanded rapidly through the Attlee years. In 1945 there were 487,047 members; by 1950 there were 908,161, at least on paper.[45] Perhaps this influx helps to explain the growing support for alternative leaders in NEC elections. For the first three years of the Labour Government, the executive contained only two Left wingers: Bevan and Laski. Foot was elected in 1948, Tom Driberg in 1949, Mikardo in 1950, Barbara Castle in 1951, Crossman and Wilson in 1952. Thereafter the seven member constituency section of the NEC, once a key instrument of Right-wing domination, always contained a majority from the Left.

This was to have dramatic effects when there was no longer a Labour Cabinet in office. Before 1951, executive discipline had been swift and uncompromising. The most famous example was the Nenni telegram affair. In April 1948, 37 Labour M.P.s had sent a telegram wishing success to Signor Nenni, Left Socialist candidate in alliance with Italian Communists. The executive treated this action as an intolerable act of rebellion. Retractions or denials were exacted from 16 of the M.P.s, and a pledge of renewed loyalty, under threat of expulsion, from the remaining 21. Bevanite revolts in the following decade were, in part, a demonstration that such a rigid insistence on orthodoxy was unacceptable and could no longer be enforced.

Bevanism, public ownership and the bomb

Bevan's decision to resign from office in April 1951, accompanied by Harold Wilson and John Freeman, inaugurated a period of factional warfare of unprecedented bitterness which for a time seemed likely to split the Party irrevocably. The immediate issue was Gaitskell's introduction of charges for false teeth and glasses, seen as a blow to the principle of a free health service. The background had more to do with defence and foreign policy – in particular, dissension over the rising cost of armaments caused by the escalating Korean war. The result was that, for the first time since Cripps's expulsion in 1939, the Left had a leader who could command wide support in the movement: a man who combined experience, great gifts of oratory and an ability to inspire personal devotion.

After the 1951 election defeat the Bevanites, based on the remnants of Keep Left, organised themselves into a parliamentary group with an elected chairman (Wilson was the first) and weekly meetings. Parliamentary support was unpredictable. Fifty-seven M.P.s (the '57 varieties') voted against the Government's defence policy in March 1952, in defiance of the Party Whip. But the number of reliable Bevanites was a much smaller hard core of 25 who had produced the pamphlet *One Way Only* in 1951.[46] German rearmament, national service and nuclear weapons, were the major causes of dissent. Until 1960 domestic socialism was far less often at the centre of controversy. Twenty-two backbench revolts involved foreign affairs and defence. One concerned membership of the Select Committee on Estimates. Only one was over nationalisation.[47]

In 1958, Bevanites reorganised themselves in a group called Victory for Socialism, the closest equivalent of a post-war ILP or Socialist League. This established 14 area groups, an annual conference and an executive, with two sub-committees. Within three years internal dissension had reduced the number of local groups to four. By then Victory for Socialism had been superseded by a new formation, the Unity Group. Both bodies survived until the mid-1960s,[48] but neither mattered as much as their leading personalities. For most of this period Left-wing dissidence was based, in the main, on a small band of intellectuals in the House of Commons and the support they could muster in the constituencies. It was a powerful combination.

Why were passions so intense? The PLP was bigger than ever before in opposition, more middle class, more articulate, less held together by a common solidarity. There was also a new world of full employment, rising incomes and a prosperity unimagined a few years before. Both 'old guard' leaders and new 'revisionists' stood for the end of a vision – placidly accepting, or indecently embracing, the rules and even the philosophy of capitalism.

Bevan had pointed to a 'basic conflict over party purpose', and argued that 'revisionism attacked Socialist ideology at its heart – the doctrine of fellowship'.[49] No doubt many felt this at the time. Was it true? It is hard to see fundamental differences of philosophy between the two sides: Bevan and Crosland shared many opinions.[50] Most of the conflicts were not of principle but of degree – how much support for American foreign policy, how many arms, how many industries to be State run. There was no unity in either camp on these issues. The conflict became increasingly symbolic. Traditions, approach and political style divided the Party into rival clans, held together by bonds of trust and friendship, or kept apart by unforgiven slights.

Labour's third successive defeat at the polls in 1959 renewed hostilities after a post-Suez, pre-election lull. Hugh Gaitskell's attempt to remove socialism from the Party constitution, in the belief that nationalisation and Labour's working-class image were out of date and lost votes, brought a predictable outcry from the Left. But it was the trade unions, not the constituency or parliamentary Left, that killed the plan, dealing Gaitskell's leadership a serious blow. How much did the issue matter? Clause Four remained in the Party Constitution. Yet despite the rhetoric of platform and manifesto, nationalisation and 'popular administration' in industry were scarcely the most notable features of policy in the ensuing years.

All the same, the decision was important in a quite different way. Martin Harrison wrote in 1960: 'If the balance of the big block votes tilted decisively the Party would have to find new leaders or the Party leaders would have to accept a far greater degree of positive union dictation of policy than has been known in recent years.'[51] The election of Frank Cousins, a Left winger, to the General Secretaryship of the Transport Workers in 1956 indicated a long-term shift of power within the largest union which shattered the old pro-right TGWU–NUGMW–NUM triumvirate.[52] The writing was on the wall. Hitherto, the Party leadership had based its power squarely on the loyalty of the big unions. Now that this protection was gone, the balance within the Party began to shift in a dramatic way.

The Clause Four controversy was soon overshadowed by the Bomb. The Campaign for Nuclear Disarmament was founded in 1957. Initially it showed little interest in political parties, though a few Left-wing M.P.s had been involved from the beginning. However, as the campaign gained momentum links with the Labour Left grew stronger. Soon the Left had adopted as its own a crusade which had a close affinity to its traditions, and which seemed to have captured a popular mood as well. With its impressive annual marches from Aldermaston to London, CND attracted more widespread and enthusiastic support than any other comparable movement since the 1930s – and it was indeed upon a pre-war heritage of disarmament and peace rallies that the campaign was able to draw. One 1960 opinion poll showed that 57 per cent of the electorate was opposed to the possession of nuclear weapons, and that one voter in three sympathised with CND.[53] At the Party Conference at Scarborough in the same year unilateral nuclear disarmament was narrowly adopted on the basis of support from the TGWU, AEU, NUR and USDAW.

Euphoria over this decision was short-lived. With no election imminent, Scarborough was merely a paper victory. CND – now firmly identified with (some felt, used by) the Labour Left – was soon torn apart by internal schisms. Unions which had backed unilateralism in 1960 had second thoughts and threw it out at Party Conference in 1961. This decision marked the end of the battle between Left and Right in its most intense form. Bevan (never a unilateralist) had died in 1960. The Labour Left now entered a period of quiescence. When Gaitskell died in 1963 he handed over to his successor a Party which was more united than at any time in the past 12 years.

The result of the leadership contest that followed showed not the strength of the Left, but the success of Harold Wilson in presenting himself as a man of the centre. Gaitskellites had little cause for complaint in the moderate, revisionist election manifesto of 1964. On the other hand, the Left was better treated in the new Labour administration in terms of ministerial posts than ever before. Crossman, Castle and Greenwood were all in the Cabinet; so was Cousins, as a gesture to the unions. This enabled the Left to identify with a Government whose slender majority provided a valid reason for a modest programme. Until 1966, the whips were more troubled by Right-wing revolt (from Woodrow Wyatt and Desmond Donnelly over steel nationalisation) than by the greatly weakened remnants of Bevanism and Victory for Socialism.

The Tribune Group

The Tribune Group (named in 1966 after *Tribune*, house journal of the Labour Left, founded by Cripps and G. R. Strauss in 1937) has maintained more cohesion over a longer period than any of its predecessors since the decline of the ILP. This is because it has preferred tactical manoeuvres to head-on collisions, and, crucially, because of increasing support from other sections of the movement. But the achievements of Tribune have been modest, and there have been few major deflections of policy as a result of its activities.

Apart from the revolution in secondary (and tertiary) education and some additions to the public sector, Labour in office in the 1960s and 1970s made no sweeping reforms of the kind that occurred in 1945–48. Yet Harold Wilson was able to treat the Left with ill-concealed contempt, a point emphasised by his monumental record of the 1964-70 years, which did not mention the Tribune group at all.[54] Opposition to the EEC (not restricted to the Left) was ignored; health charges were reintroduced; restrictions on immigration tightened. The Left also proved wholly ineffective in checking official expressions of support for American offensives in Vietnam. Vietnam became an issue which was more important outside the Labour Party than within it, drawing together the New Left (Marxist intellectuals who followed continental models) and student militants, influenced by events in Berkeley, Paris, Bonn. The Aldermaston marches, though inspired from outside, had swept up and incorporated the Labour Left; the great Vietnam rally in London in October 1968 seemed to pass the Labour Party by. The late 1960s saw the emergence for the first time since the 1920s of an important non-communist extra-parliamentary Left, and also the growth of radical pressure groups like Shelter and the Child Poverty Action Group, pragmatic, policy-orientated, impatient of party ritual and preferring to work directly with Ministers and departments. At the same time, Labour constituency activists fell rapidly away.

But there was one major defeat for the Government and success of a kind for the Left in the Parliament of 1966. Barbara Castle, Minister of Employment and Productivity, published *In Place of Strife* in January 1969, setting out a policy designed to limit the number of strikes. The Prime Minister gave his full backing. In June, after the Chief Whip had reported that a House of Commons majority could not be guaranteed, the proposed legislation was withdrawn. *In Place of Strife* had been bitterly resisted by the Tribune Group, and the prospect of a backbench revolt forced the Prime Minister's hand. Yet it was not the rebellion of established Left wingers Wilson feared so much as that of trade union M.P.s, not normally associated with the Left, backed by trade unions that were themselves implacably opposed.

The retreat over *In Place of Strife* was therefore a union, not a Labour Left, victory, reflecting union interests which had little connection with traditional socialist demands. But it was important for the Left nonetheless, marking the culmination of a shift in alliances within the movement which profoundly affected Labour politics throughout the following decade. The strength of the Left within two unions, the Transport Workers and Engineers (which together controlled almost a third of the total vote at Conference), determined the issue. Since the early 1950s a solid phalanx of constituency-elected Left wingers had served on the Executive. Nevertheless McKenzie's view that 'Leadership and initiative within the NEC has almost invariably been retained by the Leader and the representatives of majority opinion within the parliamentary party'[55] held broadly true until the late 1960s because of the loyalty or indifference of trade union members. By the early 1970s, however, the Party Executive had moved decisively away from the parliamentary leadership. After 1974, for the first time ever, a Labour Government faced more or less consistent Left-wing opposition from the NEC.

A tendency for unions and the Labour Left to be regarded as on the same side was paralleled by a change in the Left's class image. As the generation of Crossman, Driberg, Foot, Castle, Mikardo was overtaken by Heffer, Skinner, Kinnock, so there arose a new association between 'Left-wing' and 'working-class' which had eluded the Left since the demise of the ILP. Defence and foreign policy, made less immediate by the end of empire and by *détente*, were replaced by rents, wages and unemployment. Only one central international concern remained: the Common Market. At first, this cut across factional lines. Then, after the

1970 election defeat, pro-Marketeers became identified with the Labour Right, while the Labour Left, led by Michael Foot, blended a liberal-constitutional fear for parliamentary sovereignty and a *marxisant* rejection of participation in a capitalist club. The TGWU and AEU were also against, and this, together with a groundswell of grass roots hostility to British entry, swung the official Party attitude over to opposition. The Labour Government's referendum on the EEC in 1975 showed that the Labour Party was now 'controlled by the Left' – with a union-based Executive and Conference, backed by constituency activists, facing one way, and a parliamentary leadership facing the other.

Meanwhile, Left-wing influence encouraged the adoption of more radical platforms. *Labour's Programme for Britain 1973,* the basis for the election manifesto of 1974, called for 'a massive and irreversible shift in the distribution of wealth and income in favour of working people',[56] a phrase which represented a different mood from that of the PLP in the 'new type of non-gladiatorial Parliament' of 1964–70.[57] *Labour's Programme for Britain 1976* called for the nationalisation of the main banks and insurance companies, and was even described by a former member of the Keep Left group as 'a Marxist and Trotskyist plan to extend the power of the State to a detailed control of the individual's activities'.[58]

The Party's shift to the Left affected the type of candidate selected. This in turn increased the size of the Tribune group in the House of Commons. It also strengthened the constituency parties *vis-à-vis* the PLP. Two prominent Right wingers, Dick Taverne at Lincoln and Reginald Prentice at Newham North-East, were rejected by their Left-wing GMCs (with the approval of the Left-leaning NEC). In 1978 the traditional relationship between CLP and Members of Parliament was almost overturned by the militant Campaign for Labour Party Democracy. Election defeat in May 1979 helped to tip the balance. In October, the Labour Left secured its greatest constitutional victory of the decade. Overturning the decision of the previous year, Conference accepted the principle of mandatory re-selection of Labour M.P.s once in every Parliament and also gave the NEC ultimate control over the contents of the Party's election manifesto. Meanwhile, the Labour Co-ordinating Committee, a new group composed of young M.P.s and candidates, pressed for a wider policy review.

When Labour had returned to power in 1974, key posts were given to the ablest figures on the Left – Tony Benn, Barbara Castle, Michael Foot, Eric Heffer, Judith Hart. Heffer, unhappy in office, soon withdrew to the backbenches. Benn developed a personal style which enabled him to combine immense ministerial power with controlled expressions of dissent or of sympathy for Left-wing causes. Foot, never before in government, became the linchpin of both Wilson and Callaghan regimes: as deputy leader and recipient of the largest vote ever received by a Left-wing candidate for the Party leadership, he provided a unique line of communication to the Labour Left. An ironic consequence was that Foot, for so long the effective leader of the Left, became, in his turn, the focus of Left-wing attack.

How does the Left stand now? The problem of being a 'party within the Party' which drove out the ILP, destroyed the Socialist League, and brought the Bevanites to the brink of expulsion, no longer exists in the old sense. One reason is that the Left – Right battle has been increasingly formalised, and the creation of the Manifesto Group in 1974 has instituted a more stable 'two-faction' system within the PLP. The power of the Left in the unions is far from safe: the election of Terry Duffy to the General Secretaryship of the AEU in 1978 indicates the uncertainty of the industrial base. But the political weight of the Left, at all levels of the movement, remains greater than ever in the past. The Left has often argued that its main task is to capture the Labour Party for socialism. 'If the political ideas of the Left are accepted by the Party,' Eric Heffer wrote before the 1974 election, 'then the leadership would be in a difficult position if it refused to carry them out.'[59] After five years in which the ideas of the Left were, in general, accepted by the Party, why did a transformation in government policy not come about?

It is true that the Left remains a minority in the PLP, and that since 1976 the PLP has been a minority in the House of Commons. Yet life within the Parliamentary Party can scarcely be seen as a bitter struggle which the Right wins through force of numbers. There is a ritual dance, an occasional engagement, and that is all. Left-wing Ministers did not behave like unhappy hostages, and there were no Left-wing resignations from the Cabinet in this decade. Would a Tribunite predominance in Cabinet change very much? Some Left wingers have advocated 'a siege economy' and import controls based on the ideas of the Cambridge group of economists, along with a full return to free collective bargaining. Whether a Left-wing Chancellor would maintain these positions for long is open to doubt. The record of Left-wing Ministers in Cabinet give grounds for believing that the differences between a Callaghan and (say) a Tribune-based Benn Cabinet would have more to do with style and symbols than with fundamental approach. If this is so, then the failure of the Left has been caused by more than just a lack of strength, or the manoeuvrings of the other side. It is necessary, therefore, to look not for betrayals or conspiracies but at the nature of British socialism itself.

British Socialism

'Socialism,' wrote Tawney, 'is a word the connotation of which varies, not only from generation to generation, but from decade to decade.'[60] Yet British socialism has been remarkable less for its adaptability than for the persistence of traditional themes. In this century there has been a socialist manifesto whose major features were the same in the 1970s as in the days of Glasier and Hardie: the abolition of capitalism through the public ownership or control of major industries and financial institutions; a redistribution of resources in favour of the poor; better health, education and social welfare as a part of that redistribution; workers' self-management or control; the extension of civil liberties; an end to privileges based on class, race and nationality; a foreign policy rejecting armed alliances in favour of international co-operation; a reduction in arms; aid to oppressed people everywhere. This manifesto was combined with an absolute and half-acknowledged conviction that little of it would ever be carried out. 'The social revolution cannot be rushed,' wrote George Lansbury, 'it is impossible to transform a society as complex as ours from competitive behaviour to co-operative civilisation in a year, or even a century.'[61] The central contradiction of the Labour Left – the pursuit of a vision and a practical belief in its remoteness – has owed much to the religious bases of British socialism.

Some historians have contested 'the common judgement that in Britain the Bible made more Socialists than Karl Marx'.[62] All British parties have a religious heritage, and, as Beer points out, the early socialists were far from unique in drawing on the scriptures, the stuff of many brands of Victorian rhetoric.[63] Hobsbawm, on the other hand, has drawn attention to a key distinction between a political demand and the tradition with which it is associated.[64] Both writers reject the simple idea that twentieth century socialism is merely an outgrowth of nineteenth century evangelism, and stress the secular aspects of British socialism. Hobsbawm points to parallel non-religious traditions; Beer argues that British socialism was a new creed, based on a 'moral collectivism' different both from Christian ethics and from conventional morality, and transcending the ethical individualism of the Radical reformers.

Yet if religion was not the only element, it was certainly the most important one. British socialists have often been accused of utopianism. But the idiom was not so much utopian as mystical. Certainly, no political leaders gave the language, or the theology, of contemporary religion as central a place as the pioneers of the ILP. Early socialist meetings reflected both the techniques and the mood of the temperance movement and revivalism. Attention has rightly been drawn to the strange phenomenon of the Labour Churches in the 1890s, set up by a former Unitarian minister called John Trevor who 'believed the Labour Movement to be God, and built his apparatus of churches, Sunday schools, hymns etc., round it'.[65] Indeed the Socialist Commonwealth was more than merely *analogous* to the Second Coming: in the imagination of speakers and audiences there was a blurring and a merging of the two. Thus Philip Snowden gave lectures on 'The Christ That Is To Be',[66] and Bruce Glasier declared that Socialism would come 'as the very breath of April, full of sweetness and strength: and, lo! in yet a little while it will cause our valleys and cities to bloom anew with the glowing faces of men and women, and to be made glad with the music of children's feet'.[67]

For some in the ILP, socialism was in the fullest sense a secular religion – a rationalist equivalent of Christianity. Fenner Brockway, whose career over three-quarters of a century reflects with a unique loyalty the strongest features of the Labour Left, described how R.J. Campbell's 'New Theology', one of a number of crusades which grew up on the Bible-thumping margins of politics and religion, marked a staging post on his own road to socialism. Campbell joined the ILP, and toured the country with Keir Hardie. Brockway felt that Campbell's speeches were politically thin and made little impression on convinced socialists, 'but upon the outside public, particularly those with a religious background, they had an extraordinary effect'.[68] It was as a journalist employed by Campbell that Brockway was sent to interview Hardie, who immediately won him to the new faith. It is clear that the path from a non-conformist background (Brockway's parents were missionaries) through the 'New Theology' to an apparently modern and godless socialism was progressive and natural.[69]

Becoming a socialist was not merely a matter of acquiring new opinions. It was to make a commitment to an ideal and to adopt an appropriate way of life. Socialism was to be found in the hearts, not in the minds, of men – with a far more immediate meaning as a moral creed than as an alternative system of government. Glasier saw socialism as fellowship ('Fellowship is heaven and the lack of fellowship is hell').[70] Lansbury stressed in 1900 that 'the moral law which I believe in should have a freer play to mould and alter our lives' if social changes were actually to occur.[71] As Party leader a third of a century later Lansbury still held what amounted to a redemptionist view of socialist advance. 'You know the saying: "God is waiting for the people who are good enough to enter and enjoy the Promised Land",' he wrote to Cripps. 'The daily question which hits me in the face is : Are we teaching and living our lives in the way calculated to produce such people?'[72] There was little essential difference between this and the attitude of non-Christians like Brockway who backed the ILP in 1932 because the Labour Party was 'spiritually dead'.[73]

What was it to be spiritually alive? One theme was stressed from the earliest days: to campaign, to raise temperatures, above all to stir up enthusiasm among the rank and file and to make converts of unbelievers. 'The purpose of the Socialist movement is to arouse the people,' Blatchford declared in 1907, 'to uplift the souls of the people, to destroy the civil theories of individualism and class-pride, to reorganise society, to establish collective ownership of the means of life, to abolish poverty and war, to convert the world to a new faith, to inspire it with a new hope, to weld the people into one human family.'[74] The failure of the official leadership to be sufficiently active in this sense was a perennial source of frustration and complaint. The writer Storm Jameson, a keen member of the Socialist League in the 1930s, gave a particularly vivid and revealing expression of a recurrent mood:

The command 'Go' is a force releasing and recreating energy. The prohibition 'Don't Go' creates nothing except apathy and the feeling of discouragement and emptiness. If our leaders said to us, 'Go and demonstrate for socialism', that would be something. They don't. They say, 'Sit at home, draw the curtains, keep calm, don't get excited, enthusiasm is unnecessary unless we happen to want it for some gesture allowed for in the plan of action we keep filed for use some time.'[75]

'Demonstrating for socialism' was something the Labour Left often felt worthwhile when the official leadership did not. Demonstrations were generally expressive, rather than instrumental: declarations of faith, rather than displays of power. *Marching* was especially popular. Peggy Duff, veteran campaigner, recalled that during her nine years of involvement with the unilateralists:

there can be few towns in Britain to, by or from which, I have not marched, no bases I have not protested outside ... We organised hundreds – indeed, over nine years, thousands of public meetings. We distributed millions of leaflets. We sold hundreds of thousands of pamphlets. We must have sold millions of our monthly newspaper *Sanity* ... But in between all this, we marched....[76]

Sometimes marching took the form of a pilgrimage, as with CND in the 1950s, whose choice of the Easter weekend for the annual Aldermaston March emphasised the religous nature of the enterprise. Marching provided a sense of progress towards a destination; it also provided comradeship, a feeling of communal endeavour and, being wearisome, a physical sacrifice. Marches were seldom violent or threatening. When violence occurred, as in the East End in the 1930s, or in some Vietnam demonstrations in the 1960s, revolutionary groups or parties outside the Labour Party were usually responsible.

It was a feature of the British socialist tradition to turn to leaders who rejected traditional authority – whether of the State, or of a Party hierarchy considered to have grown complacent and reactionary. Such leaders – Hardie, MacDonald, Lansbury, Cripps, Bevan – were the more revered for having resigned office, or for having suffered dismissal or expulsion. Left-wing leaders sometimes seemed to welcome – even eagerly to seek – their own political calvary. Sir Stafford Cripps, who sought in his politics to give expression to deep religious convictions, was probably the most strikingly 'messianic' figure. There were those (such as Bevin) who saw in Cripps not only the class background but also the personal ambition of Sir Oswald Mosley in earlier days. In fact Cripps in the 1930s was a man of narrower vision and greater purity of heart who was ready to pursue a principle unflinchingly with little concern for outcomes or results. For such a man, to be defeated and to suffer penalties while doing what he believed to be right was not to fail: it was to be exalted. The political costs for the Left were sometimes high.

Cripps's campaigns were conducted at a time when the theme of expiation – the need to suffer and be punished – was particularly strong on the Labour Left. The events of 1931 had been regarded as a chastisement, well deserved. 'We have been beaten,' declared G. D. H.

Cole, 'no doubt, thoroughly, devastatingly, overwhelmingly beaten . . . But all the same, the predominant feeling in my mind, and in the minds of most of those whom I meet, is not depression, but rather elation and escape.'[77] The Spanish conflict was a holy war, offering purification and a release from guilt. That Bevan, Strauss and Trevelyan should have followed Cripps out of the Party, embracing their own expulsion, at the precise moment that Franco's troops were entering Madrid. had an appropriateness in imagery that was certainly not coincidental.

If British socialism was imbued with transcendentalism, this did not mean that no thought was given to the problem of implementation. After the *débacle* of 1931, the certainty of capitalist and ruling class obstruction featured prominently in socialist writings and speeches. Were socialism and the King in Parliament politically incompatible? When Cripps predicted 'opposition from Buckingham Palace' to socialist measures, he quickly yielded to critics by adding the loyal qualification that he was 'most certainly not referring to the Crown'.[78] Churchill responded to this apparent retreat by accusing him of 'leading the excited crowd forward to overturn the British institutions and then when somebody says "Order, order" running away like a whipped cur'.[79] But the suggestion that Cripps ever favoured dictatorship was wide of the mark. *Can Socialism Come by Constitutional Means?* was the title of a pamphlet by Cripps in 1933.[80] Cripps's own answer, like that of most people on the Labour Left in every period, was unhesitatingly affirmative.

How then was opposition to be overcome and socialism achieved? Cripps was in favour of the immediate abolition of the House of Lords, and an Emergency Powers Act to facilitate socialist legislation. But he also saw as an essential requirement the creation of the kind of socialist support for a future Labour Government that would make a socialist programme possible, given the inevitability of resistance. What mattered was socialism at the base. In other words, it was necessary to 'Make socialists'.

This was evangelism pure and simple. Thus (according to its own prospectus) the Socialist League was:

an organisation of convinced Socialists pledged to devote themselves to one object, and one object only, the achievement of the Socialist Commonwealth in this country, within a worldwide system of Socialism. The League, convinced that this Socialist Commonwealth can only be established by a working class which is Socialist, seeks the co-operation of all Socialists . . . Members of the League are pledged to work within and through the wider movements, and to place all their talents, their energies and their devotion at the disposal of the Movement for one specific purpose, the making of Socialists.[81]

'Making socialists' involved giving and not counting the cost, seeking and not asking for any reward. Lansbury invoked 'the lonely Nazarene' who preached 'the only gospel whereby man can be saved from the power of evil', namely 'not servant in order to rule, but to serve'.[82]

MacDonald stressed the rejection of personal ambition: 'There is no movement which lays down with such uncompromising fidelity in secular affairs the creed that it profits a man nothing to gain the whole world if he loses his own soul.'[83] Socialism for the individual was about self-abnegation – largely for the purpose of creating more socialists, in the belief that, when enough had been created, the Socialist Commonwealth would ensue. There was to be no revolutionary vanguard or elite corps, no bloody struggle, no barricades, no wrestling with intransigent bureaucracies. Capitalism could be destroyed by legal means given the support of a socialist working class.

Thus the problem of how actually to implement socialism was effectively pushed back into the moral domain: for the workers to get socialism, they needed to deserve it. Courage, conviction, commitment – these were the watchwords of the Left. Policy plans – the precise way in which socialist proposals were to be administered – were seldom presented in detail. It is true that from time to time individual Left wingers showed an interest in policy-making as opposed to the simple articulation of demands. This was especially so in the 1920s, when ILP policy documents incorporated the ideas of some of the most advanced economists of the day: drawing on J.A. Hobson's underconsumptionism and anticipating Keynes on the need to stimulate demand in conjunction with planning and controls. In the 1930s G. D. H. Cole's Society for Socialist Inquiry and Propaganda catered briefly for those on the Left who saw a need for the detailed study of particular problems. In the mid and late 1970s there has probably been a greater interest in detailed policy-making for the Labour Party among Left-wing economists and others than at any time since the Second World War. Eric Heffer recently argued that 'there should be a left-wing society similar to the Fabians and doing a similar job'.[84] In fact, Fabianism has been a broad church: from Cripps to Benn, there have been leaders normally associated with the Left who have taken a keen interest in Fabian organisations and studies. Nevertheless, concern on the Left about the nuts and bolts of future legislation has always been comparatively slight.

One reason for this was a feeling that to give close thought to administrative means was to adopt an uncomfortably 'gradualist' approach, in direct conflict with a belief in the need for a rapid transition to socialism. Creating the political will to nationalise the banks or seize the commanding heights of the economy was what mattered; given the will, a way could be found. 'The research worker is still the architect and builder of our future society,' Evan Durbin wrote in 1940.[85] The Left regarded this attitude as politically effeminate. Bevan was particularly impatient of those who felt that careful planning was necessary, as the following extract from Crossman's diary illustrates:

17 March 1952: At our New Statesman lunch we had Aneurin Bevan; not much came of it, except that Aneurin, across the table, rebuked me lightly for stating that I would not mind if the Party stayed out of power for a few months in order

to work out an agreed policy on the next stage of Socialism. 'It isn't a new policy we want', said Aneurin, 'we've got one. What we want is the victory of one tendency in the Party over another.' This is typical Bevanism. He really hates policy-making, and thinks that is what you do when you are in power. Before that moment you worry about getting the power, and even that you don't worry about very much except by making speeches which help the tide along.[86]

As has already been pointed out (and as Crossman's own comment indicates) this was not the only view on the Left. Yet it remains true that the published work of Left-wing leaders and thinkers contains remarkably little on policy that rises above the level of sophisticated propaganda, despite the voluminous pamphleteering of the Left and the brilliance of Left-wing intellectuals like Cole, Laski, Strachey, Crossman and Foot in many of their critical and analytical writings. Those within the Labour Party who adressed their minds to the practical difficulties of future implementation tended to belong to the 'reformist' tradition: writers and politicians such as Morrison, Dalton, Jay, Durbin and Crosland who rejected many of the demands of the socialist Left as unrealistic or even in principle undesirable, and who were against what Dalton called 'theatrical nightmares of violent head-on collisions'.[87]

Here then was a paradox. For the Left was equally opposed to violent collisions, and even at its most radical never favoured instant revolution. There was vagueness about the nature of the transition, but also an insistence that it should be carried out by peaceful and legal means. Thus, while the Left might scorn 'the inevitability of gradualness' it was itself gradualist none the less. The difference between Left and Right in the Labour Party was not of method, but of speed and degree. The instrument of change was to be a Labour Government, based on a parliamentary majority, and working through existing institutions. Yet in its rhetoric and in its traditions the Left barely moved from a vision of socialism coming 'as the very breath of April' once the conquest of familiar enemies had been achieved.

Why did the Labour Left not have more effect? It would be absurd to point to one cause. The rules of the political game repeatedly changed and so did the balance of forces. Before 1945, Labour held office for only three years and never as a majority Government: well over half of Labour's 20 years of government occurred after 1964. It is not possible to erect a theory which will serve with equal validity for an opposition within the Opposition during most of the inter-war period and for the Tribune Group facing Labour Governments in the 1960s and 1970s. Nevertheless, it may be suggested that a persistent philistinism in respect of future policy has been an obstacle to socialist influence.

This is not to make a familiar point about alleged Left-wing 'fundamentalism'; still less is it to disregard the importance of opposition from vested interests. Nor is it to say that Left-wing demands failed because they were wrong. It is rather to suggest that the rightness or wrongness of particular proposals may not have been the most important factor. Heffer, following a long tradition, argued that the task

186 The Labour Party

for the Left was to 'win the whole Party for a genuine socialist policy'.[88] To some extent this has been achieved, and its insignificance is apparent. For it has not been the Party that carries out policy, but a hard pressed Cabinet upon whom Party influences compete with the advice of an experienced Civil Service whose inherent tendency is towards scepticism and caution. Against this, a socialism based on principle and commitment alone was scarcely enough. Winning over the Party or even the movement could not be a substitute for examining the machinery and making efforts (in the words of the Socialist League in 1932, before it abandoned research for the politics of confrontation) 'to inform ourselves *how* we intend to achieve what we mean to do'[89] – once Labour had obtained office.

Notes

1. W. Pickles in J. Gould and W. M. Kolb (Ed.), *A Dictionary of The Social Sciences*, Tavistock, (London) 1964, p. 383.
2. 'Left' was first widely used in British politics in the 1920s (ibid.).
3. E. F. M. Durbin, *The Politics of Democratic Socialism*, The Labour Book Service (London), 1940, p. 226.
4. Ibid., p. 312.
5. See for example R. Miliband, *Parliamentary Socialism*, Merlin Press (London) 1961, pp. 194, 339.
6. R. Williams, *May Day Manifesto 1968* Penguin (Harmondsworth), 1968, p. 173.
7. D. Coates, *The Labour Party and the Struggle for Socialism* (Cambridge) 1975, p. 207.
8. H. Pelling, *Origins of the Labour Party 1880-1900*, Clarendon Press (Oxford) 1954, p. 225.
9. S. D. Shalland in *ILP News*, Aug. 1901; cited in P. P. Poirier, *The Advent of the Labour Party*, Allen & Unwin, (London) 1958, p. 24.
10. Cited in P. P. Poirier, op. cit., p. 26.
11. *Socialism and Society* (1908 edn), p. 146; cited in R. Barker, 'Socialism and Progressivism in the Political Thought of Ramsay MacDonald', in A.J.A. Morris (Ed.), *Edwardian Radicalism 1900–1914*, Routledge & Kegan Paul (London) 1974, p. 125.
12. K. O. Morgan, *Keir Hardie – Radical and Socialist*, Weidenfeld & Nicolson (London) 1975, p. 22.
13. Cited in L. Thompson, *Robert Blatchford: Portrait of an Englishman*, Gollancz (London) 1951, p. 165.
14. Ibid.
15. Cited in ibid., p. 187.
16. P. Stansky (Ed.), *The Left and War: The British Labour Party and World War I*, 1969, p. 319.
17. R. McKibbin, *The Evolution of the Labour Party 1910-1924*, 1974, pp. 88–111.
18. R. H. Tawney, 'The Choice Before the Labour Party', *Political Quarterly*, July-Sept. 1932, vol. 3, no. 3, p. 330.
19. Or so McKibbin argues (op. cit., p. 97).

20. R. E. Dowse, *Left in the Centre*, Longmans (London), 1966, p. 70.
21. M. Cowling, *The Impact of Labour 1920-1924*, CUP (Cambridge) 1971, p. 39.
22. Cited in H. Pelling, *The British Communist Party: An Historical Profile*, Black (London) 1958, p. 25.
23. Ibid., p. 40.
24. Cited in M. Cowling, op. cit., p. 372.
25. M. Gilbert (Ed.), *Plough My Own Furrow*, Longmans (London) 1965, p. 191.
26. Cited in E. Wertheimer, *Portrait of the Labour Party*, G. P. Putnam's & Sons (London) 1929, p. 159.
27. Ibid., p. 160.
28. Cited in G. D. H. Cole, *History of the Labour Party from 1914*, Routledge & Kegan Paul (London) 1948, p. 203.
29. Cited in R. E. Dowse, op.cit., p. 160.
30. E. Wertheimer, op.cit., p. 130.
31. A. J. P. Taylor, *English History 1914-1945*, Clarendon Press (Oxford) 1965, p. 349.
32. M. Foot, *Aneurin Bevan*, Vol. I, New English Library (London) 1966, p. 155.
33. S. Spender, *The Thirties and After: Poetry, Politics, People 1933-1975*, Fontana, (London) 1978, p. 13.
34. *Unity Manifesto* (London) 1937.
35. Trevelyan papers, 21 October 1939.
36. M. Foot, op.cit., p. 347.
37. Hugh Dalton's unpublished diary, 16 August 1940.
38. Cited in A. Calder, *The People's War*, Cape (London) 1969, p. 548.
39. D. Rubinstein, 'Socialism and the Labour Party' in D. E. Martin and D. Rubinstein (Eds), *Ideology and the Labour Movement*, Croom Helm (London) 1979, p. 234.
40. Ibid.
41. Cited in B. Jones, *The Russia Complex: The British Labour Party and the Soviet Union*, Manchester University Press (Manchester) 1978, p. 213.
42. Cited in ibid., p. 138.
43. L. Hunter, *The Road to Brighton Pier*, Barker (London) 1959, p. 41.
44. D. Rubinstein, op.cit., p. 233.
45. Labour Party Annual Conference Reports (London, The Labour Party).
46. L. Minkin, *The Labour Party Conference*, Allen Lane (London) 1978, p. 28n.
47. R. Jackson, *Rebels and Whips*, Macmillan (London) 1968, pp. 114, 152.
48. L. Minkin, op.cit., p. 35n.
49. S. Beer, *Modern British Politics*, Faber (London) 1965, pp. 227-38.
50. See R. Barker *Political Ideas in Modern Britain*, Allen & Unwin (London) 1978, p. 186.
51. M. Harrison, *Trade Unions and the Labour Party since 1945*, Allen & Unwin (London) 1960, p. 251.
52. Ibid., p. 250.
53. G. Thayer, *The British Political Fringe*, Blond (London) p. 167.
54. H. Wilson *The Labour Government of 1964-1970. A Personal Record.* Weidenfeld & Nicolson (London) 1971.
55. R. T. McKenzie, *British Political Parties*, Mercury Books (London) 1963 (2nd edn.), p. 520.
56. *Labour's Programme 1973*, Labour Party (London) 1973, p. 7

188   *The Labour Party*

57. B. Lapping, *The Labour Government 1964-70*, Penguin (Harmondsworth) 1970, p. 21.
58. W. Wyatt *What's Left of the Labour Party?* Sidgwick & Jackson (London) 1977, p. 126.
59. E. Heffer, *The Class Struggle in Parliament*, Gollancz (London) 1973, p. 273.
60. Cited in C. A. R. Crosland, *The Future of Socialism*, Cape (London) 1956, p. 44.
61. G. Lansbury, *These Things Shall Be*, Swarthmore Press (London) 1920, p. 13.
62. S. Beer, op.cit., p. 28n.
63. Ibid.
64. E. J. Hobsbawm *Labouring Men*, Weidenfeld & Nicolson (London) 1964, p. 378.
65. Ibid., pp. 375-6. See also K. S. Inglis, 'The Labour Church Movement', *International Review of Social History*, III, 1958.
66. Cited in C. Cross, *Philip Snowden*, Barrie & Rockliff (London) 1952, p. 38.
67. Ibid., p. 53.
68. F. Brockway, *Inside The Left*, Allen & Unwin (London) 1940, p. 16.
69. Ibid., pp. 12–18.
70. Cited in S. Beer, op.cit., p. 128.
71. R. Postgate, *The Life of George Lansbury*, Longmans (London) 1951, p. 56.
72. Ibid., p. 285.
73. F. Brockway, *Workers' Front*, Secker & Warburg (London) 1938, p. 19.
74. Cited in L. Thompson, op.cit., p. 194.
75. 'To a Labour Party Official,' *Left Review*, No. 2, Nov. 1934, pp. 32-3. Cited in N. Wood, *Communism and Britisn Intellectuals*, Gollancz (London) 1959, p. 107.
76. P. Duff, *Left, Left, Left*, Alison & Busby (London) 1971, p. 145.
77. *New Statesman and Nation*, 14 Nov. 1931.
78. Cited in C. A. Cooke, *The Life of Richard Stafford Cripps*, Hodder & Stoughton, (London) 1957, p. 159.
79. Cited in P. Strauss, *Cripps: Advocate and Rebel*, Gollancz (London) 1943, p. 70.
80. London, The Socialist League, 1933.
81. J. F. Horrabin and G. D. H. Cole, *Socialism in Pictures and Figures*, Socialist League (London) (no date).
82. G. Lansbury, op.cit., p. 15.
83. J. R. MacDonald, 'Religion and the Labour Movement', *The Constructive Quarterly*, Dec. 1913, in A. Beattie (Ed.), *English Party Politics*, Vol. II, Weidenfeld & Nicolson (London) 1970, p. 303.
84. E. Heffer, op.cit., p. 276.
85. E. F. M. Durbin, op.cit., p. 320n.
86. M. Foot. *Aneurin Bevan Vol. II 1945–1960*, Davis-Poynter (London) 1973, p. 374.
87. H. Dalton. *Practical Socialism for Britain*, Routledge (London) 1935, p. 15.
88. E. Heffer, op.cit., p. 266.
89. *New Clarion*, 17 Dec. 1932.

Notes on contributors

Chris Cook: Since January 1976, Editor of *Pears Cyclopaedia.* Educated at St Catharine's College, Cambridge and Oriel College, Oxford. Research Student at Nuffield College, Oxford, 1968–70. Senior Research Officer at the London School of Economics, 1970–76. His previous publications include the five-volume *Sources in British Political History* and, with co-authors, *The Slump, Post-War Britain: A Political History* and *Trends in British Politics.* A Fellow of the Royal Historical Society, he has contributed articles and reviews to the *Guardian, TLS* and *THES.*

Anthony Fenley: Since 1977, Lecturer in the Department of External Studies, University of Oxford. Educated at Swansea University and the London School of Economics, specialising in industrial relations, with particular emphasis on trade union studies.

Iain McLean: Since October 1978, Fellow and Praelector in Politics, University College, Oxford. Educated at Christ Church, Oxford; Student and Research Fellow, Nuffield College, Oxford, 1967–71. Lecturer in Politics at the University of Newcastle-upon-Tyne, 1971–78. His previous publications include a biography of Keir Hardie.

Ben Pimlott: Since 1979, Visiting Research Associate in the Department of International History, London School of Economics. Lecturer in Politics, University of Newcastle-upon-Tyne, 1970–79. Educated at Worcester College, Oxford. His previous publications include *Labour and the Left in the 1930s.*

David Roberts: Since 1978, on the administrative staff of the University of Bangor. Formerly Research Assistant in the Department of Politics, Kingston Polytechnic. Completed his doctorate on the Labour movement in the 1930s.

David Steel: Since 1972, Lecturer in Politics at the University of Exeter. Educated at Jesus College, Oxford. Research Student of Nuffield College, Oxford, 1969–72. His previous publications include (with R. G. S. Brown) *The Administrative Process in Britain* and *Nationalisation and Public Ownership* in *Trends in British Politics.*

Ian Taylor: Since October 1978, Lecturer in Politics at the University of Aston, having previously taught at Bristol Polytechnic and Exeter University. His doctoral thesis (completed at the London School of Economics) was concerned with the impact of the Second World War on the domestic policies of the Labour Party.

Chronology of principal events

1900 (27 Feb.) Formation of Labour Representation Committee. Two M.P.s elected in 1900 election.

1902 Taff Vale Decision.

1903 Gladstone–MacDonald electoral pact.

1906 29 LRC M.P.s returned in the General Election. After the election, LRC group of M.P.s assumed title of 'Labour Party'.

1910 40 Labour M.P.s returned in January election, 42 in December.

1914 Arthur Henderson becomes Chairman of the Parliamentary Party.

1917 W. Adamson becomes Chairman of the Parliamentary Party.

1918 Labour Party Constitution promulgated; 63 Labour M.P.s elected in 'Coupon Election'.
Labour and the New Social Order published.

1921 J. Clynes becomes Chairman of the Parliamentary Party.

1922 Ramsay MacDonald becomes Chairman of the Parliamentary Party; 142 Labour M.P.s returned in the General Election (November).

1923 (Dec.) Labour returns 191 M.P.s in the election.

1924 (Jan.) First minority Labour Government.
1924 (Oct.) Defeat of Labour Government followed by 'Zinoviev Letter' election. 151 Labour M.P.s returned.

1926 General Strike: formal understanding with Cooperative Party.

1929 Labour formed second minority Government, returning 288 M.P.s in the election.

1931 MacDonald's betrayal; formation of National Government. Henderson becomes Party leader after MacDonald's defection. Labour reduced to 52 M.P.s in the election.

1932 George Lansbury elected Party leader. ILP disaffiliates.

1934 *For Socialism and Peace* published.

1935 Clement Attlee elected leader; Labour returns 154 M.P.s in the General Election.

1937 Modification of Party constitution to give more power to local constituency parties.

1940 Labour leaders join Churchill's war-time Coalition Government. Electoral truce.

1942 *The Old World and The New Society* published.

1945 Sweeping Labour victory (393 seats) results in first majority Labour Government. Major programme of nationalisation and establishment of National Health Service amongst objectives.

1950 Labour narrowly returned to power (315 seats).

1951 Resignation of Wilson, Bevan and Freeman from Government; Labour defeated in General Election (295 seats).

1955 Hugh Gaitskell elected leader; second successive election defeat for Labour (277 seats).
1956 Publication of Anthony Crosland's *The Future of Socialism.*

1959 Labour's third successive election defeat (258 seats).

1960 Death of Aneurin Bevan.

1961 *Signposts for The Sixties* published.

1963 Hugh Gaitskell dies. Harold Wilson elected leader.

1964 Narrow election victory for Labour (317 seats).

1966 Labour returned to power (363 seats); its second best performance.

1970 Labour loses election (287 seats).

1973 Publication of *Labour's Programme 1973.*

1974 (Feb.) Stalemate election (Labour 301 seats) but Wilson forms government. Social Contract with trade unions.
1974 (Oct.) In a second close election, Labour increases its representation to 319 seats.

1975 Publication of Stuart Holland's *The Socialist Challenge*. EEC Referendum.

1976 Resignation of Harold Wilson. James Callaghan elected leader.

1977 Lib–Lab pact to ensure Government's survival.

1979 (May) Defeat of Labour in General Election (268 seats).

Select bibliography

Addison, P. *The Road to 1945*, Cape (London), 1976.

Allen, V. L. *Trade Unions and the Government*, Longman (London), 1960.

Attlee, C. R. *The Labour Party in Perspective*, Gollancz (London), 1937.

Balogh, T. *Labour and Inflation*, Fabian Trust (London), 1971.

Barker, B. *Ramsay MacDonald's Political Writings*, Allen Lane (London), 1972.

Barker, R. S. *Political Ideas in Modern Britain*, Allen & Unwin (London), 1978.

Bealey, F. and **Pelling, H.** *Labour and Politics 1900–1906*, Macmillan (London), 1958.

Beattie, A. *English Party Politics*, Vol. 2 Weidenfeld (London), 1970.

Beer, M. *A History of British Socialism*, Vol. 2 G. Bell & Sons (London), 1919.

Beer, S. H. *Modern British Politics*, Faber (London), 1969.

Bevan, A. *In Place of Fear*, Heinemann (London), 1952.

Birch, L. (Ed.) *The History of the TUC 1868–1968*, TUC (London), 1968.

Blatchford, R. *Merrie England*, Clarion (London), 1894.

Branson, N. and **Heinemann, M.** *Britain in the Nineteen Thirties*, Panther (London), 1971.

Briggs, A. and **Saville, J.** (Eds) *Essays in Labour History*, Vol. 1 Macon (London), 1967.

Brockway, F. *Inside the Left*, Allen & Unwin (London), 1940.

Brockway, F. *Workers' Front*, Secker & Warburg (London), 1938.

Bullock, A. *The Life and Times of Ernest Bevin*, Heinemann (London), 1960.

Butler, D. E. *The British General Election of 1955*, Macmillan (London), 1955.

Butler, D. E. (Ed.) *Coalitions in British Politics*, Macmillan (London), 1978.

Butler, D. E. and **Kavanagh, D.** *The British General Election of February 1974*, Macmillan (London), 1974.

Butler, D. E. and **Kavanagh, D.** *The British General Election of October 1974*, Macmillan (London), 1975.

Butler, D. E. and **King, A.** *The British General Election of 1964*, Macmillan (London), 1965.

Butler, D. E. and **King, A.** *The British General Election of 1966*, Macmillan (London), 1966.

Butler, D. E. and **Pinto-Duschinsky, M.** *The British General Election of 1970*, Macmillan (London), 1971.

Butler, D. E. and **Rose, R.** *The British General Election of 1959*, Macmillan (London), 1960.

Butler, D. E. and **Stokes, D.** *Political Change in Britain*, Macmillan (London), 1974.

Calder, A. *The People's War*, Cape (London), 1969.

Campbell, J. *Lloyd George: The Goat in the Wilderness*, Cape (London), 1977.
Coates, D. *The Labour Party and the Struggle for Socialism*, CUP (Cambridge), 1975.
Cole, G. D. H. *The World of Labour*, G. Bell & Sons (London), 1917.
Cole, G. D. H. *The Principles of Economic Planning*, Macmillan (London), 1935.
Cole, G. D. H. *The Machinery of Socialist Planning*, Hogarth Press (London), 1938.
Cole, G. D. H. *Plan for Democratic Britain*, Labour Book Service (London), 1939.
Cole, G. D. H. *A History of the Labour Party from 1914*, Routledge & Kegan Paul (London), 1948.
Cook, C. *The Age of Alignment*, Macmillan (London), 1975.
Cook, C. and **Ramsden, J.** *By-Elections in British Politics*, Macmillan (London), 1975.
Cowling, M. *The Impact of Labour, 1920–1924*, CUP (Cambridge), 1971.
Craig, F. W. S. *British Parliamentary Election Results, 1950–1970*, Macmillan (London), 1974.
Craig, F. W. S. *British Electoral Facts 1885–1975*, Macmillan (London), 1976 (3rd edn).
Craig, F. W. S. *Britain Votes*, Parliamentary Research Services (Chichester), 1977.
Crosland, C. A. R. *The Future of Socialism*, Cape (London), 1956.
Crosland, C. A. R. *Socialism Now*, Cape (London), 1974.
Crossman, R. H. S. *New Fabian Essays*, Turnstile Press (London), 1952.
Crossman, R. H. S. *Planning for Freedom*, Hamish Hamilton (London), 1965.
Dalton, H. *Practical Socialism for Britain*, Routledge (London), 1935.
Dowse, R. E. *Left in the Centre*, Longman (London), 1966.
Drucker, H. M. *Doctrine and Ethos in the Labour Party*, Allen & Unwin (London), 1979.
Duff, P. *Left, Left, Left*, Alison & Busby (London), 1971.
Durbin, E. F. M. *The Politics of Democratic Socialism*, Routledge (London), 1940.
Elliott, J. *Conflict or Co-operation, The Growth of Industrial Democracy*, Kogan Page (London), 1978.
Flanders, A. *Management and Unions*, Faber & Faber (London), 1970.
Flanders, A. 'The Tradition of Voluntarism', *British Journal of Industrial Relations*, Vol. XII, No. 3, Nov. 1974.
Foot, M. *Aneurin Bevan*, Vol. I, New English Library (London), 1966.
Foot, M. *Aneurin Bevan*, Vol. II, Davis-Poynter (London), 1973.
Heffer, E. *The Class Struggle in Parliament*, Gollancz (London), 1973.
Hobhouse, L. T. *The Labour Movement*, Fisher Unwin (London), 1912.
Hobsbawm, E. *Labouring Men*, Weidenfeld & Nicolson (London), 1964.
Hobsbawm, E. *Industry and Empire*, Weidenfeld & Nicolson (London), 1968.
Hobson, J. A. *The Science of Wealth*, Home University Library (London), 1911.
Holland, S. *The Socialist Challenge*, Quartet Books (London), 1975.
Howell, D. *British Social Democracy*, Croom Helm (London), 1976.
Hughes, I. and **Moore, R.** *A Special Case*, Penguin (Harmondsworth), 1972.
Independent Labour Party, *Let us Reform the Labour Party*, ILP (London), 1910.
ILP, *Moscow's Reply to the ILP*, ILP (Glasgow), 1920.
Jackson, R. *Rebels and Whips*, Macmillan (London), 1968.
Jenkins, P. *The Battle of Downing Street*, Charles Knight (London), 1970.
Jenkins, R. *The Pursuit of Progress*, Heinemann (London), 1953.

Jones, B. *The Russia Complex: The British Labour Party and the Soviet Union*, Manchester University Press (Manchester), 1978.

Labour Party, *Labour and the New Social Order*, Labour Party (London), 1918.

Labour Party, *Labour and the Nation*, Labour Party (London), 1927.

Labour Party, *For Socialism and Peace*, Labour Party (London), 1934.

Labour Party, *Labour's Immediate Programme*, Labour Party (London), 1937.

Labour Party, *The War and After, Labour's Home Policy*, Labour Party (London), 1940.

Labour Party, *Labour's Peace Aims*, Labour Party (London), 1940.

Labour Party, *The Old World and the New Society*, Labour Party (London), 1942.

Labour Party, *Let us Face the Future*, Labour Party (London), 1945.

Labour Party, *Signposts for the Sixties*, Labour Party (London), 1961.

Labour Party, *Labour's Programme*, Labour Party (London), 1973.

Labour Party, *Labour's Programme*, Labour Party (London), 1976.

Lansbury, G. *These Things Shall Be*, Swarthmore Press (London), 1920.

Lapping, B. *The Labour Government 1966–1970*, Penguin (Harmondsworth), 1970.

Laski, H. *The Crisis and the Constitution*, L. & V. Woolf Fabian Society (London), 1932.

Laski, H. *The State in Theory and Practice*, Allen & Unwin (London), 1935.

Lee, J. *This Great Journey*, MacGibbon & Kee (London), 1963.

Lovell, J. *British Trade Unions 1875–1933*, Macmillan (London), 1977.

Lovell, J. and **Roberts, B. C.** *A Short History of the TUC*, Macmillan (London), 1968.

MacDonald, J. R. *Socialism and Society*, Socialist Library (London), 1905.

MacDonald, J. R. *The Socialist Movement*, Williams & Norgate (London), 1911.

MacDonald, J. R. *Parliament and Revolution*, National Labour Press (Manchester), 1919.

MacDonald, J. R. *Parliament and Democracy*, Social Studies Press (London), 1921.

MacKenzie, N. *The Letters of Sidney and Beatrice Webb 1912–47*, CUP and London School of Economics (Cambridge), 1978.

MacKenzie, N. and **MacKenzie, J.** *The First Fabians*, Weidenfeld & Nicolson (London), 1977.

Martin, D. E. and **Rubinstein, D.** *Ideology and the Labour Movement*, Croom Helm (London), 1979.

Marquand, D. *Ramsay MacDonald*, Cape (London), 1977.

McCarthy, W. E. J. (Ed.) *Trade Unions*, Penguin (Harmondsworth), 1972.

McKenzie, R. T. *British Political Parties*, Mercury Books (London), 1963.

McKenzie, R. T. and **Silver, A.** *Angels in Marble*, Heinemann (London), 1968.

McKibbin, R. *The Evolution of the Labour Party 1910–1924*, OUP (London), 1974.

McKie, D. and **Cook, C.** (Eds.) *The Decade of Disillusion*, Macmillan (London), 1972.

McLean, I. S. *Keir Hardie*, Allen Lane (London), 1975.

McLean, I. S. *Elections*, Longman (London), 1976.

Miliband, R. *Parliamentary Socialism*, Merlin Press (London), 1961.

Milne, E. *No Shining Armour*, John Calder (London), 1976.

Minkin, L. *The Labour Party Conference*, Allen Lane (London), 1978.

Moore, R. *The Emergence of the Labour Party 1880–1924*, Hodder and Stoughton (London), 1978.

Morgan, K. O. *Keir Hardie – Radical and Socialist*, Weidenfeld & Nicolson (London), 1975.

Morgan, K. O. (Ed.) *Lloyd George Family Letters 1885–1936*, University of Wales Press (Cardiff), 1973.

Morrison, H. *An Easy Outline of Modern Socialism*, Labour Party (London), 1935.

Muller, W. D. *The Kept Men*, Harvester (London), 1977.

Pelling, H. *The Origins of the Labour Party 1880–1900*, Clarendon Press (Oxford), 1954.

Pelling, H. *A Short History of the Labour Party*, Macmillan (London), 1961.

Pelling, H. *A History of British Trade Unionism*, Macmillan (London), 1963.

Phelps-Brown, S. (Ed.) *The Growth of British Industrial Relations*, Macmillan (London), 1959.

Pimlott, B. *Labour and the Left in the 1930s*, CUP (Cambridge), 1977.

Pollard, S. *The Gold Standard and Employment Policies Between the Wars*, Methuen (London), 1970.

Postgate, R. *The Life of George Lansbury*, Longman (London), 1951.

Ranney, A. *Pathways to Parliament*, Macmillan (London), 1965.

Robertson, D. B. *A Theory of Party Competition*, John Wiley (London), 1976.

Roskill, S. *Hankey, Man of Secrets: 1918–31*, Collins (London), 1972.

Rush, M. *The Selection of Parliamentary Candidates*, Nelson (London), 1969.

Shaw, G. B. *Fabian Essays in Socialism*, Fabian Society (London), 1888.

Sked, A. and **Cook, C.** *Post-War Britain: A Political History*, Pelican (London), 1979.

Snowden, P. *Socialism and Syndicalism*, Collins Clear Type Press (London), 1913.

Spender, S. *The Thirties and After: Poetry, Politics, People 1933–1975*, Fontana (London), 1978.

Stevenson, J. and **Cook, C.** *The Slump*, Cape (London), 1977.

Strauss, G. *Cripps: Advocate and Rebel*, Gollancz (London), 1943.

Tawney, R. H. *The Acquisitive Society*, G. Bell & Sons (London), 1921.

Tawney, R. H. *The Radical Tradition*, Allen & Unwin (London), 1964.

Thayer, G. *The British Political Fringe*, Anthony Blond (London), 1965.

Thompson, E. P. *The Making of the English Working Class*, Gollancz (London), 1963.

Thompson, L. *Robert Blatchford. Portrait of an Englishman*, Gollancz (London), 1951.

Wallas, G. *The Great Society*, Macmillan (London), 1914.

Webb, S. *Socialism in England*, Swann, Sonnenschein and Co. (London), 1889.

Wedgwood Benn, A. *The New Politics*, Fabian Society (London), 1970.

Wertheimer, E. *Portrait of the Labour Party*, G. P. Putnam & Sons (London), 1929.

Williams, R. *May Day Manifesto 1968*, Penguin (Harmondsworth), 1968.

Wilson, H. *The Labour Government 1964–1970*, Weidenfeld & Nicolson (London), 1971.

Windlesham, Lord *Communication and Political Power*, Cape (London), 1966.

Winter, J. M. *Socialism and the Challenge of War*, Routledge & Kegan Paul (London), 1974.

Wyatt, W. *What's Left of the Labour Party*, Sidgwick & Jackson (London), 1977.

Index

Bold type indicates most important entries.
Abbreviations: Con, Conservative; Lab,
Labour; Lib, Liberal; PM, Prime Minister;
tu, trade union(s).